PODIUM HUMOR

Books by James C. Humes

Podium Humor
Instant Eloquence

PODIUM HUMOR

A RACONTEUR'S TREASURY OF WITTY AND HUMOROUS STORIES

James C. Humes

HARPER & ROW, PUBLISHERS

NEW YORK, HAGERSTOWN,
SAN FRANCISCO, LONDON

1817

Designed by Sidney Feinberg

Library of Congress Cataloging in Publication Data

Humes, James C

  Podium humor.

  Includes index.

  1. Public speaking.   2. American wit and humor.

I. Title

PN4193.I5H8   808.5'1   74–15832

ISBN 0–06–011999–3

77 78 79 10 9 8 7 6 5 4 3

To Roger Whittlesey,
whose charm and good humor lightened
the lives of his friends

Contents

Acknowledgments

If, as Ben Franklin said, "At twenty years of age, the will reigns; at thirty, the wit; and at forty, the judgment," I want to thank my editor, Joe Vergara, for pushing me to write this book on wit before my fortieth-birthday deadline. The main credit for making that deadline belongs to my assistant, Stephanie Laszlo, who for close to a decade has worked for me in my various assignments. Other friends who have put up with me and my stories include Don Whitehead, Jim Greenlee, J. D. Williams, Victor Lang, Bob Smith, Trevor Armbrister, Dick McCormack, and, of course, my two brothers, Sam and Graham, and my wife, Dianne.

Introduction

How many times have you wished for a little humor in your speech —some story or anecdote that will demonstrate a point, yet make the audience laugh? You may be facing a hostile audience, such as a Catholic group on abortion. Or you may have to address your party workers after a defeat. Or maybe you're accepting an award after a glowing testimonial. Perhaps you're a moderator who has to soothe tempers after a bitter debate. Or you're a best man who feels more comfortable with humor than sentimentality. Or maybe you feel that it would be better to sharpen a point with wit than statistics.

So you think to yourself, I want a humorous story. You first try a friend. Then you take out a joke book from the library or buy one at the local bookstore. But you find nothing but old gags—two-line exchanges between women and their sons-in-law or fathers and their teenagers—or tired jokes about hillbillies, drunks, or talking horses. They are stories that will both demean you and insult your audience's intelligence. Maybe a comedian with his deadpan face and deliberate timing can make such stories funny, but you know if you try to you will embarrass yourself as well as your audience. And you will end up not easing audience tension but increasing it.

What you should be looking for is not jokes but humor. A joke is verbal slapstick—it lacks both build-up and believability. It doesn't come out of your own experience. It has been mass-manufactured, not tailor-fit to your occasion. It is, at best, a fifth-hand commodity worn down by use into a bare two-line exchange.

Humor flows out of the person or the moment. Humor builds

suspense and tension, then releases it, sometimes by presenting the unexpected or the familiar in an unfamiliar context. Humor demands something from the audience as well as from the speaker. It is the flash anticipation or sudden insight by the audience that triggers laughter. Humor is build-up, bomb, and burst.

In this book you are going to learn all about humor—its inside and its outside, what humor is made of and how to make it yourself. You will learn how to write your own humor to fit any occasion—from the topical one-liner to warm up a formal speech to the groom's toast to open a wedding luncheon.

From my cross-indexed collection of humor you will be able to find the story to fit any audience or any subject. And I will give you the "lead-in" lines, getting you into telling the story, and the "bridge" lines, getting you back to the speech. With these "lead-ins" and "bridges" you will see how to use the humorous story to open a speech or to close a program, to introduce a speaker, or to introduce a key point.

You are going to learn in this book how to be a funny speaker and you are going to have a lot of fun in learning how.

Humor is emotional chaos remembered in tranquility.

—JAMES THURBER

PODIUM HUMOR

PART ONE

1   The Laugh-Trigger

*I said of laughter; it is mad; and of mirth; what
doeth it?*

—Ecclesiastes II:2

I would no more compile a joke book than I would visit a burlesque show. Somehow the gags you read in those joke collections remind me of those fading "queens" doing their bumps and grinds before a few old men. That's how those old jokes seem—tired from being overworked, raw from too much handling, and bare from overexposure.

But though standard jokes turn me off, I enjoy humor because humor is as different from a joke as a love story is from pornography. Good literature—erotic or otherwise—asks some imagination from the reader.

Jokes, however, may insult your intelligence. What adult likes verbal slapstick? If you tend to run when a vendor says, "Do you want to see a French postcard?" then you will also want to run when a salesman says, "Hey, did you hear the one about the drunk in the elevator?" That's because jokes are often stripped from their context. It is like the school boy who thumbs through a paperback looking only for the dirty parts. Sex becomes dull as well as trite when lifted out of the emotional interplay between two human beings. So often the jokes you read are the bare gag lines lifted from a real humorous situation.

One of my favorite stories is Winston Churchill's run-in with the Labourite, Bessie Braddock. It was in 1959 and the fat Bessie was waddling toward the House of Commons Chamber as Sir Winston Churchill, who had been in the antechamber where they dispense liquid libations, was wobbling toward the same door. In the inevitable clash—down went Bessie for the count. She pulled herself up off the floor and said, "Sir Winston, you are drunk. What's more, you are disgustingly drunk." The old Prime Minister looked at the obese Bessie and replied, "And you, Mrs. Braddock, are ugly. What's more, you are disgustingly ugly. Furthermore, tomorrow, I, Winston Churchill, shall be sober."

As one who has enjoyed telling this story you can imagine my dismay when I hear a nightclub comedian say, "Did you hear the one about the drunk and the fat lady? The fat lady says, 'Hey, mister, you're drunk.' 'Yeah,' replies the drunk, 'but tomorrow I'll be sober, lady.' "

The bare gag line has been robbed from a richly comic situation. Good humor has been reduced to a mere gag. Humor needs development and build-up.

Joke books are mostly a collection of stories stripped down. Glance through one and you will hardly find any that are really funny and usable. You ask why people buy such books? There must be some market for them. Nightclub comedians, entertainers, and professional public speakers buy them, but they know how to use them. The story they tell will come out a lot different from the original joke-book gag they adapted.

A law colleague of mine in Philadelphia who died a few years ago was renowned as a raconteur. He kept a loose-leaf notebook full of jokes. A lawyer in the same firm always envied his partner's storytelling gift. He thought the secret was in his little black notebook. Yet some months after his partner died, his friend came to me and said, "I found Bill's joke book and, you know, the jokes really weren't that funny."

I read the stories too, and they weren't that funny if you told them the way they were written down. But Bill had the knack of making the story his own by adapting it to his own experience. The bare-bones joke was only the skeletal structure. Adding his own details, he could flesh out a humorous anecdote.

For example, on one of his loose-leaf pages he had noted, "A civic leader visits a local branch of the Florence Crittendon Home for Unwed Mothers. One of the young residents rushes up to him and says 'Oh, Mr. Adams, if it weren't for you, many of us wouldn't be here.' " But I recall the way he actually told the story:

"Ladies and gentlemen, I want to thank you for that nice welcome and all those nice things the chairman said about me in the introduction. You have made me feel very comfortable and very much at home being with you. You know that is not always the case. I recall an introduction some years ago when I was heading a United Fund drive in the city. One of my responsibilities was to visit the various institutions the United Fund supported, award them the check denoting our annual contribution and say a few words. On this particular occasion I was visiting the Florence Crittendon Home for Unwed Mothers and a resident had been selected to introduce me. The young girl came up to the podium and said, 'We have looked forward to your being at the home today. After all, if it weren't for you, Mr. Adams, many of us wouldn't even be here.' "

Probably the incident didn't actually happen to him. Most likely he heard the story from someone else and then wove it into his own pattern of experience. The point is it came out as believable.

The first stories I ever filed in my own collection were not from joke books but from biographies. In the biographies of Churchill, Disraeli, and Franklin Roosevelt I would come across a humorous incident and note it down. These anecdotes were far more hilarious than any gag I ever found in a joke book. The reason is that they really happened; they were not artificial or contrived.

To that collection I added stories I had heard at political dinners —stories by master raconteurs such as Everett Dirksen, Thruston Morton, and Sam Ervin. The stories they told, however, were about incidents that happened to them or their friends. With this believability the joke assumes the texture of humor.

Great storytellers like Sam Ervin know another secret that raises a joke to the level of humor. Ervin's stories have a point. Whether he is quoting the Bible, reciting Shakespeare, or telling about a preacher he once knew in North Carolina, old Sam has a message he wants to give. For instance, the senator was telling some reporters how even the most prejudiced person thinks he is fair-minded. "One time when I was presiding over a murder trial in Burke County, they had a special jury summoned in from another county to make sure that the accused got a fair hearing. I asked one of those jurors if he could be fair and he answered, 'I think he is guilty of murder in the first degree and he ought to be sent to the gas chamber, but I can give him a fair trial.' "

By itself the story might fall flat. But in the context of a speech on justice or the need for fair play, it is a humorous insight into human nature.

No matter how funny it is, a story told without a purpose is a joke. When you read an anecdote in a person's biography it is humor, and when you hear a funny story with a point to emphasize it is also humor. In this book you will find over five hundred humorous stories, all labeled and subtitled by the points you may want to illustrate in a speech—"action," "budget," "commitment," "decisiveness," etc.

Now the opening lead-in words that connect the point to the story may, in this book, detract from the anecdote, but before an audience it will add humor to a speech. And the better it is woven into the warp and woof of your speech, the more humorous your story will sound.

If there are two things to remember about telling a story in a speech, they are these: build the story into your speech and build up to the punch line. Build in and build up!

A joke becomes humor when it is part of something else—a biography, a narrative, or a speech. A joke also becomes humor when it is more than a thrust-and-response gag line.

For the technique of "build-up," let me give you a story Maxwell Droke once told:

"Solomon Finkelstein, of the firm of Finkelstein and Goldfarb, died rather inconveniently in the midst of the fourteenth annual 'Going-Out-of-Business Sale.' Abraham Goldfarb called promptly on the widow. 'Rachel,' he said, 'I don't want, in your great grief, you should be bothered with business matters. You are leaving to me the funeral arrangements. Everything is being done in an elegant, first-class manner. And also the expenses will be paid by the firm Finkelstein and Goldfarb, of which I am respectfully reminding you I am now the senior partner.'

"Concluding that Brooklyn funeral parlors were lacking in some measure of class, Abie betook himself to a fashionable Manhattan mortuary, presented his business card, and asked to look at the best available offerings. He was shown a collection of caskets priced around eight hundred dollars. 'No,' said Mr. Goldfarb impatiently. 'I am not making myself clear. This casket is for Solomon Finkelstein, late senior partner of the firm Finkelstein and Goldfarb. I am wanting something really first class.' On the second floor of the establishment he was shown caskets ranging in price up to fifteen hundred dollars. 'Very nice,' said Abie appreciatively, 'but are you maybe having something a little better?' On the third floor, in solitary splendor, reposed a single casket fashioned of rare imported woods, lined with brocaded satin, plenished in gleaming gold, air-conditioned, termite-proof—in every way a supercolossal casket. 'Well,' said Abie after a critical inspection, 'if you are having this model in a forty-four stout, maybe we can do business.'

"With the casket purchased and all arrangements completed, Mr. Goldfarb proudly ushered in the widow Finkelstein. 'Oh, Abie,' she gasped, 'it is a wonderful funeral you are arranging. Everything is beautiful.' 'Well,' agreed Abie, 'we are sparing no expense. That casket alone is costing seventy-seven hundred dollars, after the cash discount!' At this revelation Mrs. Finkelstein began sobbing softly. 'Now, now, Rachel,' soothed the distressed Mr. Goldfarb, 'you shouldn't be minding the expense. Already I am telling you everything is paid for by the firm Finkelstein and Goldfarb, of which I am now the senior partner.' 'I know, Abie, I know,' wailed the widow Finkelstein, 'but I was just thinking, for only fifty dollars more, you could have buried poor Solly in a Cadillac.' "

The origin of this story, said Droke, was a two-line joke he read somewhere that went like this:

"Ike: They gave Solly Finkelstein a wonderful funeral. I hear the casket alone cost seventy-seven hundred dollars!

"Abe: Seventy-seven hundred dollars? Why, for fifty dollars more they could have buried him in a Cadillac."

A humorous story is like a balloon: you pump it up with details and then puncture it with a punch line. It is another way of saying build-up before a fall.

Some storytellers like the "Rule of Three" as a method of build-up.

Three businessmen sitting together on a suburban train got to discussing their respective mates. Each of them was saying how lucky he was to have a wife who appreciated him. The first husband said, "My wife tells me I'm so distinguished that I look like an ambassador." The second one said, "My wife tells all my friends that I am the best-read man she ever met." The third one said, "My wife really appreciates me. I remember one time when I had to stay home from the office she was so excited that every time a mailman or delivery man arrived at the door she shouted, 'My husband's home! My husband's home!' "

Another example of the Rule of Three is the story that defines what *savoir-faire* is.

An American professor who wanted to find out all the nuances of such a phrase for his about-to-be published dictionary recently flew to Paris to question members of the Académie Français.

"It is not difficult to define," one said. "If I go home and find my wife sleeping with another man and I tip my hat to him and say, 'Excuse me,' that is *savoir-faire.*" "Not quite," said a second member. "If I go home and find my wife with another man and I tip my hat and say, 'Excuse me. Please continue,' that is *savoir-faire.*" "Oh no," said a third, fingering his beard. "If I go home and find my wife with another man and I tip my hat and say, 'Excuse me. Please continue' and he *can* continue, *he* has *savoir-faire.*"

If the sexual situation is the best way to describe *savoir-faire*, it may also be the best analogy to humor. Sigmund Freud was not the first, only the most famous, writer to see the comparison. The build-up and release pattern is in both sex and humor.

Freud carried it further. He found in humor the aggressive release of pent-up frustrations. The subject of humor, to Freud, was always the cuckolded, henpecked, or impotent husband—the drunk, the tramp, the miser, the dunce.

Certainly the Jewish humor in this country is rooted in Eastern European origins. The Jew in the ghetto needed someone to look down on and make fun of even if it was a caricature of himself. In the oppressive states humor may be one of the only releases. In most Eastern European humor there is a Charlie Chaplin quality to the butts of a comic situation, whether they be the "Good Soldier Schweik" in Czechoslovakia or Gogol's Russian clerk in *The Overcoat*. You laugh at the guy worse off than yourself.

When I was in Czechoslovakia a few years ago my guide (whose son-in-law, after the uprising of 1968, had been demoted from professor to janitor at the University of Prague) told me the latest story making the rounds:

"A man seeking a minor bureaucratic post was asked to fill out a questionnaire. After he did, a party official asked him what he meant in his reply to this question: 'What is your attitude toward the Soviet Union?' The applicant replied, 'As I wrote in the space, I feel deeply about the Soviet Union. It's like the way I feel about my own wife.' 'What do you mean?' said the official. 'Well,' the little man replied, 'I wouldn't say like my own mother—because my motherland is Czechoslovakia—but I do believe my attitude is the same as that toward my own wife.'

"Afterward, when he got the job, friends chided the meek clerk for ingratiating himself that way with the officials. He explained, 'But I really do feel toward Russia the way I feel toward my wife. I don't love it, I can't change it, and I can't help dreaming of something better.' "

When we laugh at the henpecked or impotent husband we feel superior—in a sense we release our own frustrations, be they about marriage, job, or growing old.

Listen to this story about a man approaching seventy years of age:

A man who was just about to celebrate his forty-fifth wedding anniversary decided to do it big with his wife. "Let's go back," he said, "to the Plaza Hotel, where we spent our wedding night, and celebrate. We'll order the same vintage French champagne and relive the whole thing." She replied, "That's wonderful, dear. And, you know, I still remember the number of the suite—705." So they went back for their forty-fifth—same hotel, same champagne, same room, even the same flowers in the room, roses. Only this time the *husband* went into the bathroom and cried.

The German philosopher Immanuel Kant has said, "The essence of humor is an expectation that comes to nothing." It is the collapse of a developed pattern. In other words, the punch line deflates the build-up. The poor guy gets his hopes up and then *pfttt*.

All of us at one time or another have had the balloon of our hopes punctured by reality. We can laugh at the expectant bridegroom who tells his best man, "This girl I'm going to marry is the perfect combination of all the qualities you'd want in a wife. She'll be an economist in the kitchen, an aristocrat in the living room, and a harlot in bed."

Later, sometime after the honeymoon, the best man asked the husband if his wife still combined the magic qualities of aristocrat, harlot, and economist. "Yes," he replied, "but not in quite the same way as I expected. "She's turned out to be an aristocrat in the kitchen, a harlot in the living room, and an economist in bed."

Along the "expectation that comes to nothing" vein, one of the funniest stories I tell is that of the frustrated eagle. The great eagle in his aerie is frustrated. He spreads his wide wings and looks down and spies a dove. He swoops down after the dove, takes it to his aerie. Following sounds of "rustle-flustle, rustle-flustle," the contented bird floats away saying, "I'm a little dove and I just had some love."

But then the great titan of the skies gets frustrated again. He spreads his wings and looks down and this time he sees a lark. He swoops down after the lark and takes it back to the nest. Once again we hear sounds of "rustle-flustle, rustle-flustle." The happy lark wafts away saying, "I'm a little lark and I just had fun in the dark."

But after a while the mighty monarch of the mountains is frustrated again [note Rule of Three]. He spreads his wings, looks down to his left, then to his right—nothing in sight, except way down in a little rivulet he sees the glimmer of a duck. The eagle swoops down after the duck and takes it to the aerie. This time there is one cloud of commotion—dust, twigs, feathers, and finally a bedraggled creature falls out of the nest saying, "I'm just a little drake and there's been one awful mistake."

Aristotle once explained humor as "the pleasurable distortion of what is expected"—the familiar in an unfamiliar place. We are embarrassedly tense expecting to hear the four-letter rhyme to "duck," and then our fears are released in laughter.

What makes the sexual-situation story funny is that it is something of a taboo subject in polite conversation. It is not that the sexual organs or processes are inherently comic. Total nudity is not as sexy as a low neckline or a wisp of panties under a short skirt and so a story is more funny when the sexual connection is more implied than spelled out. You leave it to the audience's imagination to think of the missing dirty word or phrase.

Did you ever hear the giggles of a couple going through a tunnel of love? Stories with overtones of sex are like that. It is the invasion of a taboo area—the act of trespass—that triggers our comic sense.

Like sex, religion is another taboo subject in polite society. I once heard former Ambassador Robert Murphy tell about his meeting with Pope Pius XII in 1944 after the Allies had entered Rome. Murphy reminded the Pope that he had first met him as a junior foreign-service officer in Berlin in 1931 when Eugene Pacelli was Vatican secretary of state. Murphy recalled the papal secretary's prediction that the newly-installed Chancellor Hitler was only a passing phenomenon. "Ah," replied the Pope, "but that was before I was infallible."

It is almost skirting irreverence to treat the Pope as humanly prone to mistakes like the rest of us. Then our nervousness is released by the Pope's comeback.

Or take another story that our reader has no doubt heard, but its familiarity proves its success in stimulating our comic sense. It is about the bishop who liked to play golf. He loved the game. He carried his clubs around in the trunk of his car, ready to tee off at the first opportunity.

One spring he decided to give up playing golf during Lent. Everything was fine for the first week. But then one Sunday he was driving by a golf course on a beautiful day. He couldn't resist the temptation. He said to himself, "I think I'll just hit a few practice balls to keep my game in shape. It isn't really the same as playing, because I'll be by myself." So he parked his car and started playing on about the fourth hole. The next thing he knew he was going the whole route, playing by himself.

He didn't know it, but he was being observed. A little angel up in heaven was watching him. Finally the angel went to St. Peter and said, "St. Peter, look down there. There's the bishop. He's breaking his vow for Lent. He should be punished." St. Peter said, "You're right. We should teach him a lesson." And the angel said, "What do you want me to do? Strike him dead with lightning?" "No," said St. Peter. "I have a better idea. Watch me. I'll punish him."

At that moment the bishop was on the sixth tee. This was a 450-yard dog leg. The bishop took a mighty cut at the ball and away it went up, up, over the trees, straight for the pin. He did it! A hole in one! The little angel said to St. Peter, "Look at that. A 450-yard hole in one. Do you call that punishment?" "Yes," said St. Peter. "For a golfer that is the worst punishment possible. The bishop has just hit one of the greatest shots in golf history and he can't tell anybody about it."

A shorter ecclesiastic tale is the one about the Bishop of Durham. As the guest speaker he was invited to a black-tie banquet at the Savoy Hotel. Just as the soup was served the waitress slipped and spilled a tureen of pea soup over the bishop's belted cassock. In agony, the bishop cried out, "Will some layman please say something appropriate to the occasion?"

It is the very augustness of the bishop's position that provides the build-up of the comic situation. As Somerset Maugham once said, "Impropriety is the soul of wit." What is irreverent or impious can be the stuff of humor.

A cousin of the taboo joke is the "great man" anecdote. As I observed earlier, stories of the famous can be funnier than stories about unknown people. One reason is that we like to see the high and mighty brought down to the everyday level of the earthy situation.

Wit can be the one-liner, the squelch or repartee. (Even the lowly pun, which is word distortion for comic effect, is a form of wit.)

The poet Dryden wrote, "Wit will shine through the harsh cadence of a rugged line." Therefore, there has to be that imaginative intelligence in the punch line to puncture the balloon build-up. An example of the witty line is a famous editorial response in the New York *Sun*.

At the turn of the century many big-city newspapers competed for the most graphic and lurid stories. One such story by the *Sun* prompted the New York *Post* in an editorial to denounce its sister paper as an exponent of yellow-dog journalism. The next day the *Sun* replied in its editorial pages, "The *Post* has called the *Sun* a 'yellow dog.' The attitude of the *Sun*, however, will continue to be that of any dog toward any post."

The punch line is the bullet, but wit triggers that bullet. Build-up, bullet, burst is the way I explain humor. But if you misfire the bullet, you are going to have a dud of a joke.

A good example of botching the punch line was the telling of a story about Lyndon Johnson when he was senator from Texas. I had heard the anecdote before. It should go like this:

Johnson, soon after he came to the Senate in 1949, tried for a minor leadership position in the Democratic caucus. He announced to the press that he had a sizable number of pledged votes based on promises personally made to him by many of his colleagues. But when the vote was taken, Johnson emerged from the Senate Caucus Chamber with only a handful of votes. A reporter cornered Johnson and said, "Senator, can you explain your overwhelming defeat?"

"Son," said LBJ, "as senator from Texas I learned a very valuable lesson."

"What was that lesson, Senator?"

"The lesson was the difference between a cactus and a caucus."

"What's the difference, Senator?"

"Well," drawled Johnson, "in a cactus all the pricks are on the outside."

The problem with our would-be raconteur was that he had LBJ close the story saying, "In a *caucus* all the pricks are on the *inside.*" In telling a story you can omit a detail in the build-up and either catch up with it later or leave it out altogether without too much damage. But if you forget or fumble a punch line, you will get a weak smile instead of a hearty laugh.

What goes up must come down, and what is built up must be brought down by the bullet burst. A story without a pointed line is like an aria or a symphony without a climax. In both humor and music there should be development and crescendo.

It was Mozart who said, "You can't teach a man how to write a symphony," and another Austrian named Freud who said, "You can't teach a man how to write a joke."

Neither might find my simple humor structure description—build-in, build-up, bullet thrust—satisfying. But perhaps they would appreciate what geniuses in the discipline of art have said.

Marc Chagall was asked once his secret to art. He replied that he would take his painting outside and if it clashed with something of nature—a tree or a flower—it was not art.

Similarly, in speech humor, don't let your story clash with your speech. Humor should blend in with your talk—give it pointed emphasis and flavor. Don't tell a story just because it is funny—only if it fits. Build it in.

A remark of Renoir may tell us about the need of build-up in humor. Renoir said he would keep adding nuances and hues to a portrait until he felt he could actually pinch her bottom. So in a story develop your build-up so it is more believable and more ripe for a thrust.

Finally, Marcel Duchamp said about artistic insight, "Unless it jolts, it is not art." The bullet of a punch line should jolt. It should knock the build-up down, breaking into laughter.

2 The One-Liner

When everything else fails shoot yourself full of jokes.

—Joey Adams

As he lay dying in 1679, the Earl of Rochester expressed the hope that his only son might never be a wit. As the greatest wit of his time, he knew the pressures of supplying daily fresh humor. The Restoration court of King Charles is a far cry from the Washington of Jerry Ford, yet increasingly the humor writers of television are being pressed into moonlighting for presidents and senators. Nixon drafted one of the *Laugh-In* writers for humor help. And now Jerry Ford uses Bob Orben, who has made the art of drafting one-liners into a million-dollar business.

A Washington lobbyist once told me, "Humes, I can produce the winning margin in any Senate vote if I have access to two things —a live-in maid for the senator's wife and a guy who can do opening one-liners for his speeches back home." Television has made show business out of politics, and now every congressman wants to look like a Cavett. To do that he needs a constant supply of funny lines.

I heard one Democratic congressman wow a partisan audience with these opening gibes at President Ford:

"When I was a boy I was told anybody could become president. Now I'm beginning to believe it.

"Yes, Jerry Ford is a man who had greatness thrust upon him— and ducked.

"I understand that just after the pardon he had a secret popularity poll taken—and it always will be."

Or listen to how a Democratic senator put down President Nixon some months earlier:

13

"Some people laugh when Nixon compares his trials of office to that of President Lincoln. But I must confess when I think of Nixon, I think of Lincoln—especially his statement, 'you can't fool all the people all the time.'

"Really, though, I am not totally negative about the President. There are only two things about him I can't stand—his face.

"Well, he may be two-faced, but he's not blind. Dick Nixon is the type of man who cannot see a belt without unerringly hitting below it."

You see why politicians like this staccato humor approach. You can build this pattern into the beginning of any speech. Once a politician finds three or four lines he is comfortable with, he can tell them to a series of different audiences, polishing his delivery and timing in the process. (Usually they are not included in the prepared text for media release.)

Old-time politicians like LBJ and Everett Dirksen preferred the anecdote to the one-liner. But in the television age the raconteur is giving way to the guest personality. As one senator told me, "I like the one-liner better than the story because I want to look more like a wit than a windbag." So we have the spectacle today of performers talking like politicians and politicians talking like performers. It gets difficult to tell the difference between a Johnny Carson or a John Lindsay.

The problem, though, is that most speakers (and that includes politicians) don't have a $75,000 writer working for them. And even when they get the chance to appropriate such material, they come off looking like second-rate nightclub comics who fill in between songs at the local dive. The first thing is to recognize the difference between the one-liner and the bare-bones joke. A joke by my definition is a conversational exchange: the wife says, "What would it take for you to go on a second honeymoon?" and the husband replies, "A second wife."

The flavor of the one-liner is more like this: "Let's face it, men, you really need a wife. Think of all the things that you can't blame on the government."

Most successful one-liners have "upbeat" and "snapper" parts. The "upbeat" is the abbreviated "buildup," and the "snapper" is the witty punch line.

To give another example on the same topic: "I don't really mind my mother-in-law living with us—but she could have at least waited until we got married."

Of course "marriage," "mothers-in-law," "drunks," and "women drivers" are topics the amateur speaker should avoid in one-liners. The best one-liner subject for the speaker to make fun of is himself. This way if he is awkward, the audience will miss it in their sympathy for the good-natured guest who does not take himself too seriously. And this image is far more appealing than the smooth one-line artist who looks a bit smart-alecky ridiculing others. And there is yet another reason for making your one-line subject yourself. One-liners are basically opening warm-ups that follow the introduction (remember how Johnny Carson's opening pattern in the *Tonight* show always follows the introduction by Ed McMahon—"Here's Johnny!").

In a speech, your opening one-liners will follow your own introduction. So try to break the ice with a bit of modest self-deprecation:

"Thank you very much for the warm reception—which I so richly deserve and so seldom get.

"Seriously, Mr. Chairman, I want to say that I truly appreciate your introduction. I especially admire your way with words—the way you don't let yourself be inhibited by the facts.

"Actually, Mr. Chairman, I'll have to say that was the second-best introduction I ever received. The best was a few weeks ago when the program chairman arrived late and I had to introduce myself."

Another way to make fun of yourself is to make light of your position. I heard a corporate vice-president describe himself this way: "I thank the chairman for his introduction, but I don't think he quite spelled out what a vice-president means. That's the title given to a corporate officer instead of a raise.

"Really, though, there is some satisfaction in being a vice-president. One thing is you can take a two-hour lunch without hindering production.

"Actually, though, being a vice-president is a real challenge. Not everyone who finds a molehill at nine can make a mountain of it by five."

Another speaker I heard used as his takeoff place for humor his

recent position in Washington, which was mentioned in the introduction.

"Thank you for your generous introduction. It's always nice to
be described as a former high public official. That sounds better
than what I really was—just another bureaucrat but without tenure.

"The chairman was also kind enough not to dwell on some of the
details of my sudden departure. But I'll tell you one thing: my brief
stint in government was actually like being a mushroom. They
kept me in the dark, they piled on a lot of crap, and then they had
me canned.

"I did, however, learn in Washington what the initials 'D. C.'
stand for: Darkness and Confusion."

Whether it's being fired from a job, losing an election or getting
panned in a review, the best one-liners make fun of the deliverer.
John Tower, the diminutive senator from Texas, talks about his
size, while Joe Garagiola, the former baseball catcher, kids about
his hair, his hitting, and the lack in either department. Sometimes
a speaker, particularly when he is the guest of honor at a testimonial dinner or a retirement ceremony, will refer to his age.

"Really, though, I am very happy to be here tonight. In fact, at
my age I'm happy to be anywhere.

"Actually, being sixty-five isn't so bad. As a matter of fact I rather
like being called a sexagenarian. At this time of life it sounds like
flattery.

"Seriously, though, being of retirement age has its advantages.
I understand from recent statistics that for every sixty-five-year-
old man there are three available women. The problem is by that
time it's too late."

As you read these one-liners you must be aware of their rhythm
—the straight sentence or two that is the upbeat, followed by the
snapper sentence that pulls it down. The one-liner is like riding on
a roller-coaster: you rise on the upbeat and fall on the snapper.

You might think I have an adverb problem. Did you notice how
many times I start with "really," "actually," or "seriously"? Bob
Hope, the old master of the one-liner, does the same thing—"but
seriously, folks . . ." By saying "seriously," Hope is trying to get his
upbeat sentence accepted as straight. The more the audience

believes his opening sentence is sincere, the more they are likely to laugh at the snapper line.

"Seriously, there are some great advantages in being sixty-five. One is that you are no longer bothered by insurance agents."

By beginning with the word "seriously" you have the audience half convinced you are about to wax philosophical on the benefits of old age. Then you deliver the funny snapper.

Whether you decide to make fun of your age, your weight or your golf score, stick to one topic. Don't jump from one to another. Even the professional comics, with the exception of Henny Youngman,* don't try the scatter-hit approach. Stick to the subject and let one joke segue into another until you have a package of two, three, or four.

A few months ago I was in Las Vegas for a convention, and I heard one of the top comics deliver this set of one-liners on the hotel accommodations:

"I can tell you I was in one of those very, very exclusive hotels. Even room service seems to have an unlisted number.

"No, really, I can't complain. The management went to great trouble to get me an air-conditioned room. I know—I was there when the bellboy pried open the windows.

"But seriously, did you ever stop to think how people want home atmosphere in a hotel and hotel service in a home?

"Yes, they even go and put Bibles in the hotel rooms. Of course, by that stage it usually is too late.

"Well, at least some of us will go out and get gifts for our wives when we return home from the convention. Others, of course, will have no reason to feel guilty."

When I was a speech writer in the White House I once had to submit a few sets of one-liners for President Nixon for delivery at a Gridiron dinner. I found it far more difficult than writing a eulogy for a former President.

Still, I developed my own system which you may find helpful. I don't say it will make you a polished comedy writer, but it will tell you where to mine the ore before it is refined.

The system is TOPICALISM. Topicalism is what a one-liner is—a

---

*Youngman likes the zany effect of mixing all his topics together. He depends on the very force of his delivery to carry the day.

subject for one-linemanship that is current and topical. I use it to trigger free thinking.

> T—television
> O—organization (host)
> P—politics
> I—international
> C—crazes
> A—advertisements
> L—literature (best sellers)
> I—introducer (program chairman)
> S—songs
> M—movies

Let's say I am to write one-liners for President Ford. He is to appear at Pinehurst, North Carolina, for one of those big golf classics. All-right golf or, rather, the president's golf game has to be the topicalism. So I first write on one side of the page all the words associated with golf. And on the other side I set down T-O-P-I-C-A-L-I-S-M.

GOLF	TOPICALISM
par	Television—*Marcus Welby, All in the Family*
bogey	Organization
ace	Politics—Watergate, pardon, plea-bargaining
eagle	International—oil, energy, Arabs
duffer	Crazes—streaking
stroke	Advertisements—"I can't believe I ate the
hole-in-one	whole thing"
irons	Literature—*Watership Down, Centennial*
woods	Introducer
sand trap	Songs—"Tie a Yellow Ribbon Round the Old Oak
putter	Tree"
handicap	Movies—*The Sting, The Godfather*
— bunker	
slice	
green	
hook	

Besides each category of T-O-P-I-C-A-L-I-S-M I wrote the first thing I thought of. If you can think of the title, program, issue, or fad quickly, that means it is likely to trigger some public awareness or identification.

Let's skip for a minute the organization that is host. I don't know whether it's Pinehurst or the PGA. Sometimes the host organization, be it Elks or firemen, is good material. Let's also not make up the name of the event chairman who will have to introduce President Ford, although names can be fun to work with too.

Now let's see what we can dig up when we look for associations with golf in the current headlines of the day.

Under "Television" *All in the Family* rings a bell. Archie Bunker—"bunker" is a golf word. In fact, maybe I could use "Archless" (skidding drive?) bunker some way.

"Politics"—Watergate? It sounds like a word you might be able to associate with golf.

"International"—oil, energy, Arabs, desert. I think of sand trap —American trapped by the Middle East situation. There must be some way to tie them together.

"Crazes"—streaking. Nothing comes immediately to mind.

"Advertisements." The only one I can think of with universal acceptance is "I can't believe I ate the whole thing." Is there some way to change that to read "I can't believe I 'aced' the whole thing"?

"Literature." What best sellers come to mind? *Centennial, Watership Down.* It could be a buried golfball, but is it too high-brow for the audience?

"Songs"—"Tie a Yellow Ribbon Round the Old Oak Tree." That's a natural. There must be some way to use the song to make fun of a Ford hook to the woods.

"Movies"—*The Sting, The Godfather.* How about *Sodfather* to describe Jerry's divoting habit? (Playing around with letters is part of the game in crafting one-liners. Many times I go right through the alphabet: *Bodfather, Codfather,* etc.)

Then when you start putting down some of the ideas, you look through the golf words again.

irons in the fire?
bald eagle
duffer (buffer) zone
can't see the woods for the trees
sand trap—we already have something to work in about the
    Middle East
handicap—"hire the handicapped"

bunker—we have that idea
slice—what about "slice guys finish last"?
hook—"you can't judge a hook by a duffer"—no, too corny.

Now you go back and gather your more promising leads. Work them into your upbeat and snapper parts. Then rewrite them until they sound crisp and sharp. Here's what I would have President Ford say:

"After all the controversy about the pardon, it is a pleasure to come down here and relax in North Carolina. You know, golf with all its subtleties—the necessary strategies, the need for finesse— is much like politics. The difference is that while the golfer strives for a hole-in-one, I'm just trying to get out of a hole.

"As you know, I did manage to get away from some of the world problems today and put in a few hours on the course. But on the fifth hole while I ran into a little trouble in a bunker, one of my aides came up to me and said that Secretary Kissinger was on the line for instructions. Henry was negotiating in the Middle East somewhere in the middle of the Saudi desert, trying to find a way out of the oil problems there. I got on the line and said, 'Henry, don't give me your problems. I'm in the middle of a sand trap, too.'

"Seriously, it is good to be back here in Pinehurst. It's been four years since I was last here. I remember it well, because on the sixth hole I had a drive there lost in the woods. Even though it has been four years the staff seems to remember my visit very well. But I didn't know how well till I got to the sixth hole and the gallery crowd began welcoming me with a song—'Tie a Yellow Ribbon Round the Old Oak Tree.'

"You have to admit that wasn't the type of message that would restore confidence in my driving game. So at the end of the day, with the score I had, I was looking for a bit of encouragement, and I'll never forget what Arnie Palmer told me. He put his arm around me and said, 'Mr. President, one thing you always got to remember—"Slice guys finish last." ' "

You will note that some of the possibilities—"Archless Bunker," "Codman"—I scratched in my final draft. Remember, all you have to do is have three or four of the best.

Perhaps as you read the lines in cold print you may not find it all that hilarious. But it would work. When the President of the

United States makes fun of himself he has to get a good response. Just consider that as the main speaker or central attraction at a dinner you will have some of the same star appeal going for you too. Secondly, when you stick to a single topic like golf you have the advantage of each successive one-liner drawing from the success of the previous. In the first sally you start to build the impression in the audience's mind of the President as a duffer golfer. If you were then to jump to another subject you would waste the momentum you have built up. But with a series of one-liners you have the audience better conditioned to react and laugh.

Remember that after one dip in the roller-coaster track you don't stop, get out, and buy another ticket for a different car ride. So keep to a single track. If you do this, you won't crash and you'll provide lots of fun.

Or to change the metaphor, I don't say that the TOPICALISM technique in developing one-liners will always get you a hole-in-one. But it *will* help get you out of a hole.

3 The Toast-Spreader

I drink to the general joy of the whole table.
—Shakespeare, *Macbeth*

Woodrow Wilson was once asked how much time he would need to prepare for an hour speech. He answered, "Five minutes." "Then," said the questioner, "you could give a short five-minute speech right off the top of your head." "No," said Wilson. "For a five-minute speech I need one hour."

What Wilson meant was that in an hour's time you can sometimes let yourself collect your thoughts as you go. But if you are going to have to compress all your thoughts into five minutes, that takes much longer preparation. I don't know if Wilson was right about planning for a long speech, but he was right in stressing at least some groundwork for brief remarks. Over the years I have heard many leaders give dull and plodding speeches. However mediocre the speech, they did not look foolish. Yet I have watched many a top executive look high-schoolish giving an introduction, delivering a toast, or awarding a plaque.

The humorous story is a good way to handle such a situation with poise and style. At one wedding I heard a venerable businessman who was great-uncle to the bride raise his glass with these words:

"When I look at this happy couple, radiant with love and excited by the promise of the future, I first think back to my own youth and then I think of the comment Bernard Baruch made on his ninety-fifth birthday to a caller. The caller asked, 'Bernie, do you think there's as much love in the world today as there was years back?' 'Yes' was the reply, 'but there's another bunch doing it.' "

How much better was this story than some trite remarks about young love from a man whose acquaintance with his niece was not all that close. As the most distinguished man at the wedding he was expected to say something—and he did it well through humor.

In my book *Instant Eloquence* I talk about how people tend to foul up introductions. An introduction should be a prologue; instead it often winds up a catalogue of statistics. ("Our speaker was born in 1934. He attended . . .") It is no great distinction to go to college, marry, have children—and have a job. My suggestion is to tell an anecdote about the speaker's life:

Ladies and gentlemen, I could spend most of the allotted time for the speech talking about our speaker's enviable academic background and record in community endeavors. However, I would rather tell you about the time I first met him because I think it shows what a great man he is to work with—his ability to think quickly as well as compassionately.

Of course, many times you don't know a humorous anecdote or, for that matter, any sort of personal vignette about the speaker. In this situation a story I have often used to introduce a speaker with impressive credentials is this:

"The many and varied talents of our speaker are well known to all of us. Brilliantly educated, he rose to the top of his profession. He is as charming as he is distinguished. His many assets remind me of an eligible young man for whom a smitten young lady was trying to buy a gift.

"In desperation she consulted her mother, who said, 'How about a record?' 'No, he has a hi-fi stereo with a library of thousands of records. I wouldn't know what to buy.' 'What about a box of cigars?' 'No, he has a whole humidor case of fine prewar Havanas.' 'What about wine?' 'No, Mother. He has his own wine cellar full of rare French wine vintages as well as expensive cognac. The question is, Mother, what do you give a man who has everything?' Her mother replied, 'Encouragement.' "

Another good introduction story is this:

Our speaker today is qualified by both background and experience. In no way is he like the son of an acquaintance of mine. This boy managed to get up sufficient courage to show his report card to his father and ask for his signature. When his father saw the grades, four D's and an F, he berated his son for such a poor record. When the reprimand was over the son asked his father, "Dad, do you think it is because of heredity or environment?"

Well, in our speaker's case, he not only comes from a distinguished family, but he has added laurels of his own to that ancestral tree.

Or, if you want to introduce a woman speaker, here is a way to lead off your introduction:

The woman we introduce tonight is successful in her own right. She is not the kind of wife Mrs. Oliver Wendell Holmes made that wonderful line about. You might remember it was at a White House dinner party shortly after her husband was appointed to the Supreme Court. President Theodore Roosevelt asked, "Mrs. Holmes, do you find the Washington ladies pleasant?" "Washington," Mrs. Holmes replied, "is full of successful men and the women they married before they were successful."

The advantage of the humorous story is that you can turn a prosaic task into a fun occasion. All you need is some time beforehand to figure out which of your best stories can be tailored into an introductory send-off.

As a speech writer at the White House I had to draft a lot of what we called the "Rose Garden Rubbish." That's when the President comes out of the Oval Office into the garden opposite to deliver some informal remarks to a gathering of assembled guests. On Monday it's the poster girl of the Crippled Children Society. Tuesday it may be the introduction of a new cabinet officer and Wednesday some U. S. Chamber of Commerce officials.

Once after I left the White House I was asked on a New York talk show by Jim Brady, "Jamie, isn't it true that you didn't really draft the really tough speeches—you did a lot of the ceremonial stuff?"

"Jim," I said in mocking tones, "I resent that. It doesn't take much brains to rewrite a draft by Henry Kissinger on foreign policy, but just you try to write a thirty-minute speech dedicating the Lady Bird Johnson Forest on the occasion of LBJ's wedding anniversary. In fact," I continued, "I liked it when the President called me his 'Schmaltz King.' "

Of course, it is not easy to come up with something new and different each year about the March of Dimes or the League of Women Voters. But I developed a formula to explore all the aspects of an occasion and to see which one would lend itself to a fascinating short presentation. The formula was PITCH.

P—purpose of the occasion
I—institution involved
T—time (what was happening the year it started)
C—city involved
H—hero (founder or great man associated with the institution)

I took the word from a ride I had once during a Presidential campaign through Pennsylvania in 1956. The speech writers for the Presidential candidate in preparing remarks for each whistle-stop delivery at the back of the train would say, "Well, what's the pitch on Altoona?" Meaning, what's its history, its industry, its background, and its famous people.

In one of John D. MacDonald's Travis McGee books, Travis's friend Meyer says that the artist in looking at a scene faces the problem of where to frame it. PITCH puts you in the position of the artist. It allows you to walk around the ceremonial setting and see which angle is best for portrayal. So let's see if we can also use the PITCH method when we want to have an opening bit of humor as our launch for a few remarks.

For "purpose of the occasion" let's try a Churchill story as a way to start off a ribbon-cutting occasion.

When people asked me what was the real purpose behind the tradition, I like to recall what Winston Churchill said to an official of the Women's Christian Temperance Union in Britain. The woman protested to Churchill, who was then First Lord of the Admiralty, saying, "Mr. Churchill, the practice of christening ships with champagne is a horrid example for temperance. We demand you discontinue this practice." Replied Churchill, "Madam, I think the Royal Navy's hallowed custom of christening ships is a splendid example of temperance. The ship takes its first sip of wine and then proceeds on water ever after." And similarly I think cutting a ribbon is a splendid symbol. It, in effect, signifies the last bit of cutting through red tape.

"Institution" is the second aspect of the formula—one way to talk about the value of an organization or association. If you are going to talk about what the Kiwanis Club means to the community you could begin this way:

When I think of your organization certain things automatically come to mind. It's like an association test a codgy old Church of

England dean once gave to a young man who was hoping to win a church-endowed scholarship to Oxford. The dean was known as a strict teetotaler and he started off with the word "Gordon," hoping to trick the wayward lad into making the wrong association —like what rhymes with sin and goes with tonic. "What does Gordon make you think of, young man?" The young applicant replied, "Gordon. I think of General Gordon, the hero of Khartoum, the great colonial statesman in the Sudan."

And the dean next said, "Haig, Haig. What does that remind you of?" "Lord Haig," the young man replied. "Earl Haig, the distinguished marshal and commander of the Allies in World War I."

Then the dean, making one last attempt to catch the student, pulled a sly one. "Vat 69. Vat 69. What does that make you think of?" The student thought for a moment and said, "Vat 69. Isn't that the Pope's telephone number?"

Well, there's no ambiguity about what the name Kiwanis means. It has always meant service—service to the community by concerned citizens for all walks of life, all professions and trades.

"Time" is the next dimensional angle in our formula:

As we gather here today I see among our many friends some of the founders of the multiple sclerosis chapter twenty-five years ago. Somehow my thoughts remind me of something my wife said a few weeks ago on my son's thirtieth birthday. My wife woke up at three A.M., called our boy on the phone and asked him how he felt, and then wished him a happy birthday. He said, "Gee, Mom, is there anything wrong?" and she said, "Why, no. Its your thirtieth birthday, so I thought I'd call you."

And he said, "Good grief, Mom, you didn't drag me out of bed at three o'clock in the morning just to wish me happy birthday, did you?" And she said, "Well, thirty years ago tonight you made me get up at three A.M. and now I'm paying you back."

And in a reverse sense I wish we could really pay back those who, twenty-five years ago, gave so much of themselves in establishing. . . .

I put "city" in my formula because at the White House Rose Garden presentations the city, state or region involved was often fertile background for vignettes or stories. The reader who speaks frequently will have to travel to some city to make ceremonial remarks.

At a Little League dinner (I was one of the first players as a boy in my home town of Williamsport) I once heard a speaker from New York allude to Williamsport's fame as the birthplace of Little League baseball this way:

"As I drove in from New York today I had the car radio on, tuned in to one of those radio shows that give prizes to those who answer the phone and answer the question right. As I was listening, one housewife answered the phone and then answered the question correctly. 'You've won,' said the MC, 'and your prize is three days' expenses paid at the glamorous Waldorf Astoria Hotel in New York City.'

" 'Oh, no,' she said. 'I couldn't go *there.*' 'Why?' he asked. 'Because I was there on my honeymoon.' 'But that's wonderful' he said. 'You can have a second honeymoon!' 'No, you don't understand. Nine months exactly to the last time I was there I had triplets.'

"Similarly Williamsport is where it all started for the Little League. They may not have had triplets—just thirty countries around the world that play Little League baseball."

"Hero" is the final facet of the occasion worth focusing on. It may be Baden-Powell of the Boy Scouts or John Paul Jones of the U. S. Navy. But if it's a local hero you may not know an anecdote about, you can try humor as a way to begin extolling the local founder or benefactor. I once heard a tribute to a retiring chairman of a hospital board beginning with this story:

"Although he is retiring as chairman today, I think you will all agree that we won't let him leave our hearts. He has been much too important to us. It's like the time I overheard two young models talking about a wealthy bachelor. 'He's rich, I know,' said the first girl, 'but he's too old to be eligible.' 'No, he isn't,' her friend said. 'I think he's too eligible to be old.'

"And so we may add that our friend is far too valuable to let him cease taking an interest. . . ."

As Cervantes' Don Quixote says, "Forewarned and forearmed" —to be prepared is half the battle. So when you think there is a chance you might be called on to speak, be thinking of a personal story or anecdote as a base for some short remarks.

If you are at a formal dinner a toast to the hostess or guest of honor is always appreciated—especially if it is brief and entertaining. I once had to be host at the American ambassadorial residence in Vienna for a small dinner for a German prince and his wife. Because we had never met, I knew the dinner might not be that relaxed. Yet I knew that his Old World manners would require him to rise with a formal toast. I was ready. The only real fact I had learned about him was that he had a castled estate and game reserve where he bred, among other things, stags. In response to the toast I made an entertaining allusion comparing the guest and his wife and their respective qualities to the native deer strain of Austria. The guest was so impressed with my knowledge of Austrian game (I had spent half an hour looking in the encyclopedia) that he asked me if I would go to Peking to negotiate the trade of a panda bear for a rare extinct herd of Milu deer that he had on his estate.

Not long ago I was seated at the head table at a function in Frankfort, Kentucky. Since I was there as a consultant to the Appalachian Regional Commission, I thought I might be called on to say a few words when introduced by the toastmaster. I had this story ready:

"While I am not a Kentucky mountaineer, or even a Southerner by background, I like to think that I am picking up some of the spirit of Kentucky. It reminds me of what Prince Philip once told me at a reception at Buckingham Palace. As an American schoolboy there I was invited to a special affair arranged by the English-Speaking Union. Having Scottish forebears, I thought it appropriate when greeting the Duke of Edinburgh to wear a Hume plaid tie. Prince Philip looked at the tie and said, 'Why do all you Americans like to proclaim your Scotch background?' Remembering what my schoolteacher mother always told me about the word 'Scotch,' I said, 'Sir, as you know, Scotch is the liquid but I am Scottish in background.' 'Young man,' replied the Duke, 'I rather think you're right but I venture to say more Scotch flows in American veins than Scottish.'

"And tonight I can say that there are many who have the spirit of Kentucky in their veins."

If you are ever going to be the honoree at a birthday affair, retirement occasion, or testimonial dinner, you might cut through the cloying sweetness with this wit from Mark Twain:

"As I look out at this motley group that has come here tonight to share the rather dubious distinction of having some association with me and my work, I can only think of the story attributed to Mark Twain. After his last controversial novel, which had bleak agnostic tones, a reporter approached him. 'Mr. Clemens, you are a man who has thought much upon all topics. I wish to ask you for your idea of Heaven and Hell.' Gazing at the earnest questioner, the man known as Mark Twain answered, 'When I think of the beauteous descriptions of the abode of saints, and when I recollect that many noble, witty and genial souls have died "unregenerate," I must answer you that while doubtless Heaven has the best climate, Hell has the best society.' "

4   The Speech-Starter

Laughter is not at all a bad beginning for a friendship.

—Oscar Wilde

In Miami Beach they tell of two middle-aged acquaintances who unexpectedly run into each other at a sea front cabana. The first asks, "Why are you here? I thought you still had that clothing store in the Bronx." "I did," replied the other. "But I had an awful tragedy—a fire. It gutted the place. I took my $70,000 insurance and decided to come south and retire. And why are you here?" he countered. "Didn't you have a clothing shop too?" "Yes, but, like yourself, I had a terrible misfortune in my Brooklyn store—a flood. It ruined everything. I cashed in my insurance—$150,000 worth —and, like you, decided to retire."

There was a significant pause. Then the first man asked the Brooklyn proprietor, "Tell me—how would you ever start a flood?"

Similarly, many people don't know how to start a speech. They would agree with Aristotle that "to be able to start is more than half the whole." If they can just break the ice, the rest will be easy sailing. Some feel they need humor like a drink before dinner. They think a story relaxes the audience as well as the speaker. No good speaker likes to approach the audience like a classroom. He wants to have a talk with the audience, not lecture down to them.

Horace Greeley once approached the campus of Philadelphia's Girard College, whose eccentric founder, Stephen Girard, had stipulated in a will that no clergyman be allowed to enter. The college guard, seeing Greeley in a somewhat clerical-looking garb, challenged him, calling out, "Hey, you can't enter here!" "The hell I can't," replied Greeley. "I beg your pardon, sir," said the guard. "Pass right in."

In the same way a speaker doesn't want an audience on guard. He wants to be accepted as a friend. Once the speaker has the audience in a friendly and relaxed mood he can deliver his message. Not only is the speaker an authority but a friend you can trust. If a doctor should have bedside manners, so should a speaker have a platform manner. One way to do that is to make some light fun of yourself with three or four one-liners, as I mentioned in Chapter 2. An easier route is the anecdote that shows you don't take yourself too seriously. A story poking fun at your title or position not only makes a good antidote to the introduction but a good anecdote as well. I once heard a distinguished general tell this story on himself:

"I thank the chairman for his generous introduction. But sometimes I would rather have someone remind me of my flaws, because people who have great-sounding titles frequently begin to believe in their own infallibility. I remember a time on a Texas base we were in a staff conference when a major entered the room and approached the front row where two other generals and I were sitting and said, 'Gentlemen, I found this gold mechanical pencil yesterday in the briefing room. I believe it belongs to one of you.' 'Yes,' I said. 'That's mine.' But then I asked, 'But I am curious. What made you so certain it belonged to one of us generals? Was it because it's gold?' 'No,' replied the major. 'It was because the pencil had an eraser that had never been used.' "

In a hospital drive I worked on, a public-relations consultant brought in from New York for the campaign opened the kickoff dinner this way:

"In the introduction you have painted a very expanded impression of what a consultant does. A better definition was made by a neighbor of mine in Scarsdale whose family pet was a very vocal tomcat. Every evening our block was accustomed to hearing his cat give oral evidence that he was indeed the cat's meow. But one day on the morning train to New York I saw my neighbor and I happened to think that his cat had been noticeably quiet lately. I went over to him and said, 'I haven't heard that tomcat of yours lately.' 'Well,' he said, 'I took the hints of friends like you and had him altered.' 'Oh, I bet he spends his nights now on the hearth before the fire getting fat.' 'No,' he said, 'he still goes out. But like you he now goes along as a consultant.' "

A successful author once opened his talk at a book luncheon with this story:

"I thank the chairman for his kind introduction. I only wish he could release a text of that to my home-town weekly newspaper. I left Iowa right after high school. But some time after my first book, which made the best-seller list, I went back without fanfare to the town. At the small railroad stop I engaged the old ticket agent in conversation without revealing my name. 'Hey, isn't this town where that author comes from?' 'Yep,' he replied. 'I understand he got a big award from some guild.' 'Yep.' 'And what do people say about it?'

" 'They don't say anything' was the reply. 'They just laugh.' "

Once the audience sees you can laugh at yourself you have their hearts. And once you have won their hearts, the winning of their minds is easy. Just ask any girl or boy in love.

I heard a psychologist address a group of college girls on marriage. He said girls in love should observe "the banana-peel test" before marrying the man of their dreams. If the fiancé could slip on a banana peel in front of her friends or family and come up laughing at himself, he would pass with flying colors. His point was that it was not hard to find successful men or potentially successful men who are accomplished in business, law, or medicine. But it is more difficult to find a successful man who doesn't take himself all that seriously and who laughs at his own misadventures.

More than once I have heard a speaker open a speech by telling of a logistical slip-up like the following:

First of all, I want to thank all of you for the nice welcome you gave me when I arrived at the airport. It was certainly better than the experience I had in another city, better left unnamed. The members of the arrangements committee had a motorcade ready to meet me at the airport and escort me to the hotel with great fanfare. But there was a mix-up. I arrived by an earlier plane and the motorcade wasn't there. After completing my address that evening I was approached by the program chairman.

"Sir," said the chairman, "we're powerful sorry that we didn't have the opportunity to escort you into the city but we'll take great pleasure in escorting you out of it."

When a last-minute change in the arrangements have made me a substitute speaker I have occasionally told this story:

"As you know I am a substitute speaker tonight. The role of being a substitute is not always an easy one. I recall a time a few years ago when I was a state legislator and was asked to fill in for Senator Hugh Scott, who was being detained in Washington for an important vote. I felt obliged to tell the audience after the introduction that I was actually a 'substitute' in the true sense of the word—at least according to my sixth-grade teacher, who lectured to our class on the difference between 'replacement' and 'substitute.' As she explained in her example, 'If when a window is broken you put in cardboard, it is a substitute, but if you put in another "pane," it is a replacement.' And so I said, 'As a state representative I am only a substitute for a U. S. senator.' With that modest disclaimer I went on to give what I thought was a good speech. Afterward the program chairman came up, a gushing lady who said, 'Oh, Mr. Humes, you weren't a substitute—you were a real pane.' "

Former Senator Kenneth Keating often uses this story about program arrangements to open a speech:

"I must thank the chairman for the arrangements he has made to make my stay as smooth as possible. You see sometimes one can be a little unclear as to what exactly your role is supposed to be. I recall last May I had an invitation to speak at a Memorial Day celebration. The program chairman in his letter of invitation had these words of counsel: 'Don't speak for more than twenty minutes or you'll run into the shooting by the honor guard.' "

Another way to poke fun at yourself is to refer to your place in the program. Back in 1910 Governor Al Smith of New York was attending a Democratic conference in New York City. A succession of speakers went over the substantive problems of the day, and finally Al, who was the last speaker, found it was his turn. Al said, "I find that everything I was going to say has been pretty well covered. That's the handicap of being the last speaker—but after all you can't be the first in everything. Even George Washington, who was first in war and first in peace, married a widow."

Once when I was appearing in a panel presentation the first of the speakers introduced his talk with this story:

"My spot in the program tonight reminds me of a letter a young friend of mine recently wrote to a television station. This station in my city had a contest inviting youngsters to write why they enjoyed the show. One honest lad who should have won the fifty-dollar prize—but didn't—wrote, 'The reason I like your show is because as soon as it's over a better one comes on.' "

Even if you don't have any experts following you on the program you may have some people in the audience who know more about the subject than you do:

"As I look out into the audience and see many experts in the field about which I am going to talk, I can't help but feel a little nervous. In that sense I feel a bit like the old man I once heard about whose proudest experience was that he was one of the few to survive the famous Johnstown flood. Now except for his harmless compulsion to tell any listener his tale, he was a good sort and eventually, when he died, he found his way to heaven.

"St. Peter, after an interview with him, said, 'Your papers are in order, so we welcome you and we want to ask you if you have any particular request.' 'Yes, I'd like to tell some people about my experiences surviving that Pennsylvania flood in 1889.' 'We'll see,' said St. Peter. After a while he returned and said, 'We have it arranged. You are expected to speak on Cloud C this afternoon.' 'That's wonderful,' said the Johnstowner. 'But just one thing,' said St. Peter. 'I just want to warn you that also in the audience will be Noah.' "

It may be uncomfortable to speak to a group that has many experts in its ranks. But it is downright embarrassing to address an organization that has taken some public positions hostile to your point of view. One speaker took this tack:

"I thank the chairman for the kind things he said about my qualifications and abilities. But even with those supposed abilities I am a little hesitant to speak on a subject on which your organization has such positive views. I feel like a man back in my home town. He was a large and husky guy looking for work. He approached the bartender and said, 'I see by the sign in your window that you're looking for a bouncer. Has the job been filled yet?' 'Not yet,' said the bartender. 'Have you any experience?' 'No,' the man admitted, 'but watch this.' He walked over to a loudmouth at the back of the room—obviously drunk—lifted him off his feet, and sent him sprawling out of the bar onto the street. Then, returning to the bar, he said, 'How's that?' 'Great,' admitted the bartender, 'but you'll have to ask the boss about the job. I only work here.'

'Fine,' said the man. 'Where is he?' The bartender replied, 'Just coming back in the front door.' "

When you are going to speak on a sensitive subject, it may help to have an ice-breaker to relieve some possible audience tension. The following is a story I have often opened with in such a situation:

"I don't mind telling you that I was advised not to make a speech on a subject that was too controversial. That type of prohibition reminds me of a remark a chairman of hospitality once made to a friend of mine, a former district attorney who had assumed leadership of a citizen effort to crack down on the numbers, narcotics, and prostitution rackets. At a reception before the dinner speech the hostess said to my friend, 'I suppose I mustn't offer you anything to drink since you are head of the Anti-temperance League.' 'Oh no,' said my friend. 'I'm chairman of the Anti-vice League.' 'Oh,' said the flustered hostess, 'I knew there was something I shouldn't offer you.'

"And I suppose this might be a subject I shouldn't offer you, but. . . ."

Sometimes the sensitive topic you are going to speak on is so euphemistically labeled as to be misleading. A friend of mine who is a doctor once had to speak on contraceptive techniques and found his speech had been billed as "Family Counseling." He opened his remarks with this story:

"As I arrived for tonight's speech, I looked at the board and saw the poster announcing the topic 'Family Counseling.' At the moment I had a doubt whether I had the right place. I'm a doctor, not a psychologist. Sometimes I think it is perhaps better even in a sensitive subject to say right out what you are going to talk about —even if it is a subject like contraception.

"I recall that a minister friend of mine was asked to speak at the Rotary Club on marital sex, but when he was asked by his wife about his speech that night he just mumbled the first thing that came into his head—yachting. Afterward, on the street, a neighbor came up to his wife and said how much they all liked the speech. 'Really,' she said. 'I'm somewhat surprised. There are only three times he tried it. Once he got sick and the other times his hat blew off.' "

If humor is a good relaxer of tensions when you have to speak on a sensitive subject of such a personal nature, it is almost a requisite when you have the job of delivering bad news. A corporate president once cushioned the shock of a bad financial report by this story:

"Gentlemen, as I begin reading our report, I would like to assure you that I included the bad as well as the good news. I don't agree with the rationale of a scientist who had been unjustly accused and convicted of some major crime and found himself imprisoned with a long-term sentence in a jail in the midst of the desert. His cellmate turned out to be another scientist. Determined to escape, the first man tried to convince his co-professional to make the attempt with him, but the man refused. After much planning, and with the undetected help of other inmates, our scientist made his escape. But finally the heat of the desert and the lack of food and water made him turn around and return to the jail. He reported his terrible experience to the other scientist, who surprised him by saying, 'Yes, I know. I tried it and failed, too, for the same reasons.' The first scientist responded bitterly, 'For heaven's sake, man, when you knew I was going to make a break for it, why didn't you tell me what it was like out there?' To which his cellmate replied, with a shrug of the shoulders, 'Who publishes negative results?' "

In a similar situation a restless group of stockholders came to hear a president who, according to speculation, was going to announce another year of no dividends:

"Ladies and gentlemen, I am sure you have heard some of the rumors about proposed dividends. The bad news is that they are true; the good news is that we have put ourselves in a strong position for next year. On that development I'll be here to answer questions as soon as I finish the financial report. But whatever your disappointment, I think you'll agree that at least we are in a better position than a company that recently held its annual meeting. The president, in the middle of his address, saw his secretary frantically signaling to him. When he tried to wave her off she said in a loud whisper, 'It's a long-distance call from Brazil. The treasurer wants to give the financial report.' "

Whether it is a bad financial report, lack of funds, or a poor public-relations image, many speeches have to begin by recognizing the problem. As Confucius once said, "I would begin by defining the problem." One story that leads into the assessment of current difficulties is this:

There comes a time when we all must make a careful audit of our situation. It reminds me of the first marital spat. Even Adam had his problems with Eve, as we know. But one of the disputes you might not have heard about was Adam's habit of going out at night. Eve was a little concerned about his "berry-picking" jaunts. "Adam, do you have to stay out late every night?" "Eve," replied Adam, "you know that's silly. Why, you're the only girl for me; in fact, you're the only girl in the world." That night when Adam fell asleep he woke suddenly when he felt a poke in his stomach. "Eve," he said, "what is it you're doing to me?" "Just counting your ribs."

The astronaut Michael Collins, when he was assistant secretary of state, used to begin his talk by getting people to be more aware of U. S. foreign-policy development with this story:

"The biggest part of our problem is getting people to recognize the situation and care about being involved. I recall the case of the young mother with a very unruly son—so unruly that she found him just about impossible to control. On the advice of her friends she took him to a psychologist, who said, 'Yes, madam, you do indeed have a problem with that child. But at the moment I am far more concerned with you. You are terribly upset and I want you to take these tranquilizers. Bring the boy back again next week.' When the mother appeared the following week the psychologist said, 'Now, tell me, has the boy improved any the past week?'—to which the mother replied, 'Who cares?' "

My own favorite all-purpose anecdote for beginning any speech is this:

America today is like the story of the late Supreme Court Justice Oliver Wendell Holmes, who once found himself on a train, but couldn't locate his ticket. While the conductor watched, smiling, the eighty-eight-year-old Justice Holmes searched through all his pockets without success. Of course, the conductor recognized the distinguished justice. So he said, "Mr. Holmes, don't worry. You don't need your ticket. You will probably find it when you get off the train and I'm sure the Pennsylvania Railroad will trust you to mail it back later." The justice looked up at the conductor with some irritation and said, "My dear man, that is not the problem at all. The problem is not where my ticket is. The problem is, where am I going?"

5 The Point-Maker

Wit is a sword; it is meant to make people feel
the point as well as see it.
                              —G. K. Chesterton

When I was in the Pennsylvania Legislature I was once appointed by Governor Scranton to the Pennsylvania Shakespeare Quadricentennial Commission. Now while I appreciated having the chance of serving with such notables as Andrew Wyeth and Conrad Richter, the appointment was not quite the great-help-to-re-election-chances in 1964 I expected for loyally supporting the governor's tax program. So in accepting the formal commission I wrote, "Will your Grace command me any service to the world's end? I will go on the slightest errand now to the Antipodes that you can devise to send me on. I will fetch you a toothpicker now from the furthest inch of Asia; bring you the length of Prester John's foot; fetch you a hair off the great Cham's beard; do you any embassage to the Pigmies." Signed, James C. Humes.

It must have taken a while for one of the Governor's aides to look up the Shakespeare quotation, because four weeks later I got a handwritten note from the governor: "James, methinks you are making 'much ado about nothing.' "

In picking Benedick's comic reply I found a humorous way to make my point—that I didn't regard the appointment as the choicest political plum. Yet I said it in a light manner. Just as I did, you can use Shakespeare or the Bible to underscore almost any point. You can use wit for the same purpose. In the back of this book there are hundreds of stories that will wittily get your point across. Remember, the story doesn't have to be uproariously funny to be humorously effective. It only has to point out a situation in a comical way.

Dr. Elton Trueblood, in his book *The Humor of Christ,* lists thirty humorous passages by Christ in the Gospels, such as camel through a needle's eye, pearls before swine, speck and log in the eye, good old wine. . . . He compares the storytelling techniques of Jesus to those of Lincoln. When Jesus said the sanctimonious Pharisees "would strain at a gnat yet swallow a camel," the man on the Midwestern frontier or Mideastern desert would readily find the earthy exaggeration comical.

Abraham Lincoln was such a storyteller that the New York *Herald* called him the "American Aesop." Like Jesus, he was a master of exaggeration and irony. He called a weak argument sophistry as thin as the boiled shadow of a homeopathic pigeon. When asked about the size of the Confederate Army, Lincoln said, "1,200,000 men." When doubt was expressed to that figure, the president went on, "1,200,000—no doubt of it. You see, all generals when they get whipped say the enemy outnumber them three to five to one, and I must believe them. We have 400,000 men in the field."

Lincoln could also relate the earthy anecdote to express a point. Once in lamenting on McClellan's slowness to commit his army, he told of hearing the sound of hammering as he was visiting army headquarters. He asked the soldiers what they were doing and they replied, "Building a privy for General McClellan." And he asked, "Is it a one-holer or two?" "A one-holer" was the reply. "Good," remarked Lincoln. "If it were two, McClellan, in trying to make up his mind, would shit himself."

But most of Lincoln's stories were not about his own experiences. As he himself once admitted, he did not make up most stories himself. "I remember a good story when I hear it, but I never invented anything original. I am only a retail dealer." Similarly, you don't have to be a born wit to make your speeches sparkle with humor. All you need to do is start developing your own collection of stories with the help of this book.

Wit can brighten the message of your speech. It can focus on a point or light up an idea. As Lincoln said, "A funny story, if it has the element of genuine wit, has the same effect on me that I suppose a good square drink of whiskey has on an old toper; it puts new life into me."

Some years ago I was asked to speak on Lincoln at a Lincoln Day Republican dinner. A biographical recital seemed too dull, and yet formal discourse on the wisdom of Lincoln seemed too pompous. What I did was to read through my anecdotes on Lincoln and try to find three that I could lump together for a speech.

There was the story about Preacher Cartright, the evangelical minister who approved Lincoln in a Congressional race. At a prayer meeting Cartright spied Lincoln and said, "All those who want to go to Heaven rise." Everybody but Lincoln rose. Then again he said, "All who do not want to go to Hell rise." Again everybody but Lincoln got up. Cartright then challenged Lincoln. "Where, Mr. Lincoln, do you want to go?" Lincoln replied, "I want to go to Congress." I used this story to show Lincoln's sense of purpose. Then I expanded on Lincoln's reply to a genealogist, "I don't know who my grandfather was and I'm more concerned who his grandson will be." This exchange manifested Lincoln's belief in the potential of the common man. Finally, I cited Lincoln's parable about the sheep. He once asked a man, "If you count the tail as a leg, how many legs does a sheep have?" "Five," the man replied. "No," said Lincoln. "Calling a tail a leg doesn't make it a leg." This story makes a good example of Lincoln's common sense.

I then had in a speech Lincoln's common sense, his belief in the common man, and his faith that his destiny lay in proving democracy.

Shakespeare's Benedick says to Margaret, "Your wit ambles well; it goes easily." Humor carries a speech easily. In my book *Instant Eloquence* I wrote that a speaker should inform while he entertains and entertain while he informs. A good way of doing this is getting together a group of stories around which to build your talk.

In 1953 I watched the coronation procession of Queen Elizabeth in London from a good viewing point in Hyde Park. But when a friend and I went to Hyde Park the night before, the lines there were already ten deep. So we went back and bought a case of English beer and spent the night in Hyde Park playing bridge with some English girls but not drinking the beer. When morning came we were about eighteenth back in the standing rows (we, of course, did not have the scarce fifty-guinea seats). We gallantly offered beer to our English friends in front of us wishing cheers to their Queen. Then about two hours later, at the time of the procession, we found ourselves in the front line. In the meantime nature had taken its inexorable course on those English standees' bladders. In the same way, the stories you offer can bring you to the head of the line. Stories with a point not only arrest the listener's attention but entertain him. As Shakespeare said, "It makes a speech amble easily."

One of the most entertaining stars on the lecture circuit today is former Senator Sam Ervin of North Carolina. His technique is often to weave a speech around stories. In a speech to the Philadelphia Bar Association, when I was executive director, Senator Sam wove in these three stories in his discourse:

"In these days it is important to speak up and say exactly what you mean in plain language. People will not be persuaded by big words, but they can be moved by gut words. I once knew this preacher back home who liked to use big words he didn't quite understand. One time he brought in a visiting minister and after introducing him to the congregation he said, 'You be sure to preach loud now because this church has very bad agnostics.' "

"Gentlemen, I think it is time for the bar to re-evaluate its case on ethics. We might follow the example of the woman in a law case I remember. She was being examined in court for jury service. She looked up at the judge and said, 'I am sorry, Your Honor, I can't serve on the jury. I don't believe in capital punishment.' 'Maybe you don't understand,' the judge said. 'This is a civil suit brought by a wife to recover five thousand dollars of *her* money spent by her husband on gambling and other women.' 'Oh,' she said, 'I'll serve on the jury. I could be wrong about capital punishment.' "

"The lawyers with specialties should not be allowed to advertise. It reminds me of a law case I heard about recently. A man went to see his lawyer and said to him, 'I want to get a divorce. My wife hasn't spoken to me for three months.' The lawyer said to him, 'If I were you, I'd think about that for a while. Don't be too hasty. Wives like that are mighty hard to find these days.' "

Some speakers think it is a cardinal rule to begin a talk with a funny story and never to use humor again. You can almost hear the grinding of gears as they switch from high to low and then plod through the rest of the speech. What a bore! See if you can weave in humor throughout your speech. I don't mean that you have to tell funny stories at varied intervals throughout your speech. That will subtract from the message of your talk. But use humor to flower your speech. Look for the amusing illustration or the warm anecdote to make your point.

Have you ever listened to a sermon by an outstanding minister or rabbi? They generally do not open with a funny story, but their talk is salted with humorous insights into life. In fact, one of the best sources for good anecdotes and stories is the good preacher. This may be a roundabout way to get you to go to your church or synagogue, but I have collected some of my best anecdotes from scribblings on Presbyterian church bulletins that I stuffed in my pocket after church. Listen to four stories I took down from Dr. Sizoo in Washington:

"Most of us are not as honest with ourselves as the famous scholar and philosopher David Hume. The political minister Lord John Russell came to Hume and asked him to explain his political philosophy.

"Lord Russell asked, 'What do you consider the object of legislation?' Hume replied, 'The greatest good to the greatest number.' 'And what,' said Russell, 'do you consider to be the greatest number?' Hume replied, 'Number one.' "

"Too often we tend to put God's work low on our list of priorities. For example, when we feel the financial pressure, it's often the church contributions that we first cut down on. It's like the young boy starting out for Sunday school one morning who was given two dimes, one for the collection plate and one for himself. As he was walking down the street he played with the coins. One of them slipped out of his hand, rolled away and disappeared irretrievably down the grates of a sewer. The lad gazed sadly down through the grates and then said, 'Well, there goes the Lord's dime.' "

"It takes a special type of courage to stand out from the crowd and do what you believe is right regardless of popular pressure. Not long ago a friend of mine who is an Episcopal bishop told me of an occasion when he went to address a private Episcopal day school. His little sermon was on moral courage. 'Ten boys were sleeping in a dormitory,' said he by way of illustration, 'and only one knelt down to say his prayers. That is moral courage.' When he had finished his talk he asked the class for an example of moral courage. 'Please, sir,' said one lad who raised his hand, 'ten bishops were sleeping in a dormitory and only one jumped into bed without saying his prayers!' "

"When I hear of people who say they don't have time to get involved, I think of Senator Charles Sumner of Massachusetts. Julia Ward Howe, who incidentally wrote 'The Battle Hymn of the Republic,' asked Senator Sumner to give his concern to the problems of an unfortunate family. The senator replied, 'I've become so busy that I can no longer concern myself with individuals.' Julia replied, 'Charles, that is quite remarkable. Even God isn't that busy.'

Or listen to these stories that came from a recent sermon:

"What with all the problems of today—the energy crisis, pollution, mugging, terrorism—the problem of daily survival gets tougher and tougher. I recently heard that when that Japanese officer was brought out after twenty-five years in a Philippine jungle, the leader of the rescue team first made the derelict read the last four weeks of the Tokyo newspapers. Then he said, 'Do you still *want* to be rescued?' "

"Acts like that make us wonder if we are such an advanced society. We recall the remark of Dr. Albert Schweitzer after he came back to Europe after a long stay in Africa. A reporter asked him, 'What do you think of civilization?' 'It's a good idea,' said Dr. Schweitzer. 'Somebody ought to start it.' "

Now, I don't mean to suggest that your speech should consist just of five or ten funny stories patched together in a loose theme. Pick the two or three that can be best woven into your talk.

When I was a seventeen-year-old schoolboy in England, my brother Graham, at Williams College, wanted to send me something unique for my birthday. He and his girlfriend (now his wife) put ads in the newspapers of nearby women's colleges (Vassar, Smith, Mt. Holyoke) asking girls to send cards to his kid brother who was "in a stuffy English public school." On the days around my birthday the house common-room table became piled high with lovey-dovey cards, passionately-worded post cards, and perfumed letters from girls I never knew. When the count went past six hundred, the housemaster called me in for a talking to. "James," he said, "we in England are more conservative about our private lives. I would suggest that you ration your love life, as we do now our jam and sugar, to two or three a week." (England was still rationing then.)

So you need only two or three stories to liven even the most dull topic. Not long ago I heard William Casey (then chairman of the Securities Exchange Commission but now head of the Export-Import Bank) speak to a group of investment bankers. These are the three stories he built into his presentation:

"We businessmen get a little uptight about our image today. We are attacked by consumer groups, environmentalists, and other groups for lacking sensitivity. It recalls to me the case of a big-business leader who went to Houston for a heart-transplant operation. He was told by the surgeon that the donors of the hearts included a twenty-four-year-old track star, a forty-year-old steamfitter and an eighty-year-old banker. Although he had only a few minutes to decide which of the three he wanted, he instantly chose the eighty-year-old banker's heart. In the recovery room his wife asked, 'Why did you choose the oldest of the three hearts?' He replied, 'I just chose the heart that had never been used before!' "

"There is only one thing wrong with the proposal and that is it's against the law. It violates a federal statute. It recalls the advice once given to J. P. Morgan, who was trying to put together one of his big cartels. His lawyers questioned the validity of some of his proposed actions. Morgan, not liking the advice he was getting, wired the eminent lawyer John Gregorious Johnson, who was vacationing in the Bahamas. The wire asked whether he thought such a merger could work out. Johnson wired back, 'Merger possible, jail certain.' "

"Everyone has tax problems these days. A friend of mine told me about an acquaintance of his—a big businessman who was being audited by the IRS. It was an all-day affair. The investigator went over his write-offs—his entertainment expenses. When it was all over he was so shaken he put a call through to his favorite call girl.

"As he finally began to unwind with his second martini in an out-of-the-way restaurant, he turned to the girl. 'Honey, you sure are in the right business. You make all that money and don't have to report it.'

" 'I'm not sure,' she replied. 'You see, I can't write anything off for depreciation.' "

In London's Victoria Embankment there is a tablet inscription to W. S. Gilbert of Gilbert and Sullivan fame. It reads, "His foe was folly and his weapon wit." Over the years I have heard many speakers—advertising men, business consultants, sociologists, educators, and politicians—use wit to underscore the dangerous implications of a certain policy or program.

I once heard a New York advertising executive use these two stories:

"On the surface it looks like a very clever promotion. But I question whether it will actually have the results we want. It's like the special half-fare rate one of the airlines recently introduced for wives accompanying their husbands on business trips. Anticipating some valuable testimonials, the publicity department of the airline sent out letters to all the wives of businessmen who used the special rates, asking how they enjoyed their trip. Responses are still pouring in asking, 'What trip?' "

"What we should ask ourselves is, who is it that we want to reach? Who is it that we want to make a favorable impression on? I recall the answer a young Marine gave to a nurse while recovering at a Navy hospital. The youthful Leatherneck was composing a letter home to his wife. A kindhearted nurse was taking down the note. 'The nurses here,' he dictated, 'are a rather plain lot.' 'Why,' exclaimed the nurse, 'don't you think that's rather unfair?' The soldier smiled and exclaimed, 'Yes, it is, but it will make my wife very happy.'

A management consultant from a Chicago firm at a conference of businessmen told this story about the necessity for planning ahead:

"The problem of supply failure would never have happened if there had been the right planning. No one at the time thought out the full consequences. Maybe that's what a doctor I know was alluding to. It was a sweltering summer day and this perspiring obstetrician was rushing frantically to examine all his patients before answering a summons from the hospital. 'These hot August days getting you down, Doc?' asked one woman sympathetically. 'No,' said the doctor, 'it's not these hot August days that are bothering me—it's those cold nights last November.' "

A sociologist like Alvin Toffler might explain the pressures of adapting to world changes with a story like this:

We live in a fast-changing world where we constantly have to adapt suddenly to new situations and change old habits. It is like the attractive blond girl a friend of mine met on the Metroliner not too long ago. He was a bit surprised when the girl lit up a cigar. Unaccustomed to seeing girls smoke cigars, he asked, "How did you ever begin smoking cigars?" "Oh, it was really quite simple. One evening my husband came home and found a lighted cigar in our living-room ashtray."

An educator speaking to the alumni on the role of the modern university used this story:

"Learning should not be a passive act—not a simple regurgitation of what the professor has said. It should be an interplay of question and answer—of challenge and response. I recall reading about a big Eastern city university. It seems that a lazy college student hated to get up in the morning, but he had an important 8:00 A.M. class, and the only way to get the information was to listen to the professor. So, the student gave his tape recorder to a classmate and asked him to turn it on each morning when the professor began his spiel. This worked very well; the recorder got the message, and the student listened to it later in the day.

"In time, a couple of other students noticed what was going on and they, too, sent tape recorders to the classroom and stayed in bed. Then, one by one, other students did the same, until finally the entire class decided to stay out, making arrangements with the janitor to turn on their machines. One day the dean walked into the classroom. Every chair was empty, but there was a tape recorder going on each desk—and up there on the platform, on the professor's desk, was another recorder—blaring forth the lecture."

A political opponent of mine once characterized my Republican background this way:

"Humes is a member of a party that hasn't had a new idea in fifty years. It has consistently opposed every progressive move. Some day when it inevitably fades out of existence because of lack of new blood, someone is going to say of its demise, as Alice Roosevelt Longworth once remarked when she heard Calvin Coolidge had just died, 'How can they tell?' "

In reply I referred to his habit of advocating everything that was popular at the time with this story:

"My opponent's habit of talking out of both sides of his mouth on the same issue reminds me of some New York friends of mine who were originally from Baltimore. They decided on their way home from their vacation that they would stop at Gettysburg. The guide who showed them around spoke eloquently about General Meade and other Union heroes. They thanked him, paid the fee and then happened to remark that they must be getting home to Baltimore before nightfall. The guide's face dropped. 'You know, from your license plates I thought you were Northern folks. I should have given you the Southern lecture. It's much better.' "

When I served in the State Department in public affairs as director of the Office of Policy and Plans, I used to make many speeches on U. S. foreign policy to audiences around the country. Often I would build my speeches around three or four stories or anecdotes. Some of the illustrations that I most often used were these:

"Like the French Talleyrand or the German Von Papen, the successful diplomat is one who can wangle himself out of any difficult situation. One of the earliest beginnings of this tradition was in the fifteenth century when citizens of Prague were demanding the expulsion of papal legates to Bohemia. The angry citizens stormed Haradry Castle, found the two ministers and threw them bodily out a second-floor window of the palace. It was their good fortune to land on a pile of horse manure. Thus, they survived. It is not the first time a diplomat was saved by a load of crap."

"There is great skepticism about summit meetings and other high-level negotiations. But I think British Prime Minister Ramsay MacDonald expressed it well to a British foreign office secretary, who derided such conferences. 'The desire for peace,' said the secretary, 'does not necessarily insure peace.' 'Quite true,' said MacDonald. 'Neither does the desire for food satisfy hunger. But at least it gets you started toward a restaurant.' "

"We Americans seem compulsively directed to find fault with ourselves. We forget that to millions we are still 'the last best hope.' I recall the experience of our attaché at the American consulate at Lisbon. A small, shy little man leaned confidentially across his desk and said, 'Please, mister, could you tell me if there is any possibility that I could get entrance to your wonderful country?' The attaché, pressed by thousands of such requests and haggard with sleepless nights, roughly replied, 'Impossible now. Come back in another ten years.' The would-be refugee moved toward the door, stopped, turned, and asked with a wan smile, 'Morning or afternoon?' "

Most speakers have a favorite story which they try to use as either opening humor or as a point-maker in the body of the talk. I was no exception. Mine was the Elbridge Gerry speech at the time of the Constitutional Convention. Seeing that it could tie into fears of a military-industrial complex, I often disarmed student audiences whose initial response to a member of the Nixon Administration was less than warm:

"We share your concerns about Pentagon dominance in foreign policy and the influence of a military-industrial complex. As a matter of fact, a close reading of American history will show you that one of our Founding Fathers' cardinal beliefs was that the civilian shall be supreme. For example, if you will read one account of the Constitutional Convention, you will note Elbridge Gerry's famous warning about the dangers of a country top-heavy in military power. In the debate on 'the standing army provision' he addressed General Washington, 'Mr. President, a standing army is like an erect member. Although it may provide excellent assurance for domestic tranquility it often invites temptation for foreign adventure.' "

If our Founding Fathers used wit to argue provisions in the Constitution, there is no reason for you not to use humor to make points in your speeches.

6 The Night-Capper

Humor is a final emotion, like breaking into tears.

—E. B. White

In December 1964 I was invited to speak in Ottawa at a conference of Canada's Conservative Party. As a conference guest I was allowed in the executive session of the party. It was supposed to be a routine business session, but one of the Conservative MPs made a motion that former Prime Minister John Diefenbaker step down as leader of the party. Although I was supposed to speak the next day to the Young Members Section, the party chairman, who was presiding at the conference, suddenly announced that the guest speaker, Mr. Humes, a state legislator from Pennsylvania, had arrived to speak. What the chairman wanted, of course, was to stall for time while they could plan a strategy to kill the motion. Even if I were a pawn of Canadian politics I had no recourse but to get up and begin speaking (my subject was the lesson of moderation in politics after the recent debacle of Goldwater). After I had spoken for about fifteen minutes the chairman slipped a note saying "finish it fast." How was I suddenly going to wind it up? I closed this way:

"And speaking of the Eisenhower brand of moderate conservatism, I think it appropriate to tell one of his stories about the Gettysburg section of the country where he lives. He tells of an Amishman, Jacob Scheider of the Pennsylvania Dutch community nearby. Now Jacob was a middle-aged bachelor who was hopelessly in love with pretty young Clara. Finally one night as he was riding along in his buggy with Clara he said, 'Clara, will ye marry me?' She mumbled, 'Ya, Jacob.' There followed a long silence till Clara said, 'Will ye not say something more, Jacob?' And Jacob said, 'Ach, I think I say too much already.'"

Sometimes humor is the only exit out of a difficult situation. It is like the drunk a hotel clerk told me about at a convention some years ago. The clerk described how he had been bothered by a call at the desk one morning asking, "What time does the bar open?" The clerk said eleven o'clock. Sometime later the voice again called and asked, "Say, what time did you say the bar opened?" The harried clerk replied, "Look, I'll repeat it once again—eleven o'clock." About half an hour later the voice called again. "Did you say I have to wait until eleven o'clock till the bar opens?" "Yes," the clerk replied. "But if you keep this up you won't be allowed in the bar." "Heck," said the distraught man, "I don't want to get in. I've been locked up in the bar all night. I want to get out!"

A good story can be your master key out of any situation. You should memorize one and keep it in your head for that moment of emergency.

In Ionesco's *Rhinoceros* the character Joan says, "I have to take a rest. It is in my program for the day." Occasionally the toastmaster or panel moderator will need a story to break a halt in the proceedings. One chairman with a "veddy" good English accent used this story at a bar-association convention:

"The program schedule today reminds me of a train schedule in England, or at least the difficulties three deaf Britishers had in knowing just exactly where they were. The first gentleman in the London suburban train looks up and says, 'I say, is this Wembley?' 'No,' says his deaf companion. 'Actually, I think it's Thursday.' 'Did you say thirsty?' said the third. 'So am I, rather. Let's take the next stop for a drink.' And I think this is the time to stop . . ."

At another convention the program chairman preceded his announcement of scheduled recreational activities with this story:

"As I look over the list of varied activities that are made available here at White Sulphur Springs, I am reminded of the time I heard a distinguished Latin American ambassador answer questions after a speech in Washington. A woman arose and said, 'Your Excellency, we Americans think bullfighting—your country's most popular sport—a bit revolting.' The ambassador replied, 'You are wrong on two counts. Bullfighting is our second most popular recreational activity—and it is not revolting. That is our first most popular sport.' Well, that is one activity that we do not have organized today . . ."

The moderator, like the bartender in T. S. Eliot's *The Waste-*

land, sometimes has to say, "Hurry up, please, it's time." Humor may be the best way to cut short the panel presentations in time for the luncheon or dinner break. One moderator told this story:

"I know we have all enjoyed ourselves—but even good things have to come to an end. At least this is the way a young father I heard about reacted. He and his young wife were into the 'natural birth' concept. A friend of his in the waiting room said, 'Where's the doctor?' He said, 'I don't need the doctor. I have gotten special permission to be a sort of midwife. I'm going to do it myself.' All of a sudden a scream came from the next room. He rushed in. Ten minutes later he came out. 'It's a boy!' All of a sudden another scream, he rushed in, came out five minutes later, said 'It's twins this time.' Another scream. He rushed in, came out and said, 'This time it's triplets!' Now, one more scream. He rushes out the front door. His friend said, 'Where are you going?' 'I want to find out how you shut the damn thing off.' "

The king in *Alice in Wonderland* advised, "Begin at the beginning and go on till you come to the end: then stop." But sometimes it is not so easy. Your outline says halfway but the clock says overtime. Remember, the mind can only absorb what the seat can endure. Don't strain the patience of the audience. Wind up your speech in a paragraph or two with a story:

Well, I have been talking for quite a while and I imagine you are all anxious to eat. So I will end by telling you a remark I heard the other Saturday night at a cocktail party. A couple I know had been hoisting the martinis rather steadily for quite sometime. Finally I heard the lady say to her mate, "Honey, you'd better stop drinking —your face is getting awfully blurred." Well, I'm afraid your faces are getting a bit blurred. . . .

My brother's father-in-law once passed on this ditty after I made too long a speech:

> A speaker should cultivate brevity
> With a suitable leaven of levity.
> In short, be terse,
> For nothing is worse
> Than interminable verbal longevity.

Now, while I don't suggest that that piece of verse is the best way to finish a talk (unless you have limerick-loving listeners), the point is clear. The audience prefers a half-developed speech that's short to a full-developed speech that's long.

Remember, a logical, fully worked-out presentation is more the aesthetic concern of the speaker than the audience. Never make the mistake of underestimating the tiredness of the audience. It reminds me of the time a woman advanced in years came into a friend of mine's law office on a domestic-relations matter. She tottered into his office asking for help in arranging a divorce.

"A divorce?" asked my friend. "Tell me, how old are you?" "I'm eighty-four," she replied. "And how old is your husband?" "My husband is eighty-seven." "How long have you been married?" "Next October will be sixty-one years." "Married sixty-one years! Why would you want a divorce now?"

"Because," she replied, "enough is enough."

If you are the last in a series of speakers on a long program, it is sometimes better not to try to compress your thirty-minute talk into the available five minutes remaining on the schedule. Once British Foreign Secretary Lord Balfour in a speech in Texas found his time had been used up by a long-winded toastmaster who closed his tedious introduction by saying, "Lord Balfour will now give his address." Balfour rose and said, "I have been asked to give my address in the remaining five minutes. That I can do! Here it is: 10 Carlton Gardens, London, England."

Another quick exit line was made by a speaker at a convention program who rose and said, "The program now calls for me to give a few remarks of advice and counsel, as I have in previous years. But I remember the example of Dr. George Harris when he was president of Amherst. One fall he rose in chapel to give the annual convocation address in the first assembly of the year, but after a sentence or two he stopped and smiled and said, 'I had intended to give you some advice, but now I remember how much is left over from last year unused.'"

Most speakers are wary of humor as a speech-ender. Sure, they will use it as a way to get out of a tight spot—to push along the program or to substitute for lack of time. But to end a formal speech—never. If they have a serious message, why end it on a light note?

At my recent fortieth-birthday party my brother was making fun of the circumstances of my birth. I was born on Halloween. My parents were going to a masquerade party. My father was dressed as an Indian chief and my mother, for obvious reasons having to do with eight and a half months' girth, was garbed as Aunt Jemima. The host of the party was the family obstetrician with the name of John V. Nutt, who was in a Cheshire-cat costume. When the "hurry" call came, there was no time to change. Off went the Cheshire cat and Aunt Jemima in one car with the Indian chief in hot pursuit in another. I was born just about in the hospital elevator with the good doctor still in the cat costume.

In reply I said I'd much rather make a funny entrance into the world than a funny exit. But in a talk, does humor as an ending detract from the dignity of the speaker? Some think so. Ted Sorensen, President Kennedy's speech writer, apparently would agree. He suggests funny one-liners at the beginning of the speech —and inspirational bits from history at the end.

Robert Frost once counseled that poems should begin in delight and end in wisdom. That is not a bad formula for a speech, too. And to end in wisdom can be to end in wit. After all, good wit is often the expression of wisdom in a striking and funny way. At one seminar I heard a businessman end his speech on investment planning with this fable:

"We have discussed a lot of ideas in today's seminar. But it is one thing to come up with new concepts and another to carry them out. From China comes the fable of a wise man noted for his insight and ability to solve problems. One day a merchant came to him seeking advice for a problem in his accounting department. 'I have six men and six abacuses, but my needs have expanded to the point where I need a 20 percent increase in output but cannot afford the capital investment of another man and another abacus. And even if I could, one man would not be enough and two men would be too much.' The wise man pondered the problem for several days and finally summoned the merchant. 'The solution to your problem,' he said, 'is simple. Each of your present accounting staff must grow another finger on each hand. This will increase your abacus output exactly 20 percent and will solve your problem.' The merchant smiled—his problem solved. He started to leave, paused, looked at the wise old man. 'Oh, wise one,' he said, 'you have truly given me the solution to my problem. But,' said the merchant, 'how do I get my people to grow extra fingers?' The wise man puffed his pipe. 'That's a good question. But, alas, I only make policy recommendations. The details of execution are up to you.' "

Surely a humorous fable is a better speech finale than some trite philosophic advice—like being told to work hard or have faith. Shakespeare said it. "All's well that ends well—still the finis is the crown." A strong close can make the audience forget a weak speech. That close might be an inspirational incident from history or a witty anecdote. It can even be both. Here are three stories I have often used to cap speeches:

"I know there are those who think I have overestimated the dangers involved—that I have exaggerated the implications of our present policy. It recalls to me the time Prime Minister Robert Pitt was cross-examined by Edmund Burke on his government policy. Said Pitt, 'I can assure you that we have no risk of danger. This country is safe even until the Day of Judgment.' Replied Burke, 'It is not the Day of Judgment that concerns me, rather it is the day of "no judgment."' "

"For too long we have tolerated a situation that could have been resolved. It is a situation that calls for the same remark John Witherspoon made at the time of the Declaration of Independence. Witherspoon, the Scottish-born Presbyterian minister who was president of what was later to be called Princeton, was elected to the Continental Congress in June 1776. Arriving in Philadelphia just in time to hear the debate over independence between John Adams and John Dickinson, he heard the remark 'The colonies are not yet ripe for a declaration of independence.' Witherspoon replied, 'In my judgment, sir, we are not only ripe but rotting.' "

"There is only one place to be in times like this and that is in the thick of the action. Remember the cable the British Ambassador to Greece sent to Prime Minister Winston Churchill in 1944: 'I feel like I'm sitting on top of a volcano.' And Churchill stingingly wired back, 'And where did you expect to be sitting in times like these?' "

If wit can be used to get people out of their seats, humor can be used to get money out of their pockets. It may not at first seem appropriate to close a speech on cancer or crippled children with a funny story. The fact is, though, that civic leaders in this role may feel uncomfortable tugging heart strings and purse strings at the same time. A funny story is a relaxed way of getting your pitch across without being too maudlin:

"I know we all have reasons for not wanting to give at this time. But usually I think the reasons are as flimsy as the rationale given by one of the tightest people in my home town. When the minister journeyed to his house on the hill to make the salutation on behalf of the community he opened his appeal saying, 'Mr. Flint, you are a man of great means. Your store has branches in seven major cities. You have this lovely house here as well as your summer home on the ocean front. You are on the board of eight major companies. Doesn't a man of your worth want to give to his community?' Mr. Flint replied, 'You are wrong on several counts. First, my store has branches in ten cities. Second, I have a home on the lake too. Third, I'm director of eleven companies. But did you know this? Did you know I have an aged mother in an expensive retirement park? Did you know my sister just underwent an expensive operation? Did you know my nephew has two more years of college and then four of medical school? And I don't give a dime to any one of them. Why should I give a pledge to you?' "

"Knowing this audience as I do, I think I can thank them in advance for their generosity in responding to this appeal. I feel lucky that I won't have the experience of an old Irish clerk of a small town in Massachusetts. After thirty-six years of service he found himself in a battle for re-election against the young son of a millionaire. In a speech to his constituents the old clerk complained of how much money his young opponent was spending and made an impassioned plea ending, 'Friends, if you haven't a thing, just put your nickels and pennies into the hat to pay for a little printing and advertising.' Then, continuing his speech, he sent a young assistant through the crowd with his hat. When the aide returned, the old clerk peered glumly into the hat, which had come back empty. Without missing a beat, the clerk said, 'And another thing. I want to thank each and every one of ye for returning me hat.' "

However T. S. Eliot has the world end, most people would rather end the speech with a bang, not a whimper. So if you are afraid of a situation becoming mawkish, try ending with humor.

Another speech lead-in can be the talk that involves reciting your own personal misfortunes. Months before White House Counsel Chuck Colson pleaded guilty to criminal complicity in Watergate he delivered this fable to describe the developing situation in the Watergate affair. I find that it is a good story to summarize the points of almost any speech.

"A small bird lay freezing to death along a country lane in the Northern steppes. A peasant came along, saw the dying bird and thought to himself, 'If only I had something—anything—in which to wrap this bird, I might save its life.' But, alas, he had nothing on him that he could spare in the face of the cold Russian winter. But then he saw some cow droppings nearby and he thought in desperation, 'Perhaps if I wrap the bird in that, it will warm it enough to save its life.' He picked up the bird, wrapped it in the cow manure, laid it gently on the ground and went on his way. Sure enough, the dung began to warm the bird and it started to come to life again. The bird felt so overjoyed at feeling warm again that it tried to sing, but all it could do in its feeble condition was some low, wobbly notes. Just then another peasant came along. He heard the bird's attempt at singing and thought, 'Poor bird, it's strangling in the cow dung.' So he picked it up, removed the dung, laid the bird back on the ground. Shortly thereafter the bird froze to death.

"There are three morals to the story. The first one is: it isn't necessarily your enemies who put you in it. The second one is: it isn't necessarily your friends who get you out of it. And the third moral is: when you're in it up to here, for heavens sake, don't sing."

7   The Tale-Spinner

The last man that makes a joke owns it.
                    —Finley Peter Dunne

Dr. Vincent Heiser, an educator who had been working among the people of Samoa, was given an outdoor feast in his honor by the native island king. When the time came to say some words of appreciation for the doctor's services His Majesty remained squatting while a professional orator, brought in for the purpose, expressed a flowery tribute. After a long speech of praise Heiser rose to acknowledge thanks, but the king pulled him back.

"Don't get up," he said. "I have provided an orator for you. In Polynesia, we don't believe that public speaking should be engaged in by amateurs."

Whatever the development of Polynesian civilization, speaking is one area where they are further advanced than we are. And as regards humor, speakers tend to be the most backward and awkward. Why? Because first of all they feel they have to tell a story. Now at the risk of inhibiting sales, I want to say right at the outset that there is no law demanding that a speaker begin a talk with a funny story. Just recently I heard a high-school football coach when called on to speak say, "I'm not that used to speaking, but I do know you are supposed to start with a funny story. So I'd like to tell you something I was told not long ago about the man who went into a psychiatrist's office . . ." Such amateur speaking will embarrass the listeners as much as it will the deliverer. Humor can be the most effective way to warm up a stiff audience—if you build it into your speech. Don't hold up a flag saying, in effect, "Now's the time for a story, folks." Make it part of your speech.

Once an editor gave to an aspiring writer the formula for an ideal opening for a commercially successful piece of fiction. The first paragraph should contain (1) sex, (2) high society, and (3) an unconventional situation. On that basis the writer came back with this unbeatable beginning: "Damn it," said the duchess to the king, "take your hand off my thigh."

My formula for successful speech humor is—build it in. And not only build it in as part of your speech but build it in as part of your experience. In the *Adventures of the Engineer's Thumb,* Sir Arthur Conan Doyle has these words of advice by the master sleuth: "Experience," says Holmes, laughing. "Indirectly it may be of value, you know; you only have to put it into your own words to gain the reputation of being excellent company for the remainder of your existence." Holmes is saying that to be a good storyteller, put the experience in your own words. Glance through the six hundred or more stories at the back of this book, and if the anecdote does not involve Churchill or Barrymore, see how I always tell it as if it happened to me or a friend of mine. I do that because making it part of my own experience—even if secondhand— makes the story more believable. When you start by saying "this salesman" or "this psychiatrist" you have already signaled the audience that this is a story coming, a joke, an untrue happening. You already have them half turned off. Lead them by the hand into your story—"an old woman in the town I grew up in" or "a lawyer I know who once had a client walk in . . ." When you find a story that fits the purpose of your speech, adopt it. It is now your story—something that happened to you or a friend of yours. Say it aloud, then close your eyes and tell it in your own words. Once you say it a few times in your own language, you are going to believe it as your own.

The late Senator Kerr used to tell the story of the farmer he knew who called the country doctor and asked him to come to the farm because a city stranger had met with a sudden accident. At first reluctant, the doctor came when he learned that the injured man was the son-in-law of the farmer. The doctor, upon arriving, immediately saw that the city slicker had been shot by a shotgun. "Tell me, why did you shoot your own son-in-law with a shotgun this morning?"

"He weren't my son-in-law this morning. He became my son-in-law just a bit ago when the parson I called came and hitched him and my daughter."

As the pressure of the speech deadline nears, you may have to adopt a strange story as your own. But when you adopt it, adapt to it. Weave into the story characters you know or places you are familiar with. At that point the story becomes your very own—and believable. Remember, the more believable a story is, the more ripe it is for the puncture of punch-line laughter.

Once I was a guest in an English country home for the weekend. My British friends owned an old Norman castle in Suffolk. The grounds were magnificent, especially the garden. The stables boasted some of the finest riding horses. Even the cattle stock was of the best breed. In short, my friends had everything you could want. The suite of rooms I was shown to had a tapestry puller which, I was told, rang the pantry if I should want to order food. When I got up the next morning, I pulled the cord to order breakfast and then dashed in to get a quick shower, thinking I would be finished before the butler arrived. I had hardly turned on the shower when the butler knocked. Through the slightly opened door he said, "Would you like orange juice or half a grapefruit?" I, with my towel around me, said, "The juice." "Would you like eggs boiled, poached, or fried?" I said "poached." "Would you like toast or crumpets?" I said "toast." "Coffee or tea?" I replied "tea." "Chinese, Ceylon or Indian?" he asked. "Ceylon," I replied. "With cream, milk, or lemon?" "Milk," I replied, closing the door, thinking I'd finished. "Just a minute, sir. Which milk—Guernsey, Jersey, or Holstein?"

In this book you have just as wide a selection. Let's say you are a lawyer speaking to a group of business executives. You can look through the section "Before the Bench" on lawyers and then through "Executive Suite" for businessmen. Or if you are Texan, scan "Deep in the Heart of Texas," or if the audience is Southern, check the "Old Plantation." Even if you don't have a background fit you can always try "Home Town," "Neighborhood Pub," or "Head Table."

And that's just the beginning. Read through the index for possible points a humorous story could make that would fit into your speech: Advice, Candor, Communication, Difficulty, Introduction, Mess, Planning, Problem, Qualifications, etc. With each of these points, you can allude to your friendship with the host organization (Friends), respond to a flattering introduction (Introduction), preface an outline of business or political situations (Difficulty,

Mess, Problem), or emphasize the need for straight talk (Communications, Candor). Before I tire you, just think how many ways points like advice, observation, or planning can be tailored to your speech.

Now most speakers want to open their speech with a story, so look at "Speech-Starter" (Chapter 4). But if you want a story to respond to a tribute or a toast, check "Toast-Spreader" (Chapter 3). Then if you want to inspire your speech with wit or close your talk with a laugh, look through "Point-Maker" (Chapter 5) or "Night-Capper" (Chapter 6). If you can't find a story here, you don't have the flair or imagination to be a good storyteller.

If you have that hard a time finding a story, you are like that actor of the Stanislavsky school. The director was patiently explaining the scene to this method actor. "You've been on this desert island for twelve years. One morning you awaken, crawl out of your hut and start strolling along the beach. Suddenly you see this beautiful blond girl lying on the sand beside her discarded life jacket. You rush forward, grab her in your arms and start kissing her." The actor nodded thoughtfully, then asked, "And what's my motivation?"

To be a good storyteller you have to want to tell stories. It's as simple as that. You can overcome initial shyness by practice. Just tell the story aloud until it becomes part of you. Remember, a storyteller is like an actor. Even if you just read the story for the first time the night before the speech, you must pretend it has actually happened to you or a friend of yours if it is not a fable or an anecdote about a notable.

If you can't bring yourself to act it, don't try. Stick to the true anecdotes about Lincoln or Shaw. But acting doesn't mean ham acting. Pretending a story about children happened to one of your own children is one thing. Pretending you're a Southerner or Frenchman is another.

When I attended the University of Madrid I hosted as a part-time venture a radio show on Spanish culture beamed on short wave to English audiences. One day my script at the close of the program had a paragraph about how Spanish society was flourishing as never before. Since the Spanish stock market had fallen that day, I made some remarks in Spanish like "What a laugh that was." After all, I thought the program was off the air. Of course, I was lucky that I was only fired and not jailed. The point is I might not have been caught if I had said it in English, but my bad Spanish accent jarred the ears of those who casually monitored the show.

If you don't know French, don't imitate a French accent. If you haven't lived in London, be careful of the British accent. Don't try a Yiddish accent if you are not Jewish or a Southern one if you weren't born there.

As Yogi Berra once observed, "There are some people who, if they don't already know, you can't tell them." You know if you can imitate a Londoner well. Say it straight if you can't. Let the audience's knowledge of the hero and the punch line carry the story.

Respect the sensitivities of the audience—their ethnic or regional background and their taste. If you are speaking to a West Virginia audience, you are better off not speaking about hillbillies, unless you yourself are one. The Bible Belt, for example, doesn't mind the earthy story about the outhouse, but they may not like the story with the suggestion of sex. If you are dubious, don't try the risqué story.

Perhaps the key element in storytelling is knowing what to say at the right time. I remember being in a Washington hotel and hearing a veteran bellhop tell me of his experience. He had been explaining the ropes to the young trainee. "This thing," he said, "isn't all carrying bags. In a big hotel you're forever encountering delicate situations and you have to think fast. For instance, I had to deliver some ice to a particular hotel room and walked into the one across the hall by mistake. The door shouldn't have been open, but it was. Inside the room the bathroom door was open, which it shouldn't have been. Inside the bathroom there was this fat lady taking a bath. In a minute I knew the fat lady was going to scream to the high heavens. Thinking fast, I said, 'Excuse me, sir,' and left. The 'excuse me' was being polite, but the 'sir' was tact, and it saved the day. She thought I hadn't been there long enough to see anything and she calmed down." The trainee got it, but the next day he was in the hospital with a black eye and assorted bruises. The veteran said, "And what happened to you?"

The trainee said, "I was following your advice. I was delivering drinks and I got into the wrong room and there were a man and a woman on the bed with almost all their clothes off. So I said quickly, 'Pardon me, gentlemen,' and the guy got off the bed and nearly killed me."

See if the story is right for your audience and right for you. Try to imagine what the audience reaction will be.

I remember a bishop who arrived in Philadelphia the night before he was to make a major speech. Earlier he had arranged for an informal get-together in his room with representatives of the local press. During the session he told several anecdotes he expected to repeat at meetings the next day. Because he wanted to use the stories again, he requested reporters to omit them from any accounts they might turn in to their newspapers. A reporter, commenting on the speech, ended his piece with the following: "The bishop told a number of stories that cannot be published."

So a test for a speaker might be how his story would look in tomorrow's paper. It all comes back to using stories you are comfortable with—the stories you can adapt from your own experiences. Then tell the story with flavor. I remember a PTA reception I went to for teachers, parents and children. My little girl, when she was offered a piece of rich chocolate cake, said, "Oh, I just love this chocolate cake! It's awfully nice." A nearby teacher corrected her. "It's wrong to say you 'love' cake, and you used 'just' incorrectly in that sentence. Besides, 'awfully' is wrong; 'very' would be much more correct. Now why don't you repeat your remark?"

The girl obediently complied. "I like chocolate cake. It is very good." "That's much better, dear," said the teacher. "But," protested the child, "it sounds just like I was talking about bread."

Tell the story in your own language. Describe the happening as if you were there or your friend who told you was. Remember in Chapter 1, "The Laugh-Trigger," I said the important thing was to build in and build up. Build up the details of the story. It wasn't just a city—it was Chicago. It wasn't just a hotel—it was the Hilton. It wasn't just a man—it was a business acquaintance. Read the following story and see how the build-up of detail lends authenticity to an improbable situation:

Not long ago a couple I know prominent in the Social Register were on their way to a masquerade party at a Main Line country club and the husband was very upset at having to wear a devil's suit and mask. His wife, on the other hand, was very perturbed over the fact that her own costume had not arrived. "You leave now," she told the husband. "I'll come along when my costume arrives." The wife then thought about her grandmother's wedding gown. She could wear it with some minor alterations, include a mask, and go as a fairy princess. As she donned the dress she realized that her husband would not be expecting to see her as a fairy princess. She would be able to see how he behaved when he thought she was absent.

At the ball she saw him sitting alone behind some potted palms. She disguised her voice and asked him if he'd like to dance. One thing led to another, and what with a full moon shining overhead, the two soon found themselves romancing in the back seat of a parked car. Finally she disentangled herself and returned home to await her erring spouse.

Eventually her husband came home, looking weary and with his red devil's suit slung over his arm. He asked his wife, "Where were you?" "Never mind me," said his wife. "What did you do while you were there?" "I tended bar mostly," replied the husband. "Tended bar?" said his wife, scarcely able to speak for fury. "You mean you didn't have a good time?" "Me? No. But I tell you—you know the old club bartender whose place I took—he complained of never getting in on the fun, so I loaned him my costume, and did he have a terrific time!"

A twenty-year Navy veteran once told me of the aura that surrounded one famous admiral of the seven seas. He had been the hero of countless heroics battling Germans in the Mediterranean and convoy landings in the South Pacific. But the great admiral had one idiosyncracy. Each morning after breakfast he would go to his stateroom and open his safe and read a message. For years those who worked with him speculated on the message. Finally one day a group dared to go into his cabin, open the safe and look at the little note he read every day. It said, "Starboard is right, Port is left."

Similarly, there are two main things to remember in the mechanics of humor—the build-up and the bullet. Deliver your punch line carefully. If you misfire, the story will be a dud.

Once I heard a storyteller butcher the punch line in this story: "Somehow we seem to have ended up with a confused situation. The mistake, I assure you, was not one of intention. We are rather like the GI in London during World War II. In those days before the Normandy invasion, trains were very crowded because of the thousands of troops stationed in Britain. A tired American soldier who had been up all night boarded the train in Bristol in the south of England. He entered a compartment where there were seated five people and one dog in the six-seat cubicle. Approaching the lady who was the owner of the little Pekinese, he said, 'Ma'am, would you mind if I sit down? I have a ticket.' 'Absolutely not,' replied the dog owner. After a while standing the tired GI again asked, 'Ma'am, if you don't mind, I have been standing up all night. I would gladly hold the dog.' 'Indeed not,' said the lady. 'Ma'am,' said the GI, 'I haven't eaten for forty-five hours. I have twenty-four hours of leave. Would you please let me rest for a minute?' 'Young man, you are absolutely impertinent,' she said as she hugged her little Pekinese. With that the soldier opened the window, grasped the Pekinese, threw it out the window and sat down. While the woman sat amazed, a distinguished Englishman sitting across from them said, 'You know that's the trouble with you Americans—you always do things the wrong way. You drive on the wrong side of the street, you hold your fork with the wrong hand, and then you throw out the wrong bitch.' "

But, unfortunately, my speaker friend said, "You drive on the right side of the street, you hold your fork in the left hand"—and by the time he got to throwing out the wrong bitch the punch line had lost its thrust.

The key word in this punch line is "wrong"—"wrong side of the street," "wrong hand," and then "wrong bitch." But sometimes a punch line has a punch word too. That is the last word of the line that triggers the laughter. Just take a look at the next story:

Planning means making sure we avoid any errors. I remember hearing about a young secretary who was propositioned by a philandering executive. He was plying the sweet young thing with food and drink. "I've rented a townhouse for you," he said, "and you shall have your own bank account and credit with all the best couturiers. I'll visit you a couple of nights during the week, and we'll spend all our weekends together. And if we find we've made a mistake, why, we can always separate."

After thinking about the idea for a moment, the girl smiled and replied, "Sounds fine, but what'll we do with the mistake?"

"Mistake" in this story is not only the key word but the punch word. Read the punch line over and over and make sure you are

going to end on the right word. In the six-hundred-plus stories in
this volume I don't claim perfection. I'm sure there are more than
a few punch lines that can be improved on by reshaping the line
to end on the right word.

See if you can find the key word and the punch word in the
following story:

There is a right time and place for everything. Harvard economist Dr. John Kenneth Galbraith found this out when he was
waiting for a plane in Washington National Airport. To pass the
time he browsed in the airport's bookshop. To his disappointment
he could not locate a copy of his latest book, *The Great Crash*—
an analysis of the Depression. The six-foot-five professor felt a bit
too conspicuous to ask for his own book. But finally he overcame
his embarrassment and approached the shop manager.

"Do you have a book on the Depression by a man named Hal-
braith or something like that?" "You must mean *Crash* by John
Kenneth Galbraith." "Yes, that's the one." "No, we don't carry it."

Galbraith started to walk away and then returned to ask, "You
mind telling me why you don't stock the book?" "You must be out
of your mind to think we are going to display a book entitled
"Crash" in an airport."

The key word in that story is "Crash," with "airport" being the
punch line. Now read the following story. The key word and the
punch word are the same. The whole story hangs on the last word:

Packaging is as important in selling a product as the idea itself.
I remember a conversation I overheard in a Manhattan bookstore.
The store had featured in the window a huge sign reading, "Newly
Translated from the Original French: 27 Mating Positions." Inside,
copies of the book—prewrapped—were selling like hot cakes. It
was only by accident that I heard one harried clerk say to another,
after ringing up his 423rd sale of the volume for the day, "This is
really the most extraordinary sale I've ever seen for a book on
chess."

The punch line, however, is just one mechanical element in the
build-up, bullet, burst. The fatter the details in the build-up, the
sharper the bullet in the punch line, the louder the burst of laughter.

But humor in speeches brings in another dimension. Here the
secret depends on finding the right story and building it into the

body of your talk. Shakespeare, who had such great advice about everything else in life, sums up my final words about speech humor. In *Twelfth Night* Sir Andrew asks Maria whether she is full of jest. "Ay sir," she replies. "I have them at my fingers' ends." So in this book you have at your fingertips hundreds of stories to match any occasion. Pick out two or three. Then choose the one that is funniest and fits. Then build it into your speech. Don't telegraph that the story you are about to tell is a joke. Don't be like the person Sebastian describes in *The Tempest:* "He's winding up the watch of his wit, by and by it will strike."

My closing counsel reminds me of the warning a biology professor of mine gave a young coed. This particularly beautiful student was stunned when the biology professor asked her, "What part of the human anatomy enlarges to about ten times its normal measurement during periods of emotion or excitement?" "I . . . I refuse to answer that question," the girl stammered as she shyly avoided looking at her male classmates sitting nearby. One of them was called upon next, and he correctly answered, "The pupil of the eye."

"Miss Rogers," said the professor, "your refusal to answer my question makes three things evident. First, you didn't study last night's assignment. Second, you have a dirty mind. And third," concluded the professor, "I'm afraid marriage is going to be a tremendous disappointment for you."

And similarly the speaker who has bought my book and then says he still feels awkward about telling a story makes three things clear. First, he hasn't read the book through and sampled the variety of anecdotes available. Second, he has a dull mind if he isn't able to build one of these stories into his speech topic. And third, speaking, instead of being a lot of fun, will be a chore and a disappointment.

PART TWO

Assembly Hall

If youth is a fault one soon gets rid of it.
—Goethe

Action—*Character*

1   *We can talk about the situation, but the real test of our commitment is going to be what we do.* A truck driver recently told me a story of a fellow driver who pulled off the highway and went into a roadside diner to have lunch. He ordered a hamburger, a cup of coffee, and a piece of pie. As his lunch was set before him three rough-looking guys in leather jackets, motorcycle helmets, and boots entered the diner and sat down beside him at the counter. One grabbed his hamburger and ate it. Another grabbed his coffee and drank it, and the third tasted his pie, then mashed the rest of it on the plate.

The man said nothing, got up, paid the cashier for the food, and walked out. The three guys turned to the cashier, and one said, "Not much of a man, is he?"

"He's not much of a driver, either," said the cashier. "HE JUST RAN HIS TRUCK OVER THREE MOTORCYCLES."

(Now although I'm not suggesting we run over anybody, I do think that we have to take positive action.)

Awareness—*Children*

2   *We constantly find out that children know more than we think.* I know a friend of mine was determined to have it out with his older boy and spent several hours painstakingly explaining sexual physiology to him. At the conclusion, feeling utterly exhausted and knowing that he did not want to go through it again with his younger son, he said, "And, Billy, now that I've explained it to you, can I count on you passing it on to Bobby?"

"Okay, Dad," said young William.

His elder son went out in search of his younger brother at once. "Bobby," he said when he found him, "I just had a long lecture from Dad and he wants me to pass on what he told me to you."

"Go ahead," said Bobby.

"Well, you know what you and I were doing with those girls behind the barn last month? DAD WANTS ME TO TELL YOU THAT THE BIRDS AND THE BEES DO IT, TOO."

Competition—*Appraisal*

3   *The time has come for us to stop and take a look at ourselves and see how we are doing with the competition.* The situation recalls the conversation of a young man in a drugstore phone booth. He had left the door of the booth ajar so the druggist couldn't help overhearing his conversation. "I want to talk to the boss" was his opening gambit. "Please connect me. This is the boss? Well, how would you like to hire a new on-his-toes office boy? . . . You already have one who is entirely satisfactory? No way to persuade you to make a change? O.K., I'm sorry. Thanks anyhow for listening to me. Goodbye."

After the young man hung up the druggist told him, "I couldn't help hearing what you said over the phone just now. I like your initiative and I'm sorry you didn't connect on that job. Better luck next time."

"Thanks," said the young man airily, "BUT EVERYTHING IS JUST DANDY. THAT WAS MY OWN BOSS I WAS TALKING TO. I WAS JUST DOING A LITTLE CHECKING UP ON MYSELF."

Criticism—*Teenagers*

4   *After a very generous introduction like that, I have heard a lot of speakers say they wished their wife or mother-in-law could have heard it.* I wish, though, that my two teenage daughters could have heard that I'm such an expert—with such wisdom and good advice. I sometimes feel like the bank customer I witnessed in the teller line of my bank the other day. The teller at the deposit window of the bank sharply reprimanded a man because he had neither filled out a deposit slip nor put his loose silver in the special little rolls of specified amounts.

"When you've done this properly, I'll be glad to accept your deposit," said the teller curtly.

The man accepted this tirade meekly and went to a counter to follow instructions. When he returned later to the window the teller half apologized.

"Oh, that's all right," said the man graciously. I'm used to being spoken to as if I were an idiot. YOU SEE, I HAVE THREE TEENAGERS."

Experience—*Practical*

5   *The kind of people we need are those who are going to keep their feet firmly on the ground.* A few years ago my nephew's fourth-grade class was studying the solar system. The teacher had permitted each pupil to select his own topic about which to study and report to the rest of the class. One took "Pluto," another "Mars," but my nephew selected "Earth," and his reason seemed most logical. Explained my nephew to his classmates, "IT'S THE ONLY PLANET I HAVE VISITED."

God—*Crisis*

6   *I read, of course, about the statistical decline in church attendance.* Yet I know too how people in despair turn to religion and look for spiritual help. I recall once seeing a sign posted in a public school: "IN CASE OF ATOMIC ATTACK, THE FEDERAL RULINGS CONCERNING PRAYER IN THIS BUILDING WILL BE TEMPORARILY SUSPENDED."

Problem—*Worry*

7   *Sometimes we waste too much effort worrying about potential problems that are never likely to come about anyway.* A neighbor of mine who is a second-grade teacher told me of a little boy, aged seven, who one day raised his right hand.

"Teacher," he asked, "suppose a man promised a girl a castle, a boat, a car, and marriage. Can she sue him for breaking his promise?"

The teacher shook her head. "No," she replied, "breach-of-promise cases are now outlawed in this state."

His friend, aged eight, who sat next to the questioner, leaned over. "THERE YOU ARE, PAL," he said. "I TOLD YOU THAT YOU HAD NOTHING TO WORRY ABOUT."

Request—*Commitment*

8   *The real test of our understanding and our sensitivity is our willingness to be involved—our willingness to commit our-*

selves. To express interest is easy when nothing is demanded or required. I remember hearing recently about an exchange. A young man said, "Excuse me, sir," nervously entering the living room, where his girlfriend's father was reading the evening paper, "but there's something kind of important that I'd like to ask you. I was wondering whether—uh—that is, if you'd be willing to, er . . ."

"Why, of course, my boy!" the father exclaimed, jumping to his feet and shaking the lad's hand vigorously. "I'll give my permission gladly, because my little girl's happiness is all that matters to me!"

"Permission?" the young man gulped, obviously confused.

"You want to marry my daughter," the father said, "and you have my blessing."

"Oh, no, sir," said the boy, "it's nothing like that. It's my car, sir. A payment was due last Thursday, and unless I can come up with seventy-five dollars right away, they're going to repossess it; so I was wondering if you . . ."

"CERTAINLY NOT," the father snapped, returning to the sofa and his papers. "I HARDLY KNOW YOU."

Trouble—*Attendance*

9   *That is one problem that doesn't seem to go away.* It seems to hit us every year almost on schedule. It's like a big-city teacher who reported to the junior-high-school principal, "This six-foot overgrown adolescent kid, I just can't handle him any more. He cheats, steals, lies, swears, smokes pot, and, what bothers me the most, HE'S THE ONLY KID IN MY CLASS WITH A ONE-HUNDRED-PERCENT ATTENDANCE RECORD."

(And this particular problem of ours has been . . .)

Youth—*Compulsion*

10   *For those who think the phrase "generation gap" is a myth, I'd like to tell you about a neighborhood friend of mine who has a sixteen-year-old daughter.* The daughter had developed a big crush on an eighteen-year-old boy who had just moved in next door. When the boy arrived for the first date, the mother made conversation during those awkward moments in the living room just before the youngsters took off for the movies. The girl's mother had asked the young man where his family lived before they moved into town. He said they lived in Boston. The mother

commented they had lived in Boston *eighteen years ago right after they were married,* while the girl's father was still finishing graduate school. The two young people seemed startled by this remark, but they said nothing.

The next morning the girl stayed upstairs a long time. When she was finally called, she came stomping down the stairs. When the mother asked what was wrong, she said with disgust, "Mother, you really stuck your foot in it last night. You told him that you lived in Boston when you got married eighteen years ago. And I told him I was eighteen years old. So, of course, I HAD NO CHOICE: I HAD TO TELL HIM I WAS ILLEGITIMATE."

(Well, as parents today we have no choice but to try . . .)

COMMENT: This story must be told as if it actually happened. Tell it as if your neighbor told you. Unless the story is told just this way, emphasizing the "eighteen years ago right after they were married," the audience can miss the point. The story can also be used to describe a "no choice" situation.

Before the Bench

If laws could speak for themselves, they would first complain of the lawyers who wrote them.
—Lord Halifax

11   As a lawyer, I am really happy to get such a fine introduction. I always think of what Dr. Samuel Johnson once said: "I would be loath to speak ill of any man, but I'm afraid this man is an attorney."

12   Seriously though, you mentioned just about everything about my background in my introduction but the advice I remember most from law school. That was the famous maxim of Dean Pound of the Harvard Law School: "Marry for money and make law your mistress"—except that I reversed it. I married my mistress and made money out of law.

13   Of course, there are those who think we lawyers make a bit too much money. But really you would have to admit, you

couldn't live without us lawyers, and most certainly you couldn't *die* without us.

14   Really, though, lawyers have to be thoroughly professional. In fact, we have often been compared to great artists. We find it easy to turn white into black.

15   You know, I have often thought it curious that Balboa wanted to call the Western Hemisphere ocean "serene" or "Pacific," but then I read that Balboa wrote King Ferdinand in 1523 asking that lawyers be barred from coming to the New World.

16   That reminds me of what old John Adams was quoted as saying in the production *1776:* "I have come to the conclusion that one useless man is called a disgrace, two men are called a law firm, and three or more become a Congress."

17   As Lord Halifax once said, "If laws could speak for themselves, they would first complain of the lawyers who wrote them."

18   Perhaps we lawyers should follow the rules in Dean Swift's fictional land where no law could exceed in length the number of letters in the alphabet.

Advice— *Value*

19   *I was asked tonight to give my comments on some of the current questions.* Now, while I am a lawyer and acting in the role of adviser, I guess I don't rate the treatment super-lawyer Clark Clifford had in Washington. The story is told of his being called by a corporation president who explained a difficult problem. Clifford told him not to do anything or say anything. Then he sent a bill for $10,000. A few days later the lawyer called back and remarked, "Clark, first, this bill is way out of line and, secondly, why should I keep quiet anyway?"

"BECAUSE I TOLD YOU SO," said Clifford as he hung up the phone and then proceeded to bill the client for another $5,000.

Advocacy— *Sympathy*

20   *I must admit that I am not impressed by the way they are articulating the case.* They are not effectively presenting their side. It reminds me of the time a young British barrister was

opposed by the brilliant Lord Ellenborough. The young barrister rose with trembling fear to begin his first speech, "My learned lord, my unfortunate client . . . My learned lord, my unfortunate client . . . My learned lord . . ."

"GO ON, SIR," said Lord Ellenborough. "GO ON, AS FAR AS YOU HAVE PROCEEDED HITHERTO, THE COURT IS ENTIRELY WITH YOU."

(And similarly I think it is unfortunate that this case has not been . . .)

Appearances—*Assumption*

21   *You can't always judge a person by his appearance.* I remember the case that resulted in Patrolman O'Shaughnessy being banished to a beat in the darkest and dreariest part of town. His sin? He inadvertently arrested a man climbing into a taxi in a convict suit, only to discover that said man was a cranky judge on his way to a fancy-dress party. Patrolman O'Shaughnessy learned his lesson. "THAT'S THE LAST TIME," he swore, "I'LL EVER BOOK A JUDGE BY HIS COVER."

COMMENT: This story is one of the genre that puts a twist on a familiar saying. Make sure you say the punch line slowly and surely.

Comeback—*Beginning*

22   *As we all know, the last few months have seen more downs than ups, but with the latest developments you are going to see a real comeback, something that is best described by the plaintiff in a recent lawsuit.* This character had brought suit against a large store, claiming he had fallen on its slippery floor and was totally paralyzed from the waist down. The insurance lawyer defending the suit was sure the injury was a fake and tried his best to prove it. But the jury brought in an award of $200,000.

After the trial, the lawyer walked over to the plaintiff and said, "You got your money. But you're never going to be able to enjoy it. I'm going to dog your steps until I prove you are a fake. Wherever you go, I'll be watching you. You'll never be able to get out of that wheelchair. You're not going to be any better off than if you really were paralyzed."

"Listen, Counsellor" said the plaintiff, "now that we're being frank, I'll tell you something. Tomorrow the sleekest ambulance in town calls for me at my home and takes me to the airport. I get on a plane for Paris. In Paris, another ambulance meets me with a pretty French nurse. That ambulance drives me, oh so carefully, down to the shrine at Lourdes, in the south of France.

"AND THEN YOU'RE GOING TO SEE THE GREATEST MIRACLE TAKE PLACE THAT THEY HAVE EVER HAD."

(And with this new opening you are going to see . . .)

ADVICE: The story rises and falls on the plaintiff's description of his trip to France. Be sure to have all those details—ambulance, plane, ambulance nurse, etc., down pat.

Concession—*Meaningless*

23   *The other side has made much of the concessions they have yielded.* But if you examine them closely, I think you'll find them almost as meaningless as the remarks made by a county judge I once heard about. The oft-convicted prisoner was before the bar for sentencing. "I find you guilty on twenty-six counts," said the judge, "and I sentence you to five years on each count, making a total of a hundred and thirty years."

The prisoner, already well along in years, burst into tears. The judge, taking this as a sign of remorse, said in a softened tone, "I didn't mean to be so harsh. I realize I have imposed an unusually severe sentence, so you don't have to serve the hundred and thirty years." With a benign smile the judge leaned toward the prisoner, whose face showed newfound hope. "JUST DO AS MUCH AS YOU CAN!"

Consistency—*Truth*

24   *I agree with Samuel Johnson that consistency is not without its defects.* Its relationship with truth may be one of these. I recall one case in Philadelphia where a not so young woman was called before the Common Pleas judge. She was charged with public drunkenness. It wasn't the first time.

"Madam," said the judge, "how old are you?"

"Twenty-nine years old, Your Honor."

"But, madam, you stood before this same bench not ten years ago and you told me then that you were twenty-nine years old."

"YOUR HONOR," she said, "I'M NOT THE KIND OF WOMAN WHO

TELLS A MAN ONE THING ONE TIME AND ANOTHER THE NEXT."
  (And I say while certain people have consistency in their opposition, they are still as wrong now. . . .)
ADVICE: Don't say "I remember a story"—say "case," which implies it really happened.

Customs—*Outsider*

25   *One of the worst mistakes an outsider can make is to be insensitive to the tastes and customs of the community.* I recall one Philadelphia lawyer who was dealing with a country lawyer colleague from upstate Pennsylvania. The Philadelphian, who was coming upstate for business, wanted to take a deposition of the opposing lawyer's client on a certain Friday one spring.
  The upstate country lawyer demurred, saying, "It would be quite impossible that particular Friday."
  "What do you mean 'impossible' that Friday?" said the Philadelphia lawyer. "I'll have the judge up there to subpoena him."
  "Well, if you want to do that, go ahead, but I want to warn you, people in these parts don't take too kindly to that kind of highhandedness. They can't help but remember that THE LAST TIME A PERSON WAS ORDERED TO BE INTERROGATED ON A GOOD FRIDAY, THEY CRUCIFIED HIM."

Distraction—*Concentration*

26   *I would hope that we will not be distracted from what we have to do.* I would hope that we would operate like the Supreme Court. It was back in the early 1930s a cowboy lawyer for Wyoming had petitioned the U. S. Supreme Court for a rehearing of his case. The Court granted it.
  The old rancher, looking up at Justice Oliver Wendell Holmes, Justice James McReynolds, and Chief Justice Charles Evans Hughes, opened his brief, declaring, "I come to you as John the Baptist saying: 'Repent ye, repent ye.'"
  Whereupon Justice McReynolds leaned forward and said, "But are you not aware of what happened to John the Baptist?"
  "Yes, I am quite aware," said the cowboy lawyer. "HE LOST HIS HEAD THROUGH THE INFLUENCE OF A HARLOT. BUT I KNOW THE SUPREME COURT WOULD NOT BE SO INFLUENCED."
  (And, gentlemen, I hope we are not going to let the sensationalism of recent events distract us from our main task.)

Expansion—*Readiness*

27   *I was asked if we intend to expand our work and move out in a new direction.* I reply by citing the words I recall in an old legal case. It involved possession of a still. The district attorney cross-examined the young defendant. "You mean to sit there and tell this jury that you had a completely assembled still on your premises and were not engaged in the illegal production of alcoholic spirits?"

"That's the truth," answered the defendant. "I acquired it as a conversation piece, just like any other antique."

"You'll have to do better than that," sneered the prosecutor. "As far as this court is concerned the very possession of such equipment is proof of your guilt."

"In that case you'd better charge me with rape, too," the defendant said.

"Are you confessing to the crime of rape, young man?" interrupted the judge.

"NO, YOUR HONOR," answered the defendant, "BUT I SURE AS HELL HAVE THE EQUIPMENT."

(And, gentlemen, we are not saying that we are going to expand in that direction, but we sure do have the equipment. . . .)

Expert—*Authority*

28   *Just to assure you that I am not advancing some wild new theory, I would like to quote some authorities in the field.* I know you will not regard my solution the way an upstate judge did to a colleague of mine. He was arguing the case for replevin for a cow before the county judge. The judge made some rulings disadvantageous to the scholarly lawyer. The angry lawyer started to wave a copy of Blackstone before the bench as he again tried to expound the law of personal property to the jurist.

"Sit down, Counselor," the judge shouted. "I know the law of replevin."

"OF COURSE YOU DO, YOUR HONOR," the angry attorney sarcastically said. "I JUST WANTED TO READ THIS TO SHOW YOU WHAT A DAMNED FOOL BLACKSTONE WAS."

Fairness—*Hearing*

29   *Ladies and gentlemen, I realize that what I have to say might not please a lot of you.* I hope, however, that you will at least give me a hearing. I know that you will not be like a frontier judge I once read about. It was when New Mexico had just been admitted to the Union, and the first court session opened in the new state. The judge, a grizzled old cowboy, took his place on the bench.

The first case charged a man with horse stealing. After much faltering and hitching the wheels of the law began turning slowly and the plaintiff and his witnesses were heard.

"Now, Judge, Your Honor," said the attorney for the defendant, "I would like to present my client's side of the case."

The old judge squirted a stream of tobacco juice at the stove, cleared his throat, and said, "TWON'T BE WORTHWHILE. IT'D ONLY CONFUSE THE JURY."

ADVICE: This is a "Sam Ervin" type story—a rustic anecdote to prove a point—in this case, a plea for fairness.

Inexperience—*Qualifications*

30   *You don't have to sit on a hot stove to know it burns.* In other words, you don't have to have actually experienced something in order to talk knowledgeably about it. I remember being in Philadelphia Municipal Court where the judge had never driven a car. Someone in his court wanted to know how he could rule on motor accidents without firsthand knowledge of driving.

"It's really no handicap," the magistrate explained. "I ALSO TRY RAPE CASES."

(Similarly, I think I can talk about . . .)

Lawyer—*Controversy*

31   *I know we lawyers are supposed to delight in stirring up controversy.* The first time I ever saw confirmation of that was when I went as a child to an revival meeting with my great-uncle. A bespectacled, earnest young man who, I afterward found out, was a lawyer was called upon to deliver a prayer. Unprepared, he gave a prayer straight from his lawyer's heart: "O LORD, STIR UP

AS MUCH STRIFE AMONGST THY PEOPLE, LORD, LEST THY SER-
VANT PERISH."

(But actually, lawyers should try. . . .)

Lawyers—*Doctor*

32   *Recently the medical doctors and lawyers of Houston decided to bury their various hatchets arising from lawsuits which
keep on splitting the two professions into hostile camps.* The doctors hosted at the local Country Club. There was first a two-hour
cocktail party, which in retrospect looked like bad planning, and
then a banquet at which the biggest doctor there welcomed the
lawyers with a stiff, formal little speech. One of the best-known
trial lawyers of the Southwest, a master of the high sardonic, who
had been in dogged attendance at the cocktail party, had been
tapped to respond on behalf of the lawyers. He made a short but
memorable speech. Rising, he dropped his voice low and said,
"During the course of these festivities I have taken judicial notice
of the arrival of our doctor-hosts and their ladies in limousines and
mink, all or most of them wearing expressions of superior knowledge or secrets known only to themselves. I FEEL MOVED TO RE-
MIND OUR HOSTS THAT WHILE THEIR PROFESSIONAL ANCESTORS
WERE BLEEDING GEORGE WASHINGTON WITH LEECHES AND
TEACHING THAT THE NIGHT AIR WAS POISONOUS, MY PROFES-
SIONAL ANCESTORS WERE DRAWING UP THE CONSTITUTION OF
THESE UNITED STATES—AS NOBLE A DOCUMENT AS KNOWN TO
THE MINDS OF MEN OR ANGELS. I THANK YOU ONE AND ALL."

(Seriously, though, I was reminded that while the doctors were
successfully making the first heart transplant, the lawyers of our
country were putting together the Watergate operation.)

Marriage—*Love*

33   *One thing that always bothered me about law is that the
lowest court has the authority to perform a marriage but not the
highest.* I always thought that it was because once you do it there's
no appeal—but Justice Felix Frankfurter had another explanation.
Asked to officiate at a friend's wedding ceremony, Justice Frankfurter explained that he did not have the authority to perform the
ceremony.

"What!" exclaimed his friend. "A Supreme Court Justice doesn't have the authority to marry people! How come?"

"I guess," replied Frankfurter, "IT IS BECAUSE MARRIAGE IS NOT CONSIDERED A FEDERAL OFFENSE."

Natural—*Pretense*

34   *You can get yourself in trouble when you don't act yourself and step out of character.* I recall the retort the Scottish barrister Erskine once made to Lord Mansfield in a London case in the House of Lords. It was a case involving the curator of a certain estate. Judge Mansfield, although Scottish by birth, adopted the fashionable English pronunciation of the word, saying curätor. After several times correcting Erskine, he told the Scottish barrister, "In this court, you must follow the Latin law, pronouncing the penultimate syllable—curätor.

Replied Erskine, "FAR BE IT FROM ME, MY LORD, TO CORRECT SUCH AN EMINENT SENÄTOR AND OUTSTANDING ORÄTOR AS YOUR LORDSHIP."

COMMENT: Try pronouncing "Se-nay'-ter" and "O-ray'-ter" aloud before trying the story.

Omission—*Token*

35   *All we really have received is a token gesture on their part.* In fact, we didn't get much more than Ralph got in a will that I heard about from a lawyer in my old home town. This rich banker had died and his family met in the lawyer's office for the reading of his will.

He left $20,000 to his wife, $75,000 to his brothers, and $10,000 each to his sisters.

Then the will read, "AND TO MY NEPHEW RALPH, WHO ALWAYS WANTED TO BE MENTIONED IN MY WILL, I SAY, 'HELLO, RALPH.' "

Opportuneness—*Acceptance*

36   *There is a right place and time for everything.* I remember my first year in law school in the course in criminal law, the professor concluded his final lecture before the holidays by observing, "Remember, gentlemen, if you have an affair with a girl under age, with or without her consent, it's rape. If you have an affair with a girl of age without her consent, that's rape. BUT IF YOU HAVE AN AFFAIR WITH A GIRL OF AGE WITH HER CONSENT, MERRY CHRISTMAS."

(And similarly you should remember, if you are getting ready to launch a big building complex, it is important to have the consent of not just the authorities but of the community. . . .)

ADVICE: On a story like this you should write down the words following "Remember, gentlemen, if . . ."

Practice—*Training*

37 *You can't expect to know all the answers overnight.* There is going to be a period of adjustment and training. It is not unlike the conversation of two young ladies who were discussing their marriage plans on a subway last week. "I understand your boyfriend graduates from law school this June. I suppose you'll be getting married then."

"Oh, no, not right away," replied the other. "I WANT HIM TO PRACTICE FOR AT LEAST A YEAR FIRST."

Question—*Prepared*

38 *Fortunately I had enough foresight to anticipate such a request.* I did bring along the statistical material. Perhaps one reason I did is my recollection of a negligence case. A witness who saw an automobile accident was out on the stand to testify when counsel said, "Did you see the accident?"

He said, "Yes, sir!"

Counsel added, "How far away were you when the accident happened?"

Witness said, "Twenty-two feet, nine and three-quarter inches."

Counsel looked at the court and looked at the jury and said, "Well, will you tell the court and jury how do you know it was twenty-two feet, nine and three-quarter inches?"

Witness replied, "When it happened, I took out a tape measure and measured from where I stood to the point of impact, BECAUSE I KNEW SOME DOGGONE LAWYER WAS GOING TO ASK ME THAT QUESTION."

COMMENT: Everett Dirksen told this story when debating the Housing Act in 1959.

Regulations—*Stickler*

39 *I don't see any reason why we can't depart from the usual procedure.* A failure to act when we have the chance would be unthinkable. Such an attitude reminds me of a judge in upstate

Pennsylvania. A couple from an out-of-the way rural area, Sam Brown and Eliza Wells, were celebrating the fourth birthday of their son, and they decided it was about time they got married.

They climbed in the old wagon and journeyed to the county seat, located the judge, and asked him to marry them. They knew nothing about the need for the marriage license, so the judge sent them to a county clerk in another office of the court house to get a license.

In due course they came back with a license, authorizing the judge to marry them. After inspecting it the judge turned to Sam and said, "Sam Brown, is your name Samuel?" "Yes, that's right." "Well, go back and get a new license." When they returned the judge inquired of Eliza if her real name shouldn't be Elizabeth. When they finally returned the judge looked at the license. "Your license is in order now and I have no choice but to marry you. But I want you to understand clearly, that boy of yours will remain a technical bastard."

"JUDGE, THAT AIN'T SO BAD. THAT'S WHAT THE CLERK SAID YOU ARE."

(And we can't be so narrowly technical . . .)

Thoroughness—*Professionalism*

40   *We lawyers pride ourselves on being thorough.* Of course, that is the hallmark of any professional discipline. I recall a young lawyer friend of mine who went to a local medical association meeting hoping to widen his professional acquaintance. At the end of the evening address the chairman called on my friend to speak, as he was the only lawyer there. He rose and stammered, trying to find some connection between the two great professions.

"As I come to think of it," he said, "there is some affinity between your great profession and mine, because I know that whenever I finish a case I say to myself, 'Now, have I left anything out?' Whereas in the medical profession, at the end of a case, you probably say, 'HAVE I LEFT ANYTHING IN?' "

(And tonight I want to ask if we are omitting anything . . .)

Welcome—*Reciprocity*

41   *As I arrived today I was immediately taken in tow by some of my colleagues of law in this city.* This extended courtesy reminds me of the time a lawyer and his wife were taking an ocean

cruise. The ship hit a storm and the lawyer fell overboard. Almost immediately eight sharks formed a two-lane escort for the guy and helped him all the way back to the ship.

"It was a miracle," the lawyer told his wife. "No," said his wife, "JUST PROFESSIONAL COURTESY."

Boudoir

Adultery is democracy in love.
—H. L. Mencken

Activity—*Results*

42   *I see an awful lot of activity, but I fail to see the results.* The announcement of programs and extended press coverage does not take the place of real accomplishments. Maxfield Parrish, the artist, was lolling around his studio, passing the time while having coffee with his model. All of a sudden he heard in the distance his wife, who knew of Parrish's capacity for inaction.

"QUICK" he said to his young model. "I HEAR MY WIFE COMING. TAKE OFF YOUR CLOTHES."

(And similarly it is time for our friends to strip down for action. . . .)

Adjournment—*Toast*

43   *At this time in the festivities I think it appropriate to offer a farewell toast.* Chauncey Depew was once asked by a beautiful woman, "Senator, what is the most beautiful thing in the world?"

"Sleep," he replied.

"But, Senator," protested the lady, "I was sure you would agree with me that a beautiful woman is the most beautiful thing in the world."

"Of course you are right," said Depew. "But next to a beautiful woman, sleep is the most beautiful thing in the world."

Administration—*Change*

44   *When someone asked me earlier whether I enjoyed making this trip out of Washington to give a speech such as this, I told*

*him I feel the way a bordello madam once expressed it to a fre-
quent visitor.*

It was the visitor's custom to have a brief chat with the madam
before calling on the girls. Once he was surprised to find the
woman absent from her post. She was back with the girls.

"What are you doing here?" asked the surprised visitor.

"OH," said the madam, "SOMETIMES I JUST GET BORED WITH
ADMINISTRATION."

(My feelings are similar. . . .)

Administration—*Responsibility*

45   *Gentlemen, as we close tonight's activities, I think we owe
a great debt of thanks to the young lady who organized this
program.* Her efficiency reminds me of a June wedding not too
long ago. The delicate young bride-to-be sighed to her mother,
"Oh, Mother, there are so many things to do before the wedding
and I want it to be perfect. I just hope that I won't overlook the
most insignificant detail."

"Don't worry your pretty little head," said her mother, "I'LL SEE
THAT HE'S THERE!"

(But seriously, our young lady tonight saw to it that we all got
here. . . .)

Advice—*Counsel*

46   *I am not sure that we should follow the advice we are
being given.* I can't help but think where it would leave us. I
remember a silver wedding anniversary in Paris. While all were
unrestrainedly merry over the ample liquor provided by the host,
the husband, René, remained in the corner, nursing a drink and
following one of the guests with mournful eyes.

A friend noticed this strange action, all the more strange on so
happy an occasion, and said, "Who you are glaring at, René?"

"At my lawyer, may his soul rot."

"But why are you so angry with him?"

"It is a sad tale. After I had been married ten years I decided
I had had enough and that the best solution would be to kill my
wife. Painlessly, of course, for I am humane. Being a methodical
man, I approached my lawyer—that one over there—and asked
him of the possible consequences. He told me that whereas killing
a husband is, here in France, a mere misdemeanor, killing a wife

is a felony, and that even with a most skillful defense I would have to count on fifteen years in jail. He urged me not to do it, and I let myself be guided by his advice."

"Well, then, why are you angry?"

"BECAUSE," said René, "IF I HAD NOT LISTENED TO THIS LAW-YER'S IDIOTIC ADVICE, ON THIS VERY DAY I WOULD HAVE BEEN A FREE MAN AT LAST."

Appreciation—*Party*

47   *I want to say thanks for the last few days.* Although I had little to do with the cost and preparation, I had a lot to do with the enjoyment. It recalls the incident of a young man and a blonde who came into a fashionable Fifth Avenue fur store on a Friday afternoon. The man told the clerk in a brusque manner that he wanted to look at the most expensive fur coat in the place. The clerk was doubtful and brought out a nice squirrel-skin job. "Take it away," said the customer. "Apparently you didn't hear what I said. I want the *most expensive* coat you have."

Next the clerk tried a beaver coat. Then a sealskin and then a sheared racoon, but each time with the same result. So finally the clerk shot the works and brought out a $5,000 mutation mink. When the man saw that, his eyes lit up. Turning to the blonde, he said, "That's the idea. Try it on and see how it looks. I want to charge it. Go ahead and check my credit. I'll be back Monday for the coat."

"Certainly, sir, anything you say."

Monday morning the man arrived at the store alone. The minute he walked in the clerk rushed up to him shaking his fist, followed by the floor walker, the chief buyer, the manager, and the credit manager. All were shouting at him angrily. "We've looked you up," said the credit manager. "You have no more credit than a mouse. You couldn't charge a toothbrush."

"Now calm yourself," said the man. "I haven't taken anything out of your store. I JUST CAME IN TO THANK YOU FOR A WONDER-FUL WEEKEND."

(And similarly I'd like to thank everybody . . .)

Businessman—*Ethics*

48   *There is no doubt that a businessman only interested in the short-term advantage can make a bigger profit.* The unethical

businessman doesn't care about his reputation. He is like a bride-to-be I heard about who was showing her friend a list of guests to be invited to the wedding.

After her friend had read the names she looked puzzled. "What's the matter?" asked the bride-to-be.

"Isn't it rather strange," queried the friend, "you have only put down the names of married couples?"

"Yes, that was my fiancé's idea. DON'T YOU THINK IT'S RATHER CLEVER? HE SAYS THAT IF WE INVITE ONLY MARRIED PEOPLE THE PRESENTS WILL BE ALL CLEAR PROFIT."

Decision—*Regrets*

49   *When I was asked whether I had any second thoughts about severing our connections with this operation, I recalled the story of a husband who sat at his dying wife's bedside.* "Darling," his wife breathed in little more than a whisper, "I've got a confession to make before I go. I . . . I'm the one who took the twenty thousand dollars from your safe. I spent it on a fling with your best friend, Bill. And I'm the one who reported your income-tax evasion to the government."

"That's all right, dearest. Don't give it a second thought," the husband answered. "I'm the one who poisoned you."

(And similarly I had no regrets about . . .)

Generosity—*Gratitude*

50   *Of course we have reason to be thankful to our honoree tonight.* He has been unfailingly generous. And I am sure he won't mind my telling about a conversation that I overheard recently on a commuter train.

Two friends—one fifty, the other sixty—were arguing about the forthcoming marriage of the latter to a young lady in her twenties. "I don't believe in these May-December marriages," said the fifty-year-old. "After all, December is going to find in May the freshness and beauty of springtime, but whatever is May going to find in December?"

The sixty-year-old replied, "CHRISTMAS!"

(But our honoree represents more than just the Christmas spirit. . . .)

Hypocrisy—*Politicians*

51   *It amazes me how public leaders can wax so eloquent against welfare chiselers and then turn around and pad expense accounts and take boondoggling trips.* They argue for fiscal responsibility while they give tax exemptions to special-interest groups. It reminds me of the Parisian lover who claimed he was just minding his own business. A Frenchman one day, suspicious of his wife, went home early. Arriving at his apartment house, he went up to his floor. Outside the door he could smell cigar smoke. He opened the door, went to the bedroom. There was his wife nude on the bed alone. But the smell of cigar smoke filled the room. He looked in the living room and then the kitchen. Still no one there. He looked outside the kitchen window. Way down, strolling down the front-lobby steps, was a man with a cigar. Furious, the husband looked around for something to hurl. The only object not stationary was the refrigerator standing next to the window. With all his might he pushed and shoved the refrigerator out the window. Down fourteen stories it hurtled, landing on the cigar-smoking stroller. Meanwhile the husband collapsed from the strain.

The scene then switched to heaven. St. Peter was examining the credentials of the new arrivals. Three waited outside the gates. To the first he asked, "How did you come here?" The man answered, "I don't know. I was walking down the steps of my apartment house for an evening walk when I was hit. Now I am here."

St. Peter nodded and let him pass.

He looked at the second and asked him the question. The second man said, "I was so enraged smelling strange cigar smoke in my apartment that I lost my temper and pushed a refrigerator out the window. I must have collapsed with a heart attack from the overexertion."

St. Peter nodded again and turned to the third. "Why are you here?"

"I don't know," said the third. "THERE I WAS, HURTING NO ONE, MINDING MY BUSINESS, JUST SMOKING A CIGAR IN THE REFRIGERATOR."

(And similarly, I don't see how our public leaders can escape responsibility . . .)

Intuition—*Obvious*

52   *You don't need much intuition to figure out what is likely to happen.* Not everyone is as unaware as the owner of a large furniture store who was in Denmark to buy some stock. While on his business he happened to meet in a hotel elevator a beautiful girl who gave him a friendly smile. The furniture store owner tried to become acquainted even though neither could understand a word of each other's language. He drew a picture of a taxi and she nodded her head in agreement, so they went for a ride in a taxi.

While riding in the cab he drew a picture of a table in a restaurant and again she nodded her head in agreement, so they went to a fine restaurant for dinner. After dinner he sketched two dancers and she was delighted. They went to a nightclub and had a lovely time.

Then the girl indicated she would like to use the pencil and paper, which he gave to her. She drew a picture of a four-poster bed. The fellow was dumfounded. As he said to a friend later, "YOU KNOW, I NEVER COULD FIGURE OUT HOW THAT GIRL KNEW I WAS IN THE FURNITURE BUSINESS."

Involvement—*Stakes*

53   *We can't feel real commitment if we are just passive observers.* We must have a stake in it. I remember a story about a husband who, arriving home unexpectedly, found his wife in the arms of his best friend.

"Well, I'm glad finally to have this out," said the friend. "I love your wife and want her for my own. Let's be gentlemen and settle this with a game of cards. Winner takes Joyce. All right? Shall we play gin rummy?"

"Sounds fine to me," replied the husband.

"BUT HOW ABOUT A PENNY A POINT JUST TO MAKE THE GAME INTERESTING?"

Life—*Inactivity*

54   *When we look at the record of this department I can't find the record of any accomplishments.* I don't see the programs or projects. The situation reminds me of a wife who in frustration went to a marriage counselor. "My husband has no outstanding vices," she said to the counselor, "but I'm going to divorce him."

"Remember," the counselor advised, "when you married this man it was for life."

"I know, I know," she replied, "BUT FOR THE PAST FIVE YEARS HE HASN'T SHOWN ANY SIGNS OF LIFE."

Misinterpretation—*Heaven*

55 *Even people close together do not always know each other's desires and dreams.* I recall the story of two lovers interested in spiritualism who vowed that if either died, the one remaining would try to contact the partner in the other world exactly thirty days after the tragedy. As luck would have it, a few weeks later the young man perished in the wreck of his new sports car, and, true to her word, his bereaved sweetheart attempted to contact him in the spirit world exactly thirty days later. She lay on her bed in the darkness and called out, "John, John, this is Martha. Do you hear me, John?"

A ghostly voice answered her. "Yes, Martha, this is John. I hear you."

Then his newly bereaved asked, "Oh, John, what is it like where you are?"

"It's beautiful, Martha. There are blue skies, a soft breeze and quiet beauty sweeping the horizon."

She exclaimed, "It sounds beautiful! What do you do all day?"

"Well, Martha, I have all I want to eat and I'm attended by a lot of bosomy females who see to all my needs."

Martha was somewhat taken aback. "But, John," she said, "is that really what heaven is like?"

"Heaven? I'm not in heaven, Martha!"

"Where are you, then?"

"I'M A BULL IN A WYOMING PASTURE."

Mistake—*Fault*

56 *It is one thing to make a mistake where no one knows about it, but I am in the situation where everyone can see and know the mistakes I have committed.* But at least I don't feel as bad as the husband I heard about. He was middle-aged and married for very nearly twenty years. He was clipping the hedges and she was pruning the rosebushes, but somehow their minds didn't seem to be on their work. The wife seemed especially discontented and was mumbling under her breath about something. Then, quite unexpectedly, she stalked over to where the husband was standing, examining his rhododendron at close range, and gave him a short kick in the leg.

"Ow-ouch!" exclaimed the husband. "What the heck was that for?"

"That," she said, stalking back to her rosebushes, "is for being such a lousy lover!"

The husband thought about this unexpected attack for a minute or two. Then he turned and—just as resolutely as she had a few moments before—stalked over and gave his wife a swift and well-placed foot to the behind as she bent over, about to pluck an American Beauty.

"Ow!" she cried. "Why did you do that?"

"THAT" he said, returning to his rhododendron, "IS FOR KNOWING THE DIFFERENCE!"

Pause—*Opportunity*

57   *I think it is appropriate on an occasion like this to give you a more intimate glimpse of the history of our country.* We all know of Paul Revere's ride, but we may not be aware of the colloquy that took place that night.

As Paul Revere's horse galloped down the country road to warn the people that the British were coming, the first place he came to was a farmhouse. "Is your husband at home?" he called to the woman feeding chickens in the yard.

"He's back in the barn, Paul," she answered.

"Tell him to get his musket and go to the village square. The redcoats are coming!"

The exchange of words had taken but an instant; Revere's horse had not broken its stride. The famous patriot thundered off toward the next farm. "Is your husband at home?" Revere called to the woman in the doorway of the next farmhouse he approached.

"He's asleep in his room, Paul," she said.

"Tell him to get on his clothes," Revere cried. "The minutemen are meeting at the village square. The British are coming!"

Horse and rider galloped on to still another home. "Is your husband at home?" he called to the handsome woman who leaned out of the window.

"He's gone to New Salem and won't be back till Sunday," she
said.

Then Paul reined his horse, saying, "WHOAAA!"

(And similarly I think we should call a halt to this evening's
festivities. . . .)

ADVICE: Like a Biblical subject, the humor in this story is the
comical if irreverent treatment of history.

Perfection—*Change*

58   *I for one am satisfied with the present situation and see no
need for change.* In fact, my feelings recall Chief Justice Salmon
Chase at a reception for the Supreme Court not too long after the
Civil War. Chase noted a very buxom Southern belle. He intro-
duced himself to her, saying, "Madam, my name is Salmon Chase."
The girl, mindful of Chase's Republican record, said, "Mr. Chief
Justice, I know who you are, but I want to warn you that I am still
a rebel who has not been reconstructed."

"MADAM," Chase replied, looking down at her low-cut hourglass
gown, "IN YOUR CASE RECONSTRUCTION WOULD BE BLASPHE-
MOUS."

(And I would also say that reconstruction or reform in this situation . . .)

COMMENT: "Reconstruction" is the key word.

Resources—*Change*

59   *I am not yet convinced for the need to change.* We can
operate on what we have. Our situation recalls that of a courting
couple. One night they were sitting on a bench in the moonlight,
and the odor of flowers permeated the atmosphere. It was a time
and a circumstance which would inevitably engender romance in
the heart of anybody. And John said to Mary, "Mary, if you wasn't
what you is, what would you like to be?"

And Mary said, "John, if I wasn't what I is, I would like to be an
American Beauty rose." Then Mary turned the question on John
and said, "John, if you wasn't what you is, what would you like to
be?"

John said, "If I wasn't what I is, I would like to be an octopus."

Mary said, "John, what is an octopus?"

John said, "An octopus is some kind of fish or an animal or
something that has a thousand arms."

Mary said, "John, if you was an octopus and had a thousand arms, what would you do with all those arms?"

John said, "I would put every one of them around you."

Mary said, "GO AWAY, JOHN. YOU AIN'T USING THE TWO YOU HAVE ALREADY GOT."

Response—*Cliché*

60   *There are some people who try to slide around a challenge.* Instead of a clear-cut answer they give you a cliché. Instead of a solution they give you a slogan.

It is like a wife I heard about recently who went one Sunday afternoon to the zoo with her husband. One of the apes broke through his bars, went right for the man's wife and put his hairy arms around her, grunting loudly.

The wife cried out, "Harry, Harry, do something, do something!"

"Why don't you try what you always say to me, 'HARRY, I FEEL I'M HAVING ANOTHER MIGRAINE'?"

Salesmanship—*Subtle*

61   *I think what we are observing is a very subtle approach.* It may be as successful as a college friend I once knew. He met a girl at a football game and they hit it off so well that he took her to a show. That went fine, so he asked her to dinner. They enjoyed a leisurely dinner at a good hotel and followed that with a night-club and dancing. Along toward midnight they were having a snack at a table for two and he said to her, "You know, I've had a wonderful time ever since I met you this afternoon. I think we've hit it off swell together, don't you?"

"Sure," she agreed. "I've enjoyed it too."

"I'd like to have breakfast with you in the morning." And he looked at her eagerly. "May I?"

"Yes," she answered. "I'd like that very much."

"ALL RIGHT. WHAT WILL I DO, CALL YOU OR NUDGE YOU?"

Undiscriminating—*Choosy*

62   *I don't think in our situation we can afford to be too choosy.* We're like that cleaning woman a colleague of mine knows. He had to go back to the office late one night. He met one of the cleaning women in the hall and stopped to chat with her a

moment. As they talked he discovered that he was out of cigarettes and would have to go back down to get some.

"That's all right," said the woman. "My oldest son is helping me and you can send him down."

"Your oldest son?" inquired the man. "Why, I thought you told me one time you were an old maid."

"I am," she replied, "BUT I'M NOT A FUSSY OLD MAID."

Caucus Room

An honest politician is one who, when bought,
will stay bought.

—S. Cameron

63   Ladies and gentlemen, your next Representative should be intelligent, industrious, and competent—but I'm running anyway.

64   Actually, I think I'm doing fairly well. We just conducted our own survey. Three out of four favored my candidacy. Next week we are going to conduct another survey—outside my own family.

65   Thank you for the introduction. The only thing you omitted was my career in uniform. But then I recognize that many of the men in the audience also have good records as Boy Scouts.

66   Really, though, when I was selected to be the honoree I was quite honored. After all, the party chairman had announced they would choose only the most promising candidate. Then my wife said, "But is there any other kind?"

67   Seriously, I want to make it clear that I intend to honor any promise I make today—but I would appreciate it if you people in the audience would stop taking notes.

68   You know, though, I'd be the first to admit I fall way short of a Lincoln. It was he who said, "You can't fool all the people all the time." But all I want is a good sizable majority.

69   I thank the chairman for his introduction. He didn't, however, go into one part of my background. He didn't tell you that I have known what it's like to be poor. And believe me, friends, after I finish paying for this campaign, I'll know what it's like all over again.

70   Actually, I have found politics to be just what G. K. Chesterton once told his son. "The pursuit of office is like the pursuit of women—the position ridiculous, the expense damnable and the pleasure fleeting."

71   First I want to thank the chairman for his generous introduction. My wife, however, has described it in different terms. As she said, greatness was just thrust upon me—and I ducked.

72   Of course, I disagree. I know some Congressmen achieve greatness—but as for myself, I have relied on the seniority rule.

73   There are occasions, though, when I feel the urge to act like a statesman, but then I sit down until I get over it.

74   First I want to say how deeply touched I am to be here at this campaign dinner—not, however, as deeply touched as some of you were.

75   Really, though, these political dinners are a strange phenomenon in American politics. A speaker eats a lot of food he doesn't want and then proceeds to talk about something he doesn't understand to a lot of people who really don't want to hear him.

76   Actually, I do better at these dinners than some. My friend next to me complained when he found out where he was sitting. He said he makes it a rule never to sit next to a legislator. They never pass anything.

77   I suppose I should make a few comments about my recent defeat, but I like the advice of the British Prime Minister Lord Melbourne, who said, "There is only one thing worse than a turned-out politician complaining about his being defeated and that is a turned-down maiden complaining about her being jilted."

78   Seriously, though, I want to take this chance to thank those who voted for me, and my wife also wants to thank those who didn't.

Attendance—*Fellowship*

79   *When I see the many friends of mine who have joined me on this occasion,* I can't help but think of the time in the Civil War when Fort Donelson fell, leaving the Union forces free to occupy Nashville. At that time the Tennessee legislature was in session. When the news reached the capital, the legislators prepared to adjourn and take to the hills. A member rose and said, "And now, gentlemen, God will take care of us. If we do not meet here again, we shall meet in heaven."

"Stop, Mr. Chairman," cried a voice in the rear of the chamber. "Don't adjourn to that place. IF WE DO, WE SHALL NEVER GET A QUORUM."

(And similarly, knowing the habits of many of my friends, I am not sure . . .)

Background—*Natural*

80   *As I understand, each of us on the panel is supposed to introduce ourselves and say something about our background.* I wish I had an illustrious name like some others on the panel. But I do feel that I can say what Everett Dirksen said once when he was first running for Congress. One of his opponents dwelt for considerable length on his antecedents. His grandfather had been a general and his uncle a state supreme-court judge. Then Ev rose to introduce himself, saying, "LADIES AND GENTLEMEN, IT HAS BEEN MY PRIVILEGE AND GOOD FORTUNE TO BE DESCENDED FROM A LONG LINE . . . OF MARRIED FOLKS."

ADVICE: To imitate Ev Dirksen, pro-nounce each word slow-ly and dis-tinc-tly in a low and hoarse whisper.

Campaign—*Defeat*

81   *Happily, I can say that my recent defeat left no scars other than financial.* Just the same I'm glad I wasn't introduced today the way I was recently. The toastmaster announced, "The next speaker bears a slight resemblance to the earth. You know the earth is not a perfect spheroid because it is flattened at the poles. SO WAS YOUR NEXT SPEAKER."

Conscience—*Expediency*

82   *Gentlemen, we can either do the hard thing or the easy, the right or the wrong.* But I don't feel like buying a lightning rod for an easy conscience like Abraham Lincoln's onetime foe. In Lincoln's campaign for re-election to the Illinois legislature, he tangled in debate with one George Forquer, a onetime Whig, who had changed his politics to Democrat in order to receive a handsome appointment from President Jackson. He had just recently built a new home, topped with a lightning rod. Forquer ridiculed and brutally attacked the young Lincoln. When it was Lincoln's turn to speak he replied to Forquer's argument clearly and effectively. Then he paused and with cutting sarcasm launched an attack on his opponent.

"Among other things, my opponent in this debate has said that 'this young man,' alluding to me, 'must be taken down.' I am not so young in years as I am in tricks of the trade of a politician, but," he said, pointing a deadly finger at Forquer, "LIVE LONG OR DIE YOUNG, I WOULD RATHER DIE NOW THAN, LIKE THE GENTLEMAN, CHANGE MY POLITICS AND WITH IT RECEIVE AN OFFICE WORTH THREE THOUSAND DOLLARS A YEAR AND THEN FEEL OBLIGED TO ERECT A LIGHTNING ROD OVER MY HOUSE TO PROTECT A GUILTY CONSCIENCE FROM AN OFFENDED GOD."

Conservation—*Requirements*

83   *Now I listened to the advice that says, "All we really need is some good men."* That's all very true, but it really begs the question. It is like the time when Arizona first came into the Union in 1912 and Carl Hayden, who was to serve until 1969, made an impassioned speech on a water bill, closing with the words, "All Arizona needs is some good men and water."

To which Senator Penrose of Pennsylvania replied, "WELL, SENATOR, YOU COULD SAY THE SAME THING ABOUT HELL."

(And similarly, we could say the same thing about . . .)

Credibility—*Rhetoric*

84   *Sometimes all the words I have been hearing from Washington remind me of the time some years back when a senator from the Interior Committee went to visit an Indian reservation*

in Arizona. The senator made a fine speech full of promises of better things. "We shall see," he said, "a new era of Indian opportunity." To this the natives gave a ringing cry of *"Hoya, hoya."* Encouraged by this, the senator continued, "We promise better schools and technical training." *"Hoya, hoya!"* exclaimed the natives with much enthusiasm. "We pledge better hospitals and medical assistance," said the senator. *"Hoya, hoya,"* cried the natives.

With a tear running down his cheek, the senator ended his fine speech. "We come to you as equals, as brothers. So trust us. We have only your best interest at heart." The air shook with one long, mighty *"Hoya, hoya."*

Greatly pleased by the reception, the senator then began making a tour over the reservation. "I see that you have fine breeds of beef cattle here," he said. "May I inspect them?"

"Certainly, come this way," said the chief. "BUT BE CAREFUL NOT TO STEP IN THE HOYA."

(And these days you have to duck what is being spread around in Washington. . . .)

Criticism—*Heckler*

85   *It is hard not to be blunt with such irresponsible and irrational critics.* When Senator McGovern in the 1972 campaign was reprimanded by his wife for using bad language to a young heckler he replied in defense, "IT WAS ONLY AN ELOQUENT ADMONITION DELIVERED IN GREAT PASSION TO THE YOUNG MAN, WHO WAS INVITED TO APPROACH A STRATEGIC PART OF MY ANATOMY WITH SOME TENDERNESS."

Criticism—*Hypocrisy*

86   *The hypocrisy of these critics reminds me of some words of former Senator Millard Tydings during the Prohibition era.* He was one of the few Senators who voted the way he drank. When some of his colleagues were piously fighting the repeal of the act, Tydings rose and said, "TO PARAPHRASE THE WORDS OF THE APOSTLE MATTHEW, LET HE WHO IS WITHOUT GIN CAST THE FIRST VOTE."

(And before we hastily judge others, let us . . .)

Criticism—*Opposition*

87   *The caliber of the opposition reminds me of a time on the Senate floor when Senator George Vest was attacked in a stupid, irrational outburst.* When the tirade ended, Vest rose and said, "Mr. President, after listening to the remarks of my learned colleague, I feel somewhat like the little corporal in the Philistinian army who, after Samson had passed through, picked himself off the ground and, holding his battered head, cried out, 'NOW I KNOW WHAT IT FEELS LIKE TO BE SMITTEN BY THE JAWBONE OF AN ASS.' "

Image—*Ignorance*

88   *Sometimes it pays to act as if you don't know everything.* I remember what a Colorado senator once said at a televised Congressional hearing on taxes of nightclubs. One of the clubs mentioned was the 21 Club. But Senator Milliken, ranking Republican member of the Finance Committee, would call it one time the 23 Club and the next time the 22 Club. Afterward an aide caught up with him and said, "Senator, there you were on national television and you couldn't get straight the name of the 21 Club. Why, we've been there many times together."

"I know," whispered the senator. "BUT IN POLITICS YOU CAN'T AFFORD TO BE TOO KNOWLEDGABLE OF THINGS LIKE THAT."

(And even if I have some experience, I am not going to act like an expert. . . .)

Incredible—*pure*

89   *We would like some pure and simple answers to our questions.* The only thing pure we are getting so far is like the stuff Senator Eugene Milliken once described in an exchange with Senator Lyndon Johnson. Johnson had just undergone an operation, but he was not letting his recovery impede his manuevering against some bills Milliken was keenly interested in.

One day Milliken approached Johnson outside the Senate chamber and said, "Lyndon, you know, I had that same operation and I want to know how you feel."

"Fine, Gene, thank you."

"Do you have traces of blood in your urine, Lyndon?"

"No, it's okay."

"Well, how about your sugar count in the urine?"

"No, it's all fine, Gene."

"Well, Lyndon what about your albumen?"

"No, it's okay, Gene, but just why do you ask?" said Johnson.

"BECAUSE I JUST WANT TO KNOW IF THE STUFF YOU'RE THROW-ING MY WAY IS 100 PERCENT PURE."

Insult—*Audience*

90   *One thing we want to make sure of is that no one is going to be insulted by this type of presentation.* I guess this was what Senator Oliver Johnston of South Carolina had in mind in his warning to his administrative aide. Johnston, who was coming up for re-election, was troubled by his lack of anything substantial to write about in his Congressional newsletter to his constituents. Finally he said to his assistant, "Why don't we write something against Communism?" His aide agreed and came back with a crackerjack column exposing the evils of "godless atheistic Communism," putting the good senator four-square for Americanism and against Communism.

Johnston read the prepared draft and nodded his approval. As the aide went out the door Johnston called him back.

"Wait a second. How many Communists do you think we have in South Carolina?"

"About five or six," said the aide.

"WELL, YOU MAKE MIGHTY SURE THAT THAT PIECE DOESN'T GET SENT TO ANY OF THEM! YA HEAR?"

Patron—*Support*

91   *I must admit I have some question about who is behind this group.* For all the piety and lofty ideals, I suspect more dubious types. It reminds me of back in 1948 when an evangelist named Reverend W. W. "Bill" Alexander called a press conference to announce that Jesus Christ had appeared from on high and had asked him to be a candidate for the United States Senate. Thereupon, with the Lord's blessing, he filed against incumbent Senator Monroney. Shortly thereafter, the good reverend decided to switch and run as the Republican candidate. As Alexander made progress, it was deemed necessary to bring Senator Bob Kerr,

Monroney's senior colleague, to the rescue.

At a Labor Day rally for thousands of picnickers Kerr annihilated Alexander with this remark: "Now, this fellow Alexander one day said to a press conference, 'After communion with the Lord, I have decided to enter the Democratic primary and run for the U. S. Senate.' Shortly thereafter he switched over and won the Republican nomination. What I'd like to know," Kerr said piously, "IF THE LORD TOLD BILL ALEXANDER TO RUN AS A DEMOCRAT, WHO THEN TOLD HIM TO RUN AS A REPUBLICAN?"

(And what I'd like to know is who are the men behind the scenes. . . .)

Practicality—*Principles*

92   *Gentlemen, when I hear the talk that it is against one's principles to take this course of action, I am reminded of the advice of an old Arizona senator, Henry Ashurst.* (Incidentally, for those who saw the movie *Advise and Consent,* Ashurst was brought out of a retirement home to play the bit part of the old senator who was always falling asleep.) But back in 1920 the senator counseled his colleague Mark Smith, "Mark, the trouble with you is that you will not submerge your principles in order to get yourself elected. YOU MUST LEARN THAT THERE COMES A TIME IN A MAN'S LIFE WHEN HE MUST RISE ABOVE PRINCIPLE."

(And in this matter, I suggest that we rise above . . .)

Preference—*Criticism*

93   *We have heard a lot of criticism of our speaker tonight.* We have heard him called a "reactionary," a "conservative" and a "mossback." But I think we will agree that he faithfully listens to the people of his district. In a different sense, I recall the time that Reed Smoot's credentials as the newly elected senator from Utah were being questioned. The Mormon Smoot was being attacked for his religion's polygamous views. Some of the senators were beating their breasts sanctimoniously about keeping inviolate the integrity of the home. Senator Boise Penrose, who was getting a little tired of some of his philandering colleagues' hypocrisy, stood up in the chamber to defend Smoot, saying, "AS FOR ME, I WOULD RATHER HAVE SEATED BESIDE ME IN THIS CHAMBER A POLYGAMIST WHO DOESN'T 'POLY' THAN A MONOGAMIST WHO DOESN'T 'MONOG.' "

(And similarly I'd rather have a conservative who represents his constituents than a liberal who didn't. . . .)

Public Office—*Criticism*

94   *One thing you learn quickly in public office is to get inured to criticism.* At least I don't have yet the problems of one French senator. The senator represented the Ivory Coast, then part of French West Africa, in the parliamentary chamber in Paris. The senator returned in 1950 to his constituency to explain his various positions on public issues. Out in the bush country he disappeared. All efforts to trace him failed. Three years later he was officially declared dead by a court, which, upon inspecting evidence, decided that he had been eaten by cannibals. Though many politicians claim to have been roasted by their constituents, IN THIS CASE IT WAS LITERALLY TRUE.

Support—*Solicitation*

95   *The fact is that such a drive demands an all-out campaign.* We must go after the doubtful as well as the convinced. I recall Benjamin Disraeli shortly after his entrance into political life when he stood for a certain Middlesex borough in the Conservative interest. It was a "personally conducted" canvass, and, among others, the future Prime Minister solicited the vote and interest of a well-to-do but somewhat contankerous farmer who was rather doubtful of Disraeli's political convictions.

"Vote for you!" he shouted when Mr. Disraeli made known the object of his call. "Why, I'd sooner vote for the devil."

"Quite so!" said Mr. Disraeli, "BUT IN THE EVENT OF YOUR FRIEND NOT STANDING, MAY I HOPE FOR YOUR SUPPORT?"

(And similarly we must go after . . .)

Dressing Room

What is the stage? It's a place, baby, you know,
where people play at being serious.
  —Luigi Pirandello,
    Six Characters in Search of an Author

96   Thank you for that warm applause. I only wish you had
been in the theater the night my last show closed.

97   Seriously, though, I think our performance the other
month was a success. It was just the audience that was a failure.

98   You might say the show received mixed notices. We liked
it—but the critics didn't.

99   But there was one critic who had words of praise. He
thought the scenery was original and beautiful—just that it was too
bad the performers had to get in front of it.

100   Of course, the critics were biased. One even admitted it.
He said he saw the play at a disadvantage—the curtain was up.

101   But even that review wasn't as bad as the time our guild
did the musical *Oklahoma!* Then a critic wrote, "The New York
Guild played *Oklahoma!* last night. *Oklahoma!* lost."

Age—*Birthday*

102   *When I was asked why I got involved in this project*—me
being an old man working with all these young people—I recalled
what Helen Hayes once said when an extra came up to her on the
movie set of *Airport.* "Why, Miss Hayes," she gushed, "what are
you doing in this picture?"

   "MY DEAR," replied the First Lady of the Stage, "HADN'T YOU
HEARD? I SUPPLY THE SEXAGENARIAN APPEAL."

Age—*Change*

103   *Even though some people are reluctant to recognize it, age
does play tricks on us.* Not long ago one of the better-known

photographers was dining at Sardi's in New York when Marlene Dietrich, making a grand exit, stopped in front of this particular theatrical photographer's table. She narrowed her eyes at the photographer and in a voice loud enough to be heard several tables away said, "Those pictures you took of me are rotten. I can't use them. They're terrible."

Nobody heard what the embarrassed photographer said, but he must have asked what was wrong.

"Everything's wrong!" cried the actress. "You've lost your eye, you've lost your skill. The pictures you took two weeks ago are nothing like the first ones you did of me. Those were beautiful. Exquisitely beautiful!"

"YES," said the photographer quite distinctly, "BUT YOU MUST REMEMBER I WAS TWENTY YEARS YOUNGER AT THE TIME."

(And when we were some years younger . . .)

ADVICE: This is a true story. Its believability will depend on a command of the details.

Appreciation—*Overtime*

104   *Thank you for the warm reception.* It was sincerely given and believe me it is sincerely felt. At any rate I hope it wasn't like the applause I heard not too long ago at a concert when two ushers were applauding harder than anybody else. We were pleased to note the enthusiasm of the two music lovers—until one of them stopped applauding and the other one was heard to say, "KEEP CLAPPING. DON'T YOU REALIZE, ONE MORE ENCORE AND WE'RE ON OVERTIME."

Brains—*Sensitivity*

105   *The person we are about to introduce is someone who is as brilliant as she is beautiful.* It does not always work out that way. I remember an occasion involving the great conductor Arturo Toscanini. It seems he had extreme difficulty rehearsing with one equally celebrated singer. This prima donna, of Wagnerian proportions, physically as well as vocally, gave the maestro great pain in her interpretation of a certain aria. Several times during the rehearsal Toscanini stopped the orchestra to correct the singer, patiently explaining what he believed was the intention of the composer in a particular passage. After numerous repetitions of the passage in which the soprano bellowed out the notes insensi-

tively, the maestro lost his cool. Putting down his baton, he approached the statuesque singer and, placing both hands on the most predominant part of her anatomy, proclaimed loudly, "MADAM, IF THESE WERE ONLY BRAINS!"

(Fortunately our friend tonight has everything in the right place, including her brains. . . .)

Children—*Hypocrisy*

106   *Adults are so hypocritical with children.* They have one standard for themselves and another for their children. It is as if we want our children to see us not as human beings but as gods. The actor Charles Coburn told how his father warned him about the evils of certain types of theaters.

"What kind of theaters, Father?" he asked.

"Burlesque theaters, son. Don't ever go in one."

Immediately Coburn asked, "Why not?" And his father answered, "Because you'll see things in a burlesque theater that you shouldn't see."

That, of course, aroused his curiosity. Not many days passed before he took in his first burlesque. Coburn remarked, "AND I FOUND OUT MY FATHER WAS RIGHT. I DID SEE SOMETHING I SHOULDN'T HAVE. I SAW MY FATHER."

Cost—*Expensive*

107   *For that cost we should be getting a lot more.* It reminds me of the time the famous Zsa Zsa Gabor went shopping at the fabulous Neiman-Marcus department store. Zsa Zsa was anxious to buy some pajamas for her uncle. She picked out a style that she liked and asked what they cost.

"Ninety dollars, ma'am," said the clerk.

"Ninety dollars!" gasped Zsa Zsa. "FOR THAT MONEY THEY SHOULD COME WITH A MAN IN THEM!"

(And for the amount we're paying, we should get . . .)

Creativity—*Switch*

108   *As I listened to the very eloquent introduction of the chairman, I couldn't help but think of the time a young aspiring composer came to Oscar Levant with an elegy he had composed in honor of George Gershwin.* Reluctantly Levant granted him a hearing. Eagerly the man rendered the piece with his own hands

and then turned expectantly toward Levant, seeking approbation.

"I think it would have been better," said Levant, "IF YOU HAD DIED AND GERSHWIN HAD WRITTEN THE ELEGY."

(And similarly I think, after hearing the eloquence of the chairman, that if he was making the speech and I did the introduction . . .)

Difficulty—*Solution*

109   *To get out of the mess we are in is not going to be easy.* It is going to take some time and some money. It recalls the time the Hungarian playwright Ferenc Molnar and his friend found themselves with two free tickets to a Budapest play. Early in the insufferable first act Molnar got up to leave.

"You can't walk out," objected his companion. "We're guests of the management."

Molnar meekly sat down, but after a few more doses of insipid dialogue he rose again.

"Now where are you going?" queried his friend.

"I'M GOING TO THE BOX OFFICE TO BUY TWO TICKETS SO WE CAN LEAVE," said Molnar.

(And so sometimes to get out of a problem you have to buy in —get involved. Even though we weren't participants in this tragedy we are going to have to spend some money to get out. . . .)

Discretion—*Impulsiveness*

110   *As I look over all the beautiful girls who are attending my niece's wedding, young virile thoughts pass through my head and other parts of my body.* But I remind myself of the time in the 1920s when Senator Chauncey Depew met Mary Garden, the magnificent Metropolitan Opera soprano whose talents in the chest department were not only musical. She was in this gown with decolletage spilling out all over, and the honorable Depew in admiration asked her what kept her gown up.

She replied, "Two things. YOUR AGE AND MY DISCRETION."

(Well, in this case my age and my discretion . . .)

Friend—*Resources*

111   *Gentlemen, looking at this audience, I see a lot of friends of our honoree.* Certainly we can't say of him what the playwright George Kaufman once said of an obnoxious colleague. It was in the

days of the five-cent telephone call. A number of Broadway lumi-
naries were gathered at a popular bistro when a particularly loath-
some leading man walked in and insisted on joining the party.
After a few moments he asked, "Has anybody got a nickel? I have
to phone a friend."

George Kaufman tossed him a coin and said, "HERE'S A DIME.
PHONE ALL OF THEM."

(Well, if we tried to call all of our honoree's friends, Bell Telephone would declare a dividend. . . .)

Involvement—*Withdrawal*

112   *Some of us don't like to be drawn in.* We refuse to get
involved. I recall once George Bernard Shaw received an invitation from a women seeking his acquaintance.

"Lady Robinson will be at home Wednesday between four and
six."

The author returned the card. Underneath he had written, "MR.
GEORGE BERNARD SHAW LIKEWISE."

(But although we may prefer to stay home uninvolved . . .)

Nerve—*Incompetence*

113   *I am rather astonished that these men in Washington expect us to believe their latest statements, considering their past record of incompetence.* It reminds me of an old opera troupe I heard
once in a small out-of-the-way town. One old tonsorial veteran
wept through shaky but loud strains of *Pagliacci.* At the close of the
aria one listener stood up and cheered—*Bravo, bravissimo.* I was
stunned that any operagoer would cheer this shoddy performance.
I turned to him and asked, "Did you like his performance?"

"I'M NOT APPLAUDING HIS VOICE BUT HIS COLOSSAL NERVE."

(And the colossal nerve of . . .)

News—*Repetition*

114   *Before the program starts I do have one bit of news.*
Though some of you may already have heard it, I know you are
going to be like the Hollywood press agent who came into the
office of one of the more notorious movie moguls, whose taste was
as coarse as his temperament.

The agent asked if he could have an appointment with the great
man the next day. The receptionist said, "That would be impossi-

ble. Didn't you know he died yesterday?"

Some hours later the man was back and again asked for an appointment. The girl replied, "Didn't you understand me—the president of the studio is dead." The agent again got up and left.

A bit later the agent came back and addressed the receptionist. "I'd like to make an appointment to see the president tomorrow."

"Look" she replied, "is there something wrong with you? I said he's dead—that he died yesterday."

"YES, I KNOW," he said, "BUT I JUST WANTED TO HEAR YOU SAY IT AGAIN."

Party—*Cocktail*

115   *I am to announce at the conclusion of this afternoon's session that before the main dinner tonight there will be a reception at six o'clock.* I assure you that those who come will not suffer the discomfort John Barrymore once felt when he visited the home of a teetotaler. The bibulous actor observed to his dismay that nothing stronger than tomato juice was served as a pre-meal stimulant.

When the dinner was announced, he got his coat and headed for the front door.

"Where are you going?" asked the hostess. "We're about to serve."

"YOU MUST EXCUSE ME," apologized the actor. "I NEVER DINE ON AN EMPTY STOMACH."

(And you needn't fear . . .)

Performance—*Mediocrity*

116   *The performance we have witnessed recently is enough to make anyone shake his head in wonderment.* It recalls to me the review of *Macbeth* a company of local amateurs put on in Richmond, a town in the north of England. The following day this account appeared in the local newspaper:

"Last night most of the leading citizens of our community gathered at the Richmond Theater to witness a performance of Shakespeare's *Macbeth.* The one benefit to be derived from the production is that it can forever settle the age-old dispute as to whether the play was written by Shakespeare or Bacon. All that has to be done is to open their respective graves in Stratford and London. THE AUTHOR IS THE ONE WHO TURNED OVER LAST NIGHT."

Presumptiveness—*God*

117   *Too many of us assume a power we shouldn't have.* We make decisions about people's lives where we shouldn't. We act like an actress Moss Hart once mentioned when she auditioned before him for a play he was producing. She said she had been the understudy in *Susan and God,* one of Gertrude Lawrence's great hits.

Hart, knowing that Miss Lawrence never had an understudy, said, "Interesting. I TAKE IT YOU WERE UNDERSTUDYING GOD."

(And we can't play God . . .)

Priority—*Basics*

118   *It is all right to speculate about what we should do if we had the money, but the first thing we must have is the basic necessities.* It reminds me of the show-business manager who had a big star who started to drink, stopped showing up for bookings, and finally ended up in the gutter. The actor went to a hotel where he used to spend lots of money and said to the proprietor, "I'm broke. Can you help me out?" The proprietor said, "Gee, I've got no place to put you. Wait, there's a kind of little storage room. I can put a cot in there." The ex-star was grateful.

The next morning, out walking, he met his manager. "Let me get back into show business," he said. "I'll do anything."

"What? Are you kidding me? You drink. You never show up for performances. I had a movie. You didn't want to do it. I got you a show. You didn't want it."

"Look, I'll do anything you want," the ex-star pleaded. "I'm living in a bare room with only a cot in it. I have no work. Please, what's the first thing you want me to do?"

The manager said, "THE FIRST THING I WANT YOU TO DO IS PUT ANOTHER COT IN THE ROOM."

(And similarly we can't afford to solve other people's problems until . . .)

Provincialism—*Specialization*

119   *The problem too often with people in my field is overspecialization.* And the problem with overspecialization is the tendency to be too often unaware of what's happening outside your own little sphere. I recall hearing about a cocktail party in New

York where an actor and an author had met for the first time. The actor asked who the good living writers were. The author answered, "Thomas Mann, Willa Cather, John Dos Passos, Ernest Hemingway, and myself."

The actor asked, "You write, Mr. Faulkner?"

And the author replied, "YES. WHAT DO YOU DO, MR. GABLE?"

Public—*Formula*

120   *I think our criterion has to be public acceptance.* It is the people who are going to be the final judge. I recall the death of one of the big movie studio heads a few years ago in Hollywood. Now, I won't tell you his name because of libel problems, but I will say that in a town that produces dirty old men he was top of the line. He was so obnoxious that he wouldn't receive in a hospital a get-well card from his own grandmother. And yet when he died the attendance at his funeral was just incredible. There must have been a hundred Cadillacs parked outside the memorial chapel, not to mention the Mercedes and Rolls-Royces. The flowers were enough to fill the gardens at Versailles. One veteran actor, as he came out of the chapel and looked at the thronged crowds held back by ropes, said to a press agent, "Look at all the people. Can you believe the way the people turned out for that old bastard?"

"Yes," said the press agent. "I BELIEVE IT. IT JUST GOES TO SHOW THAT IF YOU GIVE THE PUBLIC WHAT IT WANTS, THEY COME OUT IN DROVES."

Qualifications—*Combination*

121   *Our speaker today is as bright as she is beautiful.* She would not have been the recipient of a remark by George Bernard Shaw about Isadora Duncan. You might recall the fervent message Shaw received from Isadora Duncan expressing the opinion that by every eugenic principle they should have a child.

"Think what a child it would be," Isadora said, "with my body and your brain."

Shaw sent the following reply: "THINK HOW UNFORTUNATE IT WOULD BE IF THE CHILD WERE TO HAVE MY BODY AND YOUR BRAIN."

(Happily, our speaker has been twice blessed. . . .)

Qualifications—*Introduction*

122 *Thank you for your very kind introduction.* Your remark about high caliber calls to mind an incident that took place in a circus that came to my home town some years ago. The impresario of the circus was upset at the thought that his human-cannonball act would have to be scrapped. It seems the aging performer was losing his nerve in the act. He came to the boss and said, "I don't think I am up to this being shot out of a cannon twice a day any more."

"But you can't leave me," his boss replied. "WHERE WILL I EVER FIND ANOTHER MAN OF YOUR CALIBER?"

Regret—*Mistake*

123 *Many of us have regrets and wish that we could have done some things differently.* But in this particular case I feel like Harry Thaw, who went to prison for shooting the architect Stanford White in jealousy over the lovely actress Evelyn Nesbitt. Shortly after his ten years in Sing Sing he attended the grand opening of the Roxy Theater in New York. As he gazed in dismay at this swirled confectionery of a Hollywood–Byzantine lobby he cried, "MY GOD, I SHOT THE WRONG ARCHITECT."

Repeat—*Invitation*

124 *It shows how generous and kind you people are.* As you know, a return engagement is not always automatic. I remember once when Winston Churchill received an invitation from George Bernard Shaw to one of his opening plays back in the early 1900s.

The note read: "Enclosed are two tickets to the first-night performance of a play of mine. Bring a friend—if you have one."

Churchill sent back this reply: "Dear G.B.S.: I thank you very much for the invitation and tickets. UNFORTUNATELY, I'M ENGAGED ON THAT NIGHT, BUT COULD I HAVE TICKETS FOR THE SECOND NIGHT—IF THERE IS ONE?"

(And so I am proud that there is one for me—a second night.)

Toastmaster—*Introduction*

125 *We have many important and distinguished guests tonight who will be introduced to you.* In order to introduce them

properly and in a manner they deserve, special talent is required, and I feel very much like the newspaper reporter who was sent to interview John Barrymore.

The newspaper reporter met Barrymore and to make a good impression, before he began his interview, he said, "I just can't tell you how much I enjoyed your performance."

The actor looked at the reporter and replied, "THEN WHY DOESN'T YOUR NEWSPAPER SEND OVER SOMEONE WHO CAN?"

(Like this newspaper reporter, I feel that I cannot do justice to our guests who are to be introduced, so I am going to call on someone who can. . . .)

Viewpoint—*Angle*

126   *One of the difficulties in the present situation is that we can't view the problem from another angle.* I recall Alfred Hitchcock, who was bothered by a famous actress about his camera angles. Day after day the actress nagged Hitchcock about photographing her from "my best side."

Finally, Hitchcock's patience was exhausted. "MY DEAR," he explained, "WE CAN'T PHOTOGRAPH YOUR BEST SIDE BECAUSE YOU'RE ALWAYS SITTING ON IT."

(And similarly, we can really see . . .)

Embassy Party

*An ambassador is an honest man, sent to lie
abroad for the good of his country.*
    —Sir Henry Wotton

127   Thank you for the nice introduction. I must admit I've always liked the ring of the phrase "career foreign-service officer." It's better than being called a bureaucrat with passport.

128   And really, "career" doesn't quite describe the sort of tenure. True, we can't be fired, but we can be sent just about anywhere.

129   Actually it is kind of thrilling to think that there are thousands of my fellow foreign-service officers stationed in every major city around the world. In a way we in the State Department have become something like American Express, except without its prestige.

130   I do hope you will be patient with me tonight. This is one of my first speeches as ambassador, and I am just learning the technique. I'm supposed to say something when I have nothing to say or say nothing when I have something to say.

131   Harold Macmillan summed it up when he said, "A diplomat is forever poised between a cliché and an indiscretion."

132   Or remember what Adlai Stevenson said were his two diplomatic worries—"protocol and alcohol."

133   I thank you for that fine introduction. Diplomats aren't always used to such praise. After all, the first person to describe an envoy was Homer, and he said Ulysses was "a man fertile in expedients."

134   And such criticism does not just come from the outside but also in the ranks. Three hundred years ago Sir Henry Wotton said, "An ambassador is an honest man, sent abroad to lie for the good of his country." King James dismissed him. He is only one of a long line of ministers who have been fired for telling the truth.

135   I get tired of people who constantly criticize the State Department. If anyone has any doubt of our effectiveness, all one has to do is look back to the winter of 1958. In the period of a week seven critical emergency problems came up and they all came out all right. In each case the State Department avoided misstep. Of course there wasn't any action because a blizzard closed down the department for five days.

136   Seriously, I don't know how that fact ever surfaced to the press. I don't like to find fault in our State Department's Planning Section, but sometimes I think there must be a leak in the think tank.

137   I can, however, report moderate success in the recent conference. We agreed on when the next meeting was to be held.

138   On a more serious note we can say the two sides had a frank and open discussion. We said we were "open" to any proposals and they "frankly" declined.

Arabs—*Middle East*

139   *To think that the problems of the Middle East can easily be solved and differences reconciled shows colossal naïveté.* I recall Abba Eban telling about a duck that was preparing to paddle across the Suez Canal one day when a scorpion appeared with a bag of grain and said, "All this is yours if you will let me ride across on your back."

"My mother always warned me to beware of the treachery of scorpions," demurred the duck. "How do I know you won't sting me in midstream?"

"Silly duck," scoffed the scorpion. "In that case wouldn't we both drown?"

So the duck said, "Hop aboard," but sure enough, halfway across the canal the scorpion stung it. As they both went under for the third time the duck gasped, "What made you do it?"

The scorpion gasped back, "WHAT ELSE COULD YOU EXPECT? THIS IS THE MIDDLE EAST!"

Change—*Switch*

140   *Diplomacy takes many turns, and in a lifetime one must be prepared for surprises.* I must confess some suspicion over the build-up and promotion we have had over the recent détente with the Soviet Union. But I was almost made a believer when President Nixon visited Moscow in the summer of 1972. One of the ceremonial highlights of any visit to the Kremlin is the visit to Lenin's tomb for a laying-on of a wreath.

I thought such a demonstration by the head of the biggest capitalist country would surely make the old revolutionary shake. But I really was taken aback when the U. S. Marines, in one of their selections for the great occasion, picked one of Stephen Foster's tunes to play. Foster is one of the American composers approved of by the Soviet hierarchy. But I'm not sure Lenin would have approved of the piece selected: "MASSA'S IN THE COLD, COLD GROUND."

(And I am sure some of our predecessors would turn over in their grave . . .)

Communication—*Interpretation*

141   *Never has communication been more important than it is today in human relations.* "It is," as the Roman author Quintilian once said, "important not only to be understood but also not to be misunderstood." In the UN they have developed computers that can translate one language into another. Ideally, if the translated passage were then translated by computer back into the first language, the original words ought to˙ be regained. This, however, does not allow for the ambiguity of languages. There is the story of the computer that was ordered to translate a common English phrase into Russian and then translate the Russian translation back into English.

What went in was "Out of sight, out of mind."

What came out was "INVISIBLE INSANITY."

Communication—*Misinterpretation*

142   *Things are not always as they appear.* I remember one diplomatic incident when one big political contributor found himself appointed ambassador to Thailand. On one of his first days in Bangkok he was giving a speech he had spent much time in preparing. When he finished no one applauded. Then a Thai got up and gave a speech in the Siamese tongue. It was cheered with much fervor by the audience, and the new ambassador, as a good sport, joined in heartily. An embassy aide nudged him, saying, "I WOULDN'T DO THAT, SIR. THEY'RE APPLAUDING YOUR SPEECH."

Competition—*Fight*

143   *Gentlemen, I don't have to tell you that we are in for a stiff race against tough competition who believe in being first at all costs.* I have no doubt about our own ingenuity and resourcefulness. I am reminded of a story I once heard from a veteran American diplomat. In one of his first assignments right after World War II he was sent to Greece. Greece, which at that time was in the middle of their civil war, was considered by the British to be in their sphere of influence. At any rate this special two-man mission went in to investigate a report on the Greek crisis. On the first night they had free in Athens they stopped by the only club in town which was under Greek auspices. Two or three bristle-mustached Englishmen at the bar began telling anti-American jokes

in loud tones for the benefit of some Greek associates, whom the British were treating as "civilized colonials." The junior partner to my friend whispered, "Let's leave. We don't have to take this crap." My friend replied, "No—that's just what they want. I'll tell a story instead."

So speaking up to the Britishers, he said, "Have you heard about that Swiss plane going to Lisbon during the war whose engines began to conk out?"

A Britisher muttered disinterestedly, but a Greek at the bar replied, "No."

"Well," said the American head of the mission, "since it was a neutral plane it carried various nationalities. When trouble developed in the engines, the pilot announced, 'We are losing altitude. We have cast everything overboard that we could. I'm afraid one of you gentlemen will have to jump.' There was a German, an Italian, a Britisher and a Greek. They drew straws and the German lost.

"The German rose stiffly, went to the open cabin door, saluted and said 'Heil Hitler' and jumped out. Sometime later the pilot again announced that the plane was losing altitude. Once again straws were drawn. This time the Italian lost. He went to the cabin door, saluted and said, 'Viva Il Duce' and he was pushed out.

"A little later the pilot again said that someone would have to go. So the remaining two drew straws. The Englishman lost. He rose primly, walked to the open cabin door and said, 'THERE WILL ALWAYS BE AN ENGLAND' AND PUSHED THE GREEK OUT."

(But the point is that we are not going to be pushed out . . .)

ADVICE: A long involved story like this is not recommended unless it fits the exact message you want to convey. You should read it over to get a proper mental picture of all the details.

Conspicuous—*Behavior*

144   *As much as I enjoy being guest of honor at this fête, being the focal point has its drawbacks.* From friends in Paris I heard what Pope John XXIII once said when he was Papal Nuncio, the Vatican's diplomatic envoy to France. At one reception where there were many well-shaped beauties he told a diplomatic colleague, "THE PROBLEM WITH THESE RECEPTIONS IS THAT IF A WOMAN ARRIVES WEARING A GOWN THAT IS CUT DARINGLY LOW, EVERYBODY GAZES NOT AT THE LADY BUT AT ME, TO SEE IF I'M LOOKING AT THE LADY."

Deficit—*Spending*

145   *Gentlemen, if we keep on spending in the future the way we have in the past, we are going to mount a huge deficit.* We will be in the situation described at an embassy luncheon many years ago in Washington.

The wife of a European nation's finance minister wore a gown very décolleté, but nature had not endowed her with the necessary assets to wear such a garment. The counselor of the German Embassy gazed at her and then undiplomatically murmured, "MADAM IS JUST LIKE HER HUSBAND—AN UNCOVERED DEFICIT."

Embarrassment—*Insolvency*

146   *I find myself a little embarrassed at the disclosure of our financial situation.* I find myself in sympathy with British Prime Minister Harold Wilson, who came to Washington to tell President Lyndon Johnson of the impending British devaluation of the pound. As happens in the case of any visiting dignitary, there was a White House dinner. Bess Abell, the White House social secretary, had asked the singer Robert Merrill to attend the dinner. It was a bit discomforting for all when Merrill expressed his feelings of honor to be able to sing in front of the British Prime Minister and then announced his song selection from *Porgy and Bess*, "I GOT PLENTY OF NOTHIN."

Mess—*Mistake*

147   *The mess we find ourselves in did not come about by accident.* It took planning. It is like the idea a sultan of a Middle East protectorate had back before the turn of the century. He wanted to put the newly arriving British minister in his place. So he had installed in the anteroom next to his throne chamber a tunnel in order that the British envoy would arrive at the sultan's on his knees. When the English diplomat arrived at the palace to present his credentials, he took one look at the waist-high tunnel and, instead of going in forward on his knees, did it the reverse way. The sultan on his throne saw emerging on the other side not a lowered head but another part of the anatomy. IT WAS NOT THE FIRST TIME A HEAD OF STATE GOT THINGS ASS BACKWARD.

Negotiation—*Love*

148   *Whether it's love or peace, it takes two to tango—two to make it work.* A good example of that was an incident that happened to former Ambassador Ellis while he was an envoy to Greece. Both he and his secretary had been preoccupied by an approaching deadline. He had to fly to Rome to give a report before a European security conference. She, a healthy, buxom lass of twenty-three, was two days away from her wedding to a handsome Marine guard after a six-month engagement. Naturally, her mind was on the state of her trousseau rather than on the state of the Greek government. Ambassador Ellis was trying to finish up his paper on Greece before rushing to the airport. He had entitled his study—a report saying that the political situation was more shaky than the economic—"Man Shall Not Live by Bread Alone." Before he had a chance to really go over the copy, he had to race to the Athens airport. He left word that the speech should be teletyped to the Rome Embassy so they could type it up for distribution for the next day's conference. When he arrived at Rome he was met by a group of foreign-service officers who were to take him to the hotel to deliver the speech. They were a bit puzzled by the printed title of the report. Ambassador Ellis looked at one of the mimeographed copies. The bride-to-be's rendition of the Ambassador's dictated Biblical saying came out not "Man Shall Not Live by Bread Alone" but "MAN SHALL NOT LOVE IN BED ALONE."

(And for the peace of nations as well as marriage it takes two . . .)

ADVICE: This can be a difficult story to tell. It works better for one to give both the intended as well as the typed title in the punch line. It is also a good story for a wedding toast.

Negotiation—*Prima Donna*

149   *When I am critical about the terms of negotiations, I like to think that in terms of whom I was working with I did fairly well.* In fact, I am reminded what French President Georges Clemenceau said of the Versailles peace-treaty negotiations between President Woodrow Wilson and British Prime Minister David

Lloyd George: "WELL, IT WAS THE BEST I COULD DO, SEATED AS I WAS BETWEEN JESUS CHRIST AND NAPOLEON BONAPARTE."

Neutrality—*Involvement*

150   *I must admit difficulty in hiding my contempt for those who won't get involved and won't commit themselves.* I find myself in sympathy with a British diplomat, Lord Bristol, at the court of Frederick the Great who was trying to persuade the old king to ally Prussia with Great Britain in an attempt to insure European stability. King Frederick, however, refused to be involved. Later at a formal state dinner the king said, "Well, my Lord Bristol, aren't you going to eat our fine capon?"

"No," replied Bristol. "I DECLINE TO HAVE ANYTHING TO DO WITH NEUTRAL ANIMALS."

Party—*Success*

151   *I want to give a toast to our hostess, whose energy along with her gift for diplomacy would put to shame any diplomat.* Surely it would surpass that one secretary of state who never provided any alcoholic sustenance at his diplomatic receptions. It was William Jennings Bryan, who, at a dinner celebrating the anniversary of the Japanese victory over the Russians, alienated Admiral Togo by not participating in the champagne toast.

Bryan, though, had enough ingenuity to explain, "SINCE ADMIRAL TOGO'S VICTORY WAS ON WATER, I'LL TOAST WITH WATER. WHEN HE WINS A VICTORY ON WINE, I'LL TOAST WITH WINE."

(Well, gentlemen, our hostess has won a singular victory with wine. . . .)

Perspective—*Viewpoint*

152   *It is only fair that we examine the situation from the other side.* From their viewpoint things might look entirely different. I remember a British diplomat telling me of a former old colleague who had been stationed in the Sudan back in the days when there was still a British Empire. In the capital city of Sudan, Khartoum, there is an imposing equestrian statue of General Gordon, the colonial statesman who died bravely in 1885 defending the city against the troops of Mahdi. Now, as one of the British Empire's greatest heroes, General Gordon sitting astride his horse will

forever look over the city that is indelibly associated with his name.

My friend's colleague worshipped the memory of General Gordon. As a British colonial servant, raised in the belief of the Empire, he would take his young boy down to the square and ask him to look at the statue of a man on horseback.

"That is Gordon," he would say to his boy, and bow his own head in a moment of reverence.

The boy loved the mounted statue, and many a day the lad would run to the square to take a look at Gordon. When the time came for the civil servant to be transferred from Khartoum to Nepal, the boy's last deed before leaving was to walk to the square to take a farewell look at the statue. His father's eyes misted over at this action of his boy, and his heart swelled at the thought that within the lad's chest there beat the heart of a true Englishman.

On board the steamer the boy turned to his father thoughtfully and said, "Father, I have a question I have always wanted to ask."

"Yes, my son?"

"It's about Gordon. There's one thing I don't understand."

"What is that, my son?"

"TELL ME. WHO IS THAT SILLY MAN WHO IS RIDING ON TOP OF GORDON?"

Preference—*Comparison*

153   *It is always nice to be compared in some way to someone great.* I will always remember what the burly, balding, and bespectacled Belgian Paul Henri Spaak had to say when he was introduced by an American toastmaster who said the Belgian diplomat looked like Winston Churchill but spoke like Charles Boyer.

In response Spaak said, "I APPRECIATE THE COMPLIMENT, BUT ACTUALLY I'D RATHER SPEAK LIKE VEENSTON CHURCHEEL AND LOOK LIKE CHARLES BOYER."

Preference—*Excellence*

154   *We are fortunate today to have as our speaker the number-one man in the field.* In that sense we understand the answer the Iranian Prime Minister recently gave to the Soviet ambassador in Teheran. It was shortly after President Nixon named former CIA director Richard Helms Ambassador to Iran. His Russian counterpart at an embassy reception asked the Prime Minister, "What do you

think about the United States sending you a spy as ambassador?"

"Well," replied the Prime Minister, "THEY ARE AT LEAST SEND-
ING US THEIR NO. 1 SPY. YOU CAN'T BE MUCH MORE THAN SPY NO.
10."

(With that the Soviet ambassador left the reception.)

Question—*Answer*

155   *As I open the question-and-answer session I hope that I
have the same help as former British Ambassador Lord Halifax.*
He was traveling through Texas and stopped at the Consolidated
Aircraft plant in Fort Worth to address the workers. The man who
introduced him seemed a bit confused as to just how he should
refer to the titled envoy. He managed to get through beautifully
until his closing remark, which was "WHEN THE SPEECH IS OVER,
IF ANYONE WANTS TO ASK QUESTIONS, THE LORD WILL PROVIDE
THE ANSWERS."

Theory—*Hypocrisy*

156   *It never ceases to amaze me how people can develop the
most high-flung rationale to disguise the most self-serving mo-
tives.* Such posturing in the name of logic and ideals reminds me
of how the late Charles "Chip" Bohlen instructed his staff to handle the French at Quai d'Orsay. The French were cutting back
their support of NATO. An embassy official worried about the
French actions wanted to see the ambassador, who had decided
on an aloof posture as the best way to maintain the respect of the
haughty de Gaulle. After being told the ambassador was not available, the staff official burst in on Bohlen to find him putting golf
balls on the embassy carpet. Without looking up Bohlen heard the
anguished appeal for advice, Bohlen finally replied, "I suppose the
French at Quai d'Orsay explain their latest moves as the only
reasonable course of action, saying, *'C'est logique.'* "

"Yes," replied the junior officer.

"Well, the next time you tell him this story about the Frenchman who came home startled to find his son in bed with his grandmother. 'Son,' he said, 'how can you do this?' 'Well,' said his son,
'YOU SLEEP WITH MY MAMA, I SLEEP WITH YOUR MAMA. *C'est
logique.'* "

(Well, how anyone can justify what . . .)

Emergency Ward

God cures and the doctor takes the fee.
—Benjamin Franklin

157   You've heard me introduced as a specialist. You know what that is? That's a doctor whose patients can be ill only during office hours.

158   Seriously, there is a difference between a physician and a specialist. One treats what you have while the other thinks you have what he treats.

159   Actually, whatever our speciality, we doctors have certain characteristics in common. We're men over thirty who still have our tonsils and appendix.

160   Really, though, I like to think of myself as a humanitarian doctor—one with a heart. I'm always willing to make a house call when my wife and children are home in bed with the flu.

161   Of course, I know American doctors come in for their share of criticism. But one thing you will have to admit is that no doctors in the world are more up to date or better informed in diagnosing problems. If we don't know what it is, we call it a virus, and if we know and can't cure it, we call it an allergy.

162   They say in the future we are going to see fewer hospitals and more outpatient treatment. That may be one solution to our growing health-care problem, but only if we doctors are forced to write our prescriptions as legibly as we write our bills.

163   That reminds me of the way Ralph Nader recently classified us doctors into three types—expensive, costly, and exorbitant.

164   Finally, that leads me to the advice I want to leave you with: don't ever leave a hospital until you're strong enough to face the cashier.

Candor—*Language*

165   *Sometimes a situation calls for language in the bluntest terms.* I remember not long ago a distinguished doctor was called in front of the county medical society for "professional conduct unbecoming a physician." The husband of one of his patients had complained that the doctor in question had used obscene language.

When the doctor was asked to explain his action, he said, "Well, you see it was this way. I got up that day, the toast was burned and the morning paper was still soggy from the rain. I went out to the car and, because of the rain, it wouldn't start. I got pushed. I got to the office and my parking place was taken. I went in and the elevator would not work. I walked up five sets of stairs. The phone was ringing, but I had left the keys in the car. I ran down the stairs and got the janitor to open the door—and answered the phone. All I did was just answer her question: 'DOCTOR, HOW DO I USE A RECTAL THERMOMETER?'"

(And although we might not have to express ourselves in such earthy terms, we must mince no words . . .)

ADVICE: Only a lengthy build-up—toast, car, parking place, etc.— can set the stage for the punch line. Good story to preface harsh examination of facts.

Conference—*Candor*

166   *I think everyone will agree that we all have had a successful conference here in Washington.* We have spoken freely—all groups. We have let our hair down. And that's when you get most productive. Such a lesson was brought home to me the other day by a medical case I heard. A married couple had tried everything but failed to have children. Finally, their doctor said, "Listen, there is absolutely no physiological reason why you should not have children. It is undoubtedly a matter of tension. You're trying too hard. Go home and forget the whole thing. Don't take temperatures. Don't worry about the time of the month. Just live a normal life as though children were the last thing that concerned you. *However,* if on any occasion you should have the impulse to make love, then don't wait—make love."

Some months later the wife was back and the tests showed that she was clearly pregnant. The doctor smiled. "Did you follow my advice?"

"Yes, we did, Doctor, and it worked. We lived a normal carefree life, and then one evening at dinner I dropped my napkin. I bent to pick it up and so did my husband. Our fingers touched beneath the table and it was like an electric shock going through the two of us. We remembered what you said, and we just stopped in the middle of dinner and made love under the table. And that's when I got pregnant."

"I'm so happy," said the doctor, "and I can imagine how happy you must be."

"Completely happy, Doctor, except for one thing."

"Oh, and what's that?"

"WELL, THEY WON'T LET US INTO HOWARD JOHNSON'S ANY-MORE."

(Well, considering how productive our conference has been, I hope the Washington Hilton . . .)

ADVICE: Obviously, this can be used only to sophisticated audiences.

Cost—*Health*

167   *When it comes to health care Americans will not accept second best.* I remember a doctor friend telling of an elderly patient who came in for an examination. After three days of intensive tests the doctor says, "Look, my nurse is out with the flu. I'll give you the bill now." The old man says, "What, are you crazy, Doctor? I can't pay that—five hundred dollars, my goodness!" The doctor says, "All right, in your case just give me half." "Half? I can't even pay half." "Well," says the doctor, "what portion of the bill do you think you can pay?" "Not a penny. I'm a poor man." Sighs the doctor: "With all due respect, why did you come to see me—one of the greatest specialists of our time?" And the patient answers, "LISTEN, WHEN IT COMES TO MY HEALTH, MONEY IS NO OBJECT!"

Cure—*Problem*

168   *I think the cure may be worse than the disease.* It's like the woman I heard about who went to one of those health clinics where they had about seven doctors. After twenty minutes in one

doctor's office she ran screaming down the hall. Another doctor, who finally got the story out of her, called the first doctor. "What's the idea of telling that patient she's pregnant? She isn't. You nearly frightened her to death."

"I KNOW," the first doctor said, "BUT I CURED HER HICCUPS, DIDN'T I?"

Doctor—*Daughter*

169   *Our speaker today is as talented as she is charming.* And looking at her, I wonder if what I overheard some neighborhood children say isn't true. A doctor lives in one of the houses on my block and he has two of the most beautiful little girls, about eight and seven years of age. One day when the two children were out walking they happened to pass quite near two small boys. One lived in the village and the other was a visitor.

"Who are those little girls?" asked the visitor.

"They're the doctor's children," replied the village boy. "HE ALWAYS KEEPS THE BEST FOR HIMSELF."

(As you might guess, our speaker is the daughter of a doctor . . .)

Doctors—*Mistake*

170   *The medical profession gets more than its share of criticism.* Doctors are often accused of burying their mistakes. I recall the case of the man who died and arrived at the gates of heaven. A messenger of St. Peter took his name and disappeared. Later, the messenger came back and told the newly arrived applicant to heaven that he was very sorry but his name was not on the books. He was not registered to be received in heaven. The messenger suggested that he try hell.

The poor fellow made his way to the gates of hell and was promptly interviewed by a representative of the devil. Here again he was informed that he was not on the books and not registered to be admitted to hell. It was suggested that he return to heaven once more.

The fellow, now thoroughly confused, returned to the gates of heaven and announced that his name had not been found on the register in hell and Satan had suggested that he try heaven again. The fellow was taken to the office outside the gates, and St. Peter himself carefully checked every name again. Suddenly, the name was discovered far down the list.

St. Peter turned to him and said, "THERE SEEMS TO HAVE BEEN A MISTAKE HERE. SOMEONE MADE AN ERROR. YOU ARE NOT DUE TO ARRIVE IN HEAVEN FOR SIX MORE YEARS. WHO IS YOUR DOCTOR?"

Doctor—*Service*

171   *Many of us often take for granted how much we depend on our family doctor.* I know my own physician. One cold winter night about 2:00 A.M. a certain patient phoned him and said, "Doc, can you come over right away? I have a terrible toothache."

As politely as he could he answered, "My dear lady, what you need is a dentist, not a physician."

To which she calmly replied, "YES, I KNOW—BUT I JUST HATED TO CALL A DENTIST AT THIS HOUR OF THE NIGHT."

Duress—*Promises*

172   *I know that I have been accused of some inconsistency of position.* I am not going to take back anything I said, but you all understand the background of those earlier statements. I guess I feel like a patient a doctor friend told me about recently. "You'll pull through," said the doctor to his patient, "but you are a very sick man."

The patient was obviously frightened, "Please, Doctor," he pleaded, "do everything you can for me. And if I get well, I'll donate thirty thousand dollars to the fund for the new hospital."

Several months later the doctor met the patient on the street. "How are you?" he asked. "Just marvelous, Doctor," replied the former patient. "I have been meaning to speak to you," continued the doctor, "about that money for the new hospital."

"What are you talking about?" "You said that if you got well," the doctor reminded him, "you would donate thirty thousand dollars to the fund for the new hospital." "IF I SAID THAT," the former patient exclaimed, "THEN I REALLY MUST HAVE BEEN SICK."

Expert—*Interpreted*

173   *I believe in going to the right man for the difficult job.* I remember one afternoon at the corner drugstore when a pretty girl, neatly dressed, came in and asked the pharmacist to read a

letter for her. It was obviously a rather intimate letter, too, because the girl blushed while she listened and gave the pharmacist a hug and a kiss before she rushed happily out of the store.

"Don't think she's an illiterate," the pharmacist hastened to explain. "Matter of fact, she's a senior at Radcliffe. BUT HER BOYFRIEND IS A DOCTOR—AND ONLY A PHARMACIST LIKE ME CAN MAKE HEADS OR TAILS OF HIS HANDWRITING."

(And only an expert like our speaker can make heads or tails . . .)

Finality—*Consultation*

174   *Of course, you may not agree with my diagnosis as I have explained it up here.* They are currently telling the story of the three scientists who were working with some highly dangerous radioactive material when a big explosion occurred in their laboratory. The three doctors were examined by the company physician, who looked very grave and said, "Gentlemen, I have bad news. Each of you has but two months to live. But since the accident happened on company time the company is willing to grant whatever last wishes you may have for the end of your lives."

The first scientist was an Englishman and he thought seriously for a few minutes and then said, "I rather imagine I would like to spend the end of my days back in old England. I shall just sit in my club and read the London *Times* and play some cribbage with friends."

The second scientist was a Russian, and he told the doctor, "My family lives on the outskirts of Leningrad, and I would like to be with them, sharing the community pleasures, visiting the Hermitage when I can, and enjoying party lectures on the radio."

The doctor then turned to the third man, who was an old scientist from Israel, and asked him for his last wish. "WELL," he replied, "TO TELL YOU THE TRUTH, I'D LIKE TO GET A SECOND OPINION FROM ANOTHER DOCTOR."

Freedom—*Doctors*

175   *We take our freedom so much for granted.* Free speech and free press are so much abstractions. We don't get alarmed on legislation proposals to inhibit the press in Florida or the government's new moves to regulate licensing of television stations. Per-

haps we should look more from the vantage point of a Solzhenitsyn. Not too long ago I heard a story emanating from an international medical convention where three surgeons were discussing who had performed the most difficult operation.

The Englishman described some delicate brain surgery he had performed in which he helped the patient regain his speech.

The Frenchman said that that was admirable but that he undertook a heart transplant and the patient with five children went on to live.

The Russian spoke up. "I know I made medical history when I performed my first operation removing a man's tonsils."

"What's so rare about a tonsillectomy?" asked the other two surgeons.

"Ah," said the Russian, "you must understand that in our country people are deathly afraid of opening their mouths. SO I HAD TO APPROACH IT FROM ANOTHER ANGLE."

Gentleman—*Snobbery*

176 *Anyone in Congress can make an officer, but only God can make a gentleman.* To be a gentleman demands some innate courtesy and respect for your fellow man. I remember a reception after a seminar on health problems. A chiropractor was introduced to a physician. The physician said, "I am glad to meet you as a gentleman, but I can't admit you are a doctor."

"And I," said the chiropractor, "am glad to meet you as a doctor, ALTHOUGH I CAN'T ADMIT YOU ARE A GENTLEMAN."

Gratitude—*Lucky*

177 *I am certainly overwhelmed by the reception all of you have given me.* I am really moved by the care and preparation that have gone into this evening. Your consideration reminds me of what a noted pop artist did for an ophthamologist. Every newspaper in New York sent a reporter and a staff photographer to his office when it was learned that he had recently performed a successful sight-saving operation on the wife of the country's most celebrated pop artist, who, in addition to paying the doctor's usual fee, had gratefully insisted on painting one of his contemporary masterpieces across an entire wall of the doctor's waiting room. The mural turned out to be an immense multicolored picture of

a human eye, in the center of which stood a perfect miniature likeness of the good doctor himself. While cameras clicked and most of the newsmen crowded around the famous artist for his comments, one cub reporter drew the eye specialist aside and asked, "Tell me, if you can, Doctor—what was your first reaction on seeing this fantastic artistic achievement covering an entire wall of your office?"

"TO TELL THE TRUTH," replied the physician, "MY FIRST THOUGHT WAS, THANK GOODNESS I'M NOT A GYNECOLOGIST!"

Interpretation—*Bias*

178   *The interpretations some of our friends in the press have put on the straightforward recommendations and findings of the committee remind me very much of the young matron who* told her husband after a visit with the doctor, "Dear, the doctor said I am in a very distraught condition and that it is essential for me to go to St. Tropez, then to Aspen, and to buy myself a new mink wrap."

The husband immediately called the doctor back. "What did you mean by all this stuff about St. Tropez, Aspen, and mink coats?"

"I JUST RECOMMENDED TO YOUR WIFE A REGIMEN OF FREQUENT BATHS, PLENTY OF FRESH AIR, AND TO BE SURE TO DRESS IN WARM CLOTHES."

Observation—*Analysis*

179   *We have seen a lot of wringing of hands over the situation.* But I wonder if we are assessing quite correctly what is going on. I recall the lecture by the famous Viennese surgeon Billroth. He had told the students that a doctor needed two gifts—the ability not to get sick and the power of observation. Billroth, to show his students, dipped his fingers into a bitterly nauseating fluid and licked it off, requesting them to do the same. All of the students did the same without flinching.

With a grin Billroth said, "You have passed the first test well but not the second, FOR NONE OF YOU NOTICED THAT I DIPPED MY INDEX FINGER IN BUT LICKED THE SECOND."

Perfection—*Worth*

180   *Words cannot express the true value to the community of the man we honor tonight.* It reminds me of some years ago when the sultan of an Arab principality came to this country for an eye operation and the doctor did not know what to charge a royal patient. If he overcharged, it would reflect unfavorably on international relationships and good will. On the other hand, if he undercharged, the sultan would feel the operation was not serious enough to have made a trip to America.

The doctor checked with some of his colleagues and was almost ready to settle for $5,000 until one colleague suggested he consult the sultan's lawyer in New York who was handling the sultan's financial affairs. The sultan's lawyer recommended that he specify no particular amount but that he submit a blank statement with the footnote "The sultan can do no wrong" and let the sultan decide what he thought it was worth. He did.

It was not long after that that the doctor actually received a check from the royal exchequer of the sultanate for $75,000. And it was not long after that that the doctor received a blank invoice from the lawyer penned with the footnote "THE SURGEON CAN DO NO WRONG."

(And while our honoree would modestly disclaim his value, we know, as far as we are concerned, he also can do no wrong. . . .)

Problem—*Awareness*

181   *Our situation today is not dissimilar to the case of the man with a great problem of forgetfulness which drove his friends to distraction.* They finally insisted that he see a psychiatrist. He said to the psychiatrist, "Doctor, I have this terrible problem with forgetfulness."

The doctor asked, "How long have you had this problem?"

To which the man replied, "WHAT PROBLEM?"

(So tonight we must ask what is the problem facing us. . . .)

Problem—*Candor*

182   *I think the time has come to face up to the problem.* We can't be like a friend of mine who went to see his doctor. He said to the doctor, "I want you to give me a thorough examination and

then tell me in plain words what's the matter with me. I don't want any of those fancy medical terms. Just tell me in plain language.

The doctor gave him a complete physical and then told him his trouble. "There's nothing wrong with you," the doctor said. "You're just lazy—plain lazy."

My friend looked at the doctor and said, "NOW, IF YOU DON'T MIND, PLEASE GIVE ME THE FANCY TERMS FOR IT SO I CAN TELL MY WIFE."

(Tonight I think we should quit kidding ourselves. I think we should tell it like it is. And that is what I am going to do.)

Problem—*Reform*

183   *As we are asked to consider this reform, I would like to tell you what happened to a friend of mine who went to the doctor for the relief of a cold he just couldn't seem to shake off.*

My friend begged the doctor to cure him of it quickly. But the doctor, as baffled as all are by the common cold, had only one suggestion. "I want you to go out into this cold winter rain," he told the patient, "and let yourself get chilled and soaked through and through."

"But," exclaimed my puzzled friend, "that would cause pneumonia, wouldn't it?"

"CERTAINLY," said the doctor. "WE CAN CURE PNEUMONIA."

(And similarly I think the cure proposed is worse than the problem we face. . . .)

Problem—*Warning*

184   *The way we've handled the problem so far reminds me of the case of this worried businessman who went to his doctor to complain of popped eyes and a ringing in his ears.* The doctor suggested the man have his tonsils out, but this did not clear the situation.

He went to a second doctor, who ordered all the man's teeth extracted. Still the condition persisted. Then the alarmed businessman went to a third doctor, who gave the man six months to live. The man decided to live out his allotted time well.

He bought a new car, hired a chauffeur, took a suite at the best hotel, and ordered a tailor to make him a dozen suits. At the same time he decided to go all the way and have his shirts tailor-made. The tailor measured him.

"Let's see," said the tailor. "Sleeve, thirty-four; collar, sixteen."

"Fifteen," said the man.

"Sixteen," said the tailor.

"Look here," said the man, "I've always worn a fifteen collar."

"O.K.," said the tailor, "But don't say I didn't warn you. IF YOU KEEP IT UP YOUR EYES ARE GOING TO POP OUT AND THERE'LL BE A RINGING IN YOUR EARS."

(And I might add that in a different sense, we might get some ringing in our ears if we don't start analyzing the situation right . . .)

Resumption—*Proviso*

185   *Gentlemen, I am happy to announce to you that we are going to be able to resume our operations.* There are, however, some qualifications. In a way it is like a medical case I recently heard about. A man had a severe coronary and was told that if he wanted to live he had to completely cut out drinking, smoking, and all forms of physical exertion. After six months he went into the doctor's office for a checkup. After he was told he was progressing fine, he said to the doctor, "You know, sometimes I want a drink so much, not a lot, just a taste of it. Couldn't I have just one drink or two? Maybe once a week on a Friday or Saturday night?" "No," the doctor said, "but I'll tell you what. I will allow you one glass of wine with your evening meal." Some months later he was back for another physical. This time he told the doctor, "You know, Doctor, sometimes I just crave for a cigarette, just if I could puff one when I wake up and another after each meal." "No," said the doctor. "You would soon be smoking a pack a day. But if you want, you can smoke one cigar a week, perhaps after your Sunday dinner." Months went by, and our friend's health as well as state of mind improved. There was only one thing that gnawed at him. When he went to the doctor again, he came out with it very bluntly. "Doctor, it's not normal to go without sexual relations. Surely I'm healthy enough to be able to resume that." "No," said the doctor. "The physical exertion as well as excitement just could be too much. BUT I'LL TELL YOU WHAT. I'LL ALLOW YOU ONCE A WEEK TO HAVE SEX—BUT ONLY WITH YOUR WIFE."

(And similarly, we can only . . .)

Self-Interest—*Change*

186   *The problem is that everyone thinks of his own self-interest; he's really not that interested in other people's problems.* I remember the psychoanalyst who was treating a kleptomaniac. "Oh, Doctor, you mean I'm finally cured!" the woman said. "Yes," said the psychoanalyst, "I believe we now have your kleptomania firmly under control, and you can go out in the workaday world just like anybody else."

"Oh, Doctor, I'm so grateful," said the woman. "I don't know how I'll ever repay you for your help."

"My fee is all the payment I expect," said the kindly analyst. "HOWEVER, IF YOU SHOULD HAPPEN TO HAVE A RELAPSE, YOU MIGHT PICK UP A SMALL TRANSISTOR RADIO FOR ME."

(The point is we must really want to help and really be committed to helping people solve their own problems.)

Services—*Prices*

187   *I don't have to tell you about the rising cost of living.* But what is rising the most is not food prices but the price of services —repair people, car, television, plumbers. A friend of mine called a plumber to make a minor repair and the plumber fixed the trouble in about five minutes. When asked his fee, the plumber said it was twenty-five dollars. The homeowner was aghast.

"Good grief," he said. "We only pay our doctor fifteen dollars for a house call. And he usually spends fifteen or twenty minutes here."

"Yes," said the plumber, "I know. THAT WAS WHAT I USED TO GET WHEN I WAS A DOCTOR."

(And we have become a service society and a high-cost service society . . .)

Specialist—*Qualifications*

188   *When I think of the qualifications of some of our so-called specialists I think of a son of a doctor I know.* The boy barely pulled through college. And it was only because the father was a former president of the state medical association that he was accepted under pressure by a medical school.

Somehow he managed to scrape through his four years, of course with lackluster grades. At the final day the dean called him for a serious talk about his future.

"You have," said the dean, "a complete lack of understanding of medicine and a general absence of knowledge about the human body. IT IS OUR RECOMMENDATION YOU BECOME A SPECIALIST."
COMMENT: You might also tell this on yourself after you are introduced as an expert or specialist.

Specialist—*Worry*

189   *The time to worry is when we begin to undergo minute inspections by so-called experts who don't know what they are talking about.* It reminds me of a little girl next door who was always playing doctor with her little boyfriend. The little girl's mother was beginning to worry, and one day she said to her daughter, "I don't think you should play doctor with Peter anymore."

"Oh, don't worry, Mother," the little girl replied. "HE'S NOT JUST A DOCTOR, HE'S A SPECIALIST."

Worry—*Change*

190   *My wife was telling me that with this new change in my life I leave behind many old worries and cares.* Perhaps I am like a young medical student who was asked by a nurse in the maternity ward why he was enthusiastic about obstetrics. He said sheepishly, "When I was on medical rotation, I suffered from heart attacks, and asthma. In surgery, I was sure I had ulcers. In the psychiatric wards, I thought I was losing my mind.

"NOW IN OBSTETRICS, I CAN RELAX."
(And in one sense I can relax now that . . .)

Executive Suite

Damn the great executives, the men of measured merriment, damn the men with careful smiles, damn the men that run the shops, oh damn their measured merriment.
—Sinclair Lewis, *Arrowsmith*

191   I thank the chairman for his generous introduction. I would like to think I have all the qualities of a top business execu-

tive—I delegate responsibility, appropriate the credit, and shift the blame.

192   Of course there are the good times when everything succeeds. But I don't let it alarm me. I know it will pass.

193   The rest of the time I just consider I'm making progress if today's problems are different from yesterday's.

194   First I want to thank you for your congratulations. As president I'll need all the help I can get. As LBJ once supposedly said, "Being president is like being a bitch in heat. If you stand still, you get screwed, and if you try to move, they bite your ass."

195   Or as President Eisenhower once said, "Only two kinds of problems ever reach my desk—those marked 'urgent' and those marked 'important'—and I spend so much time on the 'urgent' I never get to the 'important.' "

196   Actually, there are times I feel that I am not quite up to the job, but then I realize I must put the company ahead of my own limitations.

Capitalism—*Consumerism*

197   *When businessmen protest the investigations of Ralph Nader,* I am reminded of what a Philadelphia businessman told his son, who had just graduated from business school and was about to leave for the West, there to engage in business on his account.

"Son," said the father, "on this the threshold of your business life, I desire to impress one thought upon your mind. Honesty ever and always is the policy that is best."

"Yes, Father," said the young man.

"And, by the way," added the father, "I would urge you to read up a little on corporation law. IT WILL AMAZE YOU TO DISCOVER HOW MANY THINGS YOU CAN DO IN A BUSINESS WAY AND STILL BE HONEST."

Contribution—*Accountability*

198   *One day we will all be held accountable on the great ledger.* Let us hope that we are not like the prominent businessman who went to heaven, met St. Peter at the gate, and gave him a list of his activities: president, director, consultant, engineer, etc. St. Peter asked, "What did you give personally?"

"Oh, my corporations took care of that. You know—there are charity groups."

"Up in heaven we look at the personal. What did *you* do?"

"Well, once there was a little old lady selling papers on a winter day. I gave her a dime and told her to keep the change."

"Well, that's fine. What else?"

"Well, once I saw a little boy begging in the streets on Christmas Eve and I gave him two cents."

"Well, is that all? Anything else?"

"No."

"Well, I must see the Big Man." St. Peter came out.

"Well, what did he say?"

"IT WASN'T GOOD. I TOLD HIM WHAT YOU DID AND THE BOSS SAID, 'GIVE HIM BACK HIS SEVEN CENTS AND TELL HIM TO GO TO HELL.' "

Delay—*Productivity*

199   *I know there is considerable criticism regarding my efforts,* but I feel the same way as one of our big business leaders, Elmer Knudsen, felt when he was taking charge of national defense production during the early phases of World War II. His efforts received considerable criticism. Finally Knudsen became exasperated by the constant bickering and charges of politicians that progress was not going ahead quickly enough in national defense. Knudsen replied to his critics in this manner: "Gentlemen, I realize that we are not doing this job as quickly as we would like. However, we must understand our limitations. Don't forget even though we have modern hospitals, the best anesthetics, the finest obstetricians and other medical workers, IN SPITE OF ALL OUR MODERN KNOWLEDGE AND RESEARCH IN MEDICINE AND SCIENCE, IT STILL TAKES NINE MONTHS."

Employment—*Connections*

200 *The fact is there is more to employment advancement than just hard work and ability.* There is often something else that is needed. I recall a young fellow who graduated from Princeton and went to work for a large corporation. For three months nobody paid any attention to him whatsoever. He was lost in the tremendous crowd of employees.

After three months of work he was called to the office of the president of the company one day. He entered the office and the president said to him, "You have been working here for three months now. Have you been getting any attention?"

The young fellow replied honestly, "I haven't received any notice from anyone—not even one little promotion or increase in pay."

"Well," said the president, "I'm going to make you a vice-president and increase your salary twenty thousand dollars a year."

"Gee, thanks," replied the young fellow gleefully.

"Is that all you can say?" asked the president.

"Oh no," answered the youthful graduate. "GEE THANKS, DAD!"

Hypocrisy—*Exploitation*

201 *When I read of some of these businessmen prayer breakfasts,* I am always reminded of the nineteenth-century industrial baron who told Mark Twain, "Before I die I mean to make a pilgrimage to the Holy Land. I will climb to the top of Mount Sinai and read the Ten Commandments aloud." "I have a better idea," said Twain. "WHY DON'T YOU STAY RIGHT AT HOME IN NEW YORK AND KEEP THEM?"

Party—*Confusion*

202 *I must confess that as we break for refreshments and relaxation I always think of that office in New York some years ago in December that was entered and robbed.* The thieves came in the front door and went into the main office. They then asked at gunpoint all the staff to strip themselves of their clothing and lie down on the floor. When they had all done so the robbers made their exit. A short time later a secretary who had been in the ladies' room all the while came back in the front room, saw all her colleagues and promptly started to undress too. Replied one of her fellow stenos, "RELAX, HONEY. THIS WAS A STICK-UP, NOT THE ANNUAL OFFICE PARTY."

(And I don't know what business some officers are up to . . .)

Profit—*Entrepreneurship*

203   *Recently business has become almost a dirty word.* "Sell" is a four-letter word, and profits spelled p-r-o-f-i-t-s are without honor. But to me the profit motive is not something to condemn but commend. In that connection I recall a college reunion I attended not long ago. One grad who was remembered as the dimmest in the class returned in a chauffeured Rolls-Royce. It seems he had become a fabulously successful president of a gasket company. Naturally, all of us as his former classmates were curious how someone that stupid had made so much money. So after we plied him with lots of drinks a friend of mine put the question to him. "Just how were you able to put together this gasket operation you run?"

"It was easy," he replied. "I found a manufacturer who could make them at one cent apiece and then I sold them at five cents apiece. AND YOU JUST CAN'T BEAT THAT FOUR PERCENT PROFIT!"

(And I don't think you can beat the profit system anywhere for making a country economically strong. . . .)

Qualifications—*Profession*

204   *Our speaker today has ample professional qualifications in a field that is so competitive that only the most brilliant can succeed.* Certainly it could not be said of him as it was of a very self-confident young man who had just submitted to a long series of aptitude tests and awaited results with lofty unconcern. "I suppose," he told the returning examiner, "I have an aptitude for so many fields that you fellows are a bit confused about it all."

"YOU HAVE AN APTITUDE FOR EXACTLY ONE FIELD," the examiner told him tartly, "AND THAT IS ANY FIELD IN WHICH YOUR FATHER HOLDS AN EXTREMELY INFLUENTIAL POSITION."

(Seriously, our speaker's aptitude for the field is not in question. . . .)

Reputation—*Association*

205   *I am happy to be asked to join such a distinguished group today.* I am glad I'm not in the position of a business acquaintance

of mine. He is one of those powerful figures in Wall Street. He fell in love with an actress and for many months squired her about in the fashionable circles of town. Deciding to marry her, he first prudently put a private detective to the job of looking into her background in order to guard himself against any rash mistake. At last he received his agent's report. "Miss Rogers enjoys an excellent reputation. Her past is spotless. Her associates have been irreproachable. THE ONLY BREATH OF SCANDAL IS THAT, IN RECENT MONTHS, SHE HAS BEEN SEEN IN THE COMPANY OF A BUSINESSMAN OF DOUBTFUL REPUTATION."

(Well, there's nothing dubious about your reputation. . . .)

Reputation—*Denial*

206   *As I heard the very flattering introduction I felt a little concerned.* There is a rumor going around about just how powerful our association is. My feelings are not unlike those of John D. Rockefeller, never considered exactly a spendthrift, when he was accosted outside his office by a smooth-talking panhandler who announced, "Mr. Rockefeller, I hiked fifty miles down here just to meet you, and everybody I met assured me you were the most generous man in New York."

Mr. Rockefeller thought this over for a minute, then asked quietly, "Are you going back by the same route?" "Probably," said the panhandler. "Aha," said John D. "IN THAT CASE, YOU CAN DO ME A GREAT FAVOR. DENY THE RUMOR."

(And similarly, I hope you deny . . .)

Resources—*Self-Made*

207   *No matter how strong our intentions are or how great our ideas are we still have to possess the necessary resources.* I remember reading of a testimonial dinner for a town's leading citizen. The successful businessman was called upon to tell the story of his life. "Friends and neighbors," he said in a shaking voice, "when I first came here thirty years ago, I walked into your town on a muddy road. I had only one suit on my back, one pair of shoes on my feet, and all my earthly possessions were wrapped in a red bandanna tied to a stick I carried over my shoulder.

"This city has been good to me. Today I'm chairman of the board of the bank, I own hotels, apartment buildings, and office buildings. I own three companies with branches in forty-nine cities. I am on the board of all the leading clubs. Yes, friends, your town has been good to me."

After the banquet an awed youngster approached the great man and asked timidly, "Sir, could you tell me what you had wrapped in that red bandanna when you walked into this town thirty years ago?"

"I THINK, SON," he said, "I WAS CARRYING ABOUT $100,000 IN CASH AND SOME $900,000 IN GOVERNMENT BONDS."

Salesmanship—*Approach*

208   *There are different kinds of ways of being persuasive.* Perhaps we can learn something from a situation I heard about in my city. This young man walked into a factory and asked for the sales manager. When the manager finally greeted him in his office the man nerviously said, "You don't want to buy any life insurance, do you?" and at the sales manager's curt "No!" started to leave, murmuring, "I thought you didn't."

"Wait—I want to talk with you," the manager said. The solicitor returned and sat down, plainly confused and frightened.

"I train salesmen," the sales manager said, "and you're the worst I've ever seen. You'll never sell unless you accentuate the positive. Now, because you're obviously new at this, I'll help you out by taking ten thousand dollars' worth. Get out your application blank."

After the blank was fumblingly produced and signed, the manager said kindly, "Young man, one thing you'll have to do is to learn a few standard organized sales talks."

The salesman smiled. "OH, I KNOW. I ALREADY HAVE. THIS IS MY ORGANIZED APPROACH TO SALES MANAGERS."

(Similarly, perhaps we want to adopt a low-key approach . . .)

Salesman—*Persistence*

209   *The type of persistence we want to see in the promotion of this product is best exemplified by the story of one departed salesman who wore down even the most reluctant prospects.* One of those was a big business tycoon who eventually died and went to his eternal resting place. When he got there he was greeted by our hero. The salesman gave him a big hello. "Harry, old boy, I'm here

for the appointment." And the businessman asked, "What appointment?" The salesman answered, "DON'T YOU REMEMBER? EVERY TIME I TRIED TO SEE YOU AT YOUR OFFICE YOU'D TELL ME YOU'D SEE ME HERE."

Support—*Flattery*

210   *One of the things a head of a company quickly learns is that the mere act of his being promoted into the board chairman's position has helped him to acquire a number of business associates whose principal activity is waiting for him to retire.* Not long ago I was laid up in bed for a couple of weeks. One day I opened an official letter with my company letterhead on it and it read, "WE WISH YOU A SPEEDY RECOVERY BY A VOTE OF FOUR TO THREE."

(Seriously, gentlemen, I feel flattered by the more decisive measure of support you have shown me. . . .)

COMMENT: This story can also be told about a politician. The Senate voted a resolution wishing a speedy recovery by a vote 52–48, for instance.

Uncomfortable—*Inappropriate*

211   *There is a time and place for everything.* A good example of this was a complaint by one of the salesladies at a department store in my city. The personnel manager suddenly ran a patriotic fever and set up United States flags all over the place, including the ladies' rest room. This particular woman approached the executive and asked that the powder-room flag be removed.

"And why," asked the personnel man, "should I take the glorious flag of our nation—the proud symbol of our freedom—out of the ladies' room?"

"Well, if you must know," said the exasperated employee, "WE DON'T FEEL COMFORTABLE FACING THE FLAG SITTING DOWN!"

Vice-President—*Reorganization*

212   *As I was introduced as a vice-president, I thought of how I heard such an officer once defined:* either a young man who is the son of the president or an old man they can't get rid of. Seriously, I take comfort that I am at least not as bad off as the situation back in my home town. A friend of mine walked into the bank and noticed an old schoolmate of his who was a bank teller.

Seeing that he appeared very preoccupied, my friend said, "What's the problem?"

"Well, there is a lot of trouble down at the bank. We are going through a complete reorganization."

"Why?"

"It seems that WE HAVE MORE VICE-PRESIDENTS THAN DEPOSITORS."

Family Room

Accidents will occur in the best-regulated families.
                                    —Dickens, *David Copperfield*

Anxiety—*Overeager*

213   *Sometimes we try too hard. We get overeager.* It is even worse when we press too hard on our children. We remember the visit of J. P. Morgan to the home of Dwight Morrow. The great American financier was noted, among other things, for a bulbous red nose of unsurpassing ugliness.

"Remember, Anne," Mrs. Morrow kept saying to her daughter, "you must not say one word about Mr. Morgan's nose. You must not even look at it very much."

Anne promised, but when Mr. Morgan arrived her mother watched and waited tensely. Anne was as good as gold, but Mrs. Morrow dared not relax. Turning to the financier with a gracious smile, she prepared to pour tea and said, "MR. MORGAN, WILL YOU HAVE ONE OR TWO LUMPS IN YOUR NOSE?"

Conscience—*Truth*

214   *We tell our children not to lie, not to compromise their ideals.* But then they compare our words with our actions. I recall the story of a son of a friend of mine. He was questioned by his mother regarding some escapade in which he had not told the strict truth. She put him on her knee and told him that people who told lies did not go to heaven.

"Mama, did you ever tell a lie?"

"Perhaps I have said some things not quite as they should have been."

"Did Papa ever tell a lie?"

"Yes, I'm afriad he has."

"Did Aunt Martha ever tell a lie?"

The mother concluded by saying that there is hardly anyone who at one time hadn't told the strict truth.

"MAMA, IT MUST BE AWFUL LONESOME IN HEAVEN—NOBODY THERE BUT GOD AND GEORGE WASHINGTON."

Decisions—*Budget*

215   *Gentlemen, there is a lot of business that has to be taken care of in today's meeting—decisions which some of you might think minor but I assure you are very important to the operations of this club.* The difficulty of making such decisions reminds me of a young man whose household was relatively placid. The man asked a friend how he and his wife managed to avoid arguments. "When Betty and I were married," he said, "I laid down the law. I told her that I would make all major decisions and that she could make all the minor decisions."

"What's your definition of a minor decision?"

"Well, what school our kids are going to, should I look for a better job, shall we take our savings and buy stocks, shall we buy a new house—those are the decisions that Betty handles."

"Then what are major decisions?"

"Oh, things like should we raise the national debt limit, should we continue subsidizing the UN, should we pull our troops out of Europe."

(And so on that basis we have only a minor decision to resolve today. . . .)

Delicacy—*Tact*

216   *The situation we face calls for some tact and persuasion.* I hope we can be as resourceful as a friend of mine who was called at his office by his wife, who said, "Darling, I've finally decided on a name for the new baby. Let's call her Penelope."

"Well," replied her dismayed but tactful husband, "that's a fine name. In fact, I used to know a lovely girl named Penelope and that name will always evoke fond memories."

There was a brief silence.

"YOU KNOW, DEAR, PERHAPS ELIZABETH IS REALLY A NICER NAME."

Independence—*Dependence*

217   *When I hear so many state officials crying for state's rights and freedom from Federal interference while at the same time petitioning for more funds from Washington, I am reminded of a little boy I saw the other day walking around the block with a suitcase.* I asked the five-year-old what the problem was. The little fellow explained that he was running away from home. He was angry with his mother.

"Then why do you keep walking around the block?" I asked. To which the boy replied, "BECAUSE I'M NOT ALLOWED TO CROSS THE STREET WITHOUT MY MOMMY."

Introduction—*Gentleman*

218   *The chairman certainly was generous in his introduction.* He sees me in a better light than my daughter, Rachel. She saw her mother's new evening gown, which had just been delivered.

"Oh, Mummy, how lovely!" she cried. "Will you wear it tonight?"

"No, dear, not tonight," replied her mother. "This is for when ladies and gentlemen come to dinner."

"OH, MUMMY, DO LET'S PRETEND JUST FOR ONCE THAT DADDY'S A GENTLEMAN," pleaded the child.

(Maybe some of you will try to pretend—just for tonight—that I am a gentleman!)

COMMENT: This is such a believable story that almost any father of young children can tell this about himself.

Optimism—*Negativism*

219   *Some people have the faculty of always seeing the negative side of any problem.* They immediately see the worst and start wringing their hands. An acquaintance of mine told me of his psychologist friend who had two boys—one who was a pessimist, the other an optimist. For an experiment he gave them these Christmas presents. It was a family custom that on one side of a tree one would find his gift, the other on the other side. The

pessimist found his, a bike—but he said that he would fall off and scratch himself. On the other side of the tree was a big package full of manure. The optimistic boy opened the package and exclaimed, "Oh, Father, you have been so good to me, but this time you outdid yourself. THIS IS THE MOST WONDERFUL GIFT YOU EVER GAVE ME—A PONY."

(Now, there is a right way to look at our present problem...)

Ordeal—*Repeat*

220   *As I face the ordeal of undergoing this experience once again,* I think of a friend of mine who at the age of forty, discovered she was going to have a baby. "I have sons of nineteen and eighteen away at college," she wailed, "and I certainly don't want another baby at this stage of the game." "You have nothing to worry about," I said. "You are still a good age to bear a child. Everything will go smoothly." "It's not the baby's birth that's upsetting me," she said. "WHAT I SIMPLY CANNOT FACE IS THE THOUGHT OF GOING THROUGH THAT WHOLE ROUTINE ALL OVER AGAIN WITH THE P.T.A."

Problem—*Candor*

221   *I don't think we can beat around the bush any longer.* We must take the direct approach. I don't believe in the approach my little boy used the other day when I overheard him talking to the kid next door. They were playing in the recreation room and didn't know that the door was open. We had just given my little boy a puppy and the kid next door was complaining to him because his folks wouldn't allow him to have a dog. "They won't let me have a puppy," he said. "I've begged and begged and they always say no."

And my boy said to him, "You just didn't go about it in the right way. You keep asking for a puppy. THE BEST WAY TO GET A PUPPY IS TO BEG FOR A BABY BROTHER—AND THEY'LL SETTLE FOR A PUPPY EVERY TIME."

(He must have learned that technique from his mother, because I believe in getting straight to the point. And that is what I am going to do tonight—get straight to the point.)

Problem—*Comparisom*

222   *Sometimes I long for the problems of yesteryear—like children smoking cigarettes too young, or the missile gap.* Energy

crisis and narcotics seem beyond our ability to cope. I heard of a family recently in California where they had been experiencing earthquake tremors. Fearful for the safety of their young child, they sent a telegram to the boy's uncle. "Imminent earthquake. We're sending your nephew." After about a week with the unruly six-year-old, the uncle wired, "AM RETURNING YOUR SON. SEND THE EARTHQUAKE."

Reconciliation—*Partisanship*

223　*While I know there are differences of opinion, I think there is enough common interest for us to work things out.* I recall the experience of friends of mine. They have a daughter who graduated from Radcliffe and who had been in most of the protest peace marches. Active with the McGovern volunteers, she became a Democratic party committeewoman. But recently she fell in love with this good-looking boy of Italian ancestry who has worked himself into a top job in a Boston brokerage firm. The problem is that he is a rabid Republican.

The mother, concerned, called her daughter to ask how they were reconciling their party differences.

"MOTHER, DON'T WORRY. WE'RE TOO BUSY LAUNCHING A THIRD PARTY."

(And I am sure we can get together and be productive in another way. . . .)

ADVICE: Think if this story could apply to anyone you know. Imagine that the story really happened and tell it as if it did without, of course, revealing names.

Success—*Humility*

224　*I am reminded of the man and his wife who went to church one day.* Out loud, the man prayed, "Oh, Lord, make me successful, and please keep me humble." His wife, kneeling beside him, chimed in with a somewhat corrective plea: "OH, LORD, YOU MAKE HIM SUCCESSFUL, I'LL KEEP HIM HUMBLE."

Transportation—*Improvement*

225　*My reaction to the new plans for the inner-city loop transportation reminds me of what a friend of mine's daughter said to her mother.* The little girl had become curious about where she had come from. "Mommy," she asked, "did you know ahead of time that I was going to be born?"

Her mother replied that she had, indeed, received advance notice.

"Where was I before I was born?" asked her little daughter.

Her mother decided the child was old enough for a forthright answer. The little girl pondered the reply, then marveled, "GEE! THAT SURE BEATS WALKING!"

Unexpected—*Tragedy*

226   *We must always be ready for the unexpected.* Not long ago I read an item about a clairvoyant little boy. It seems this boy had premonitions. Once while reciting prayers he said, "God bless Mommy, God bless Daddy, God bless Grandma, goodbye, Grandpa." The next day Grandpa died of a stroke.

Then later on the little boy said, "God bless Mommy, God bless Daddy, goodbye, Grandma." Then Grandma was hit while crossing the street.

Some time later in his prayers he said, "God bless Mommy, goodbye, Daddy."

The father was really upset. He had himself driven to work; he couldn't work at the office. Finally he decided to come home early. He took a taxi home and rushed in. He was greeted by his wife, who said, "WHAT DO YOU THINK HAPPENED TODAY, DEAR? THE MOST AWFUL THING—THE MILKMAN DROPPED DEAD ON THE BACK PORCH."

(And while we may not expect this kind of happening, we . . .)

Wife—*Marriage*

227   *As those who have been my friends will tell you,* I owe the great measure of my success from following my version of some advice that Henry Ford once gave. The founder of the Ford empire was a hard-working, simple man. At his fiftieth wedding anniversary he was asked by a reporter, "How do you account for your happy marriage?"

Henry Ford replied, "BY STICKING TO ONE MODEL."

First-Class Lounge

*In America there are two classes of travel—first
class and with children.*
　　　　　　　　　　　—Robert Benchley

Adjustment—*Rescue*

228　*It is my hope that once you adjust to the situation you will
have a different outlook.* I remember the case of a high-school
teacher who had saved money for several years and was finally
aboard a sleek ocean liner for her long-anticipated trip to Europe.
On shipboard she wrote: "Dear Diary: Monday. I felt singularly
honored this evening. The captain asked me to dine at his table.

"Tuesday. I spent the entire morning on the bridge with the
captain.

"Wednesday. The captain made proposals to me unbecoming an
officer and a gentleman.

"Thursday. Tonight the captain threatened to sink the ship if I
do not give in to his indecent proposals.

"Friday. THIS AFTERNOON I SAVED 1,200 LIVES."

Choice—*Alternative*

229　*Of course, it's not as if we don't have a choice.* I recall the
time Groucho Marx was traveling by air and requested permission
to smoke a cigar. There's a fairly strict regulation on commercial
airlines against this particular aromatic indulgence. But the hostess felt that perhaps in the case of a passenger as famous as Groucho Marx the rules might be relaxed.

"I suppose you can smoke a cigar if you don't annoy the lady
passengers," she said.

To which Groucho replied, "YOU MEAN I'VE GOT A CHOICE?"
(And so do we have a choice. . . .)

Disaster—*Test*

230　*One test of character is how a man would act in an emergency—under fire.* Back in the old days of the Pennsylvania Rail-

road there was a test they used to give to each applicant for district engineer. To test him, the boss asked what he would do if he saw two trains coming at each other on a single track at sixty miles an hour. The fellow thought about it for a while and said, "I'd go home and get my brother."

"Why would you do that?" the boss asked.

He replied, "MY BROTHER AIN'T NEVER SEEN A TRAIN WRECK." COMMENT: This is one of Lyndon Johnson's old favorites.

Frustration—*Misled*

231   *I think the country is getting tired of rhetoric—tired of being misled and misdirected.* I remember hearing from a conductor once about a man who got on a train, a sleeper, in New York City. He goes up to the porter and he says, "Look, I want to get off in Richmond, Virginia, but once I'm asleep it's very difficult for me to wake up. Sometimes I'm nasty and I don't know what I'm saying. Here's fifteen dollars. Please, no matter what I say, wake me up and get me off the train in Richmond, Virginia."

The man wakes up in Raleigh, North Carolina, and he's furious. He finds the porter, gets off the train. The conductor sees what's going on, goes up to the porter and says, "What happened? I've never seen anyone get that mad." The porter answers, "THAT'S NOTHING. YOU SHOULD SEE THE GUY I PUT OFF IN RICHMOND, VIRGINIA."

(And we are tired of being misled . . .)

Grievance—*Satisfaction*

232   *There are some people who can't be satisfied.* They don't want to be satisfied. I remember a porter on the old Broadway Limited, a sleeper that went from New York to Chicago. He told me about a wealthy businessman who insisted on every courtesy and convenience. One evening after he had dinner he asked for pistachio ice cream. When he was told they didn't have it he yelled, "No pistachio! I always have pistachio." "I'm sorry, sir," said the waiter. "We have chocolate, vanilla, strawberry, banana, cherry, mint, fudge ripple." "I want pistachio," cried the businessman, banging the table and turning red. "I have always had pistachio and I won't have anything else." Finally, when the train stopped at Pittsburgh a word to the conductor kept it there while

the crew amazingly found some pistachio. Finally, a whole pint of the delicious concoction was obtained and presented to the businessman together with a sliced banana and a swirl of whipped cream.

"Here is your pistachio ice cream, sir." said the waiter.

The businessman looked at it with a snarl, then with a sudden swipe of his arm hurled it to the floor, shouting, "I DON'T WANT IT NOW. I'D RATHER HAVE MY GRIEVANCE."

Location—*Convenience*

233   *In picking the right location we should look for convenience and accessibility.* We should follow the example of two young lovers trying to find a secluded spot for a long embrace. Everywhere they found people, people, people. Suddenly the man had an idea and he led the girl to the railway station. Standing beside the door of a car as though seeing her off, he kissed her fondly. After the couple had repeated the experiment at four or five different platforms, a sympathetic conductor strolled up and whispered to the young man, "Why don't you take her around to the bus terminal? THEY GO EVERY FOUR MINUTES FROM THERE."

Problem—*Interpretation*

234   *It is one thing to be aware of a problem but it is another to interpret the problem correctly.* A classic case of misreading the problem was a businessman years ago in a plane scheduled to arrive at La Guardia. It was right after the first four-engine jobs took to the skies. The captain said over the intercom, "I'm sorry to say that one of our engines has conked out. There's no cause for alarm, however, because the other three can more than do the job. However, we'll be about twenty minutes late reaching La Guardia."

A little later the captain came on again, announced a second engine had failed, and again said there was no cause for alarm. The other two engines were more than sufficient. "However," he added, "we'll now be an hour late at La Guardia."

A few minutes later the captain reported a third engine had pooped out but that the remaining engine would fly the plane. "But," he said, "we'll be about two hours late reaching La Guardia."

"Ye gods!" cried the businessman. "IF THAT FOURTH ENGINE GOES, WE MAY BE UP HERE ALL NIGHT."

Purpose—*Change*

235   *The situation we are in reminds me of a captain's airplane announcement I once heard about on one of those transatlantic flights.* His voice suddenly came over the PA system.

"Ladies and gentlemen," the pilot said, "I have two pieces of news for you. One of them is good, and one of them is not so good. So I'll tell you the bad news first. The bad news is that we are lost. We don't have any idea where we are. But as I told you, there's good news, too. The good news is that we have a two-hundred-mile-an-hour tail wind. IN OTHER WORDS, WE DON'T KNOW WHERE WE'RE GOING, BUT WE'RE GETTING THERE AWFULLY FAST."

(And that nicely describes . . .)

Rhetoric—*Action*

236   *I think we have heard enough speeches on energy to satisfy a couple of lifetimes.* What we really want to see is not more talk but some action—some constructive accomplishments. It reminds me of a dinner in Paris for the Wright brothers after their success at Kitty Hawk. At this banquet there were speeches by prominent statesmen. One of the speeches was a long flowery dissertation by a Frenchman on the great genius of the French in pioneering certain achievements in the fields of science and engineering. Hardly any mention was made of the Wright brothers, who were after all the guests of honor.

When it came Wilbur Wright's turn to speak, he said, "As I sit here listening to the eloquent speaker who preceded me, I heard eloquent illusions made to the eagle, the swallow, and the hawk, as embodying the skills of speech and flight, but somehow my thoughts kept coming back to the bird which in all the ornithological kingdom is the worst flier but the best talker—THE PARROT."

(And now is the time to stop talking, act quick and fly right. . . .)

Sincerity—*Service*

237   *I can't help but wonder how sincere this expression of concern and offer to rectify matters is.* It reminds me of the gentle-

man who found himself bitten by bugs on an overnight railroad trip. Arriving at his destination, he wrote the company an indignant letter and received a prompt reply. "Dear sir, your letter was a source of great concern to our railroad. You must realize this is the very first complaint we have ever received of this nature. Inquiry has failed to reveal any explanation for this unprecedented occurrence. Nevertheless, a number of new precautions are being taken to make absolutely certain such an unfortunate incident never happens again." The letter was signed by a high official of the railroad.

The gentleman was well satisfied with this reply and was returning it to its envelope when a slip of paper fell out onto the floor. The hastily scribbled note on it read, "SEND THIS GUY THE BUG LETTER."

Standstill—*Progress*

238   *The complete lack of progress reminds me of an excuse a husband gave to his wife recently for coming home too late.* The poor man had imbibed a bit too freely and told his angry wife that he had taken the wrong bus.

His wife said, "That's easy to understand—considering the shape you're in—but how did you know you were on the wrong bus?"

The husband said, "Well, it seemed strange when it stood on one corner for a couple of hours, but what finally convinced me was the fact that PEOPLE KEPT COMING IN AND ORDERING HAMBURGERS AND COFFEE."

Wait—*Excuse*

239   *I apologize for the delay in our program this evening.* You wouldn't believe all the difficulties we encountered—what with the traffic tie-ups and lack of communication. But at least our excuses sound a bit better than those of a house builder I heard about recently. He was telephoned by a woman to complain about the vibrations that shook the structure of her new house when a train passed by three blocks away. "Ridiculous," he told her. "I'll be out to check it."

"Just wait until a train comes along," said the woman when the builder arrived for his inspection. "Why, it nearly shakes me out of bed. Just lie down there; you'll see."

The builder scoffed but accepted her challenge. He had just stretched himself out on the bed when the woman's husband came home. "What are you doing on my wife's bed?" the husband demanded.

The terrified builder shook like a leaf. "WOULD YOU BELIEVE," he said, "I'M WAITING FOR A TRAIN?"

Witness—*Inauguration*

240   *As we gather here for this opening day I am reminded of a situation I once saw in an Atlanta airport.* There was an old fellow in line from back in the hills who wanted to go to New Orleans, so he went to the Atlanta airport. He was fascinated by all the people, the vastness of the large terminal, and most of all by the big jets. When he got to the ticket counter he asked about the next flight to New Orleans. The ticket agent told him the plane left at 9:25 and arrived at 9:30. The agent didn't think it necessary to explain about the change in time zones.

The old fellow didn't think the agent knew what he was talking about but was too polite to protest. He just waited until another man arrived to take the agent's place at the counter. He again asked about the flight to New Orleans. "Look, mister, the plane leaves at 9:25 and arrives at 9:30." He then asked for the manager. The manager said, "Look here, you're becoming a nuisance. For the last time, the plane leaves at 9:25 and arrives at 9:30. Do you want a ticket or don't you?"

"Nope," said the old fellow, "BUT I'M SURE AS HECK GOING TO STICK AROUND AND WATCH THAT SON-OF-A-GUN PLANE TAKE OFF!"

(And we are also going to enjoy . . .)

COMMENT: Tell the story as if you saw it happen or at least as if a friend of yours saw it happen.

Women—*Priority*

241   *Every organization has its priorities*—problems that *have to be taken care of first no matter how we would wish it differently.* I remember the interview the late Sir Winston Churchill had when he was boarding an Italian liner for a transatlantic voyage to the United States. A British journalist asked the Prime Minister why he was choosing an Italian ship over one of the

queens of the British Cunard line.

Said Sir Winston, "First, the cuisine on the Italian line is superb. Second, their service is unsurpassed. And, finally, on an Italian line THERE IS NONE OF THIS NONSENSE ABOUT WOMEN AND CHILDREN FIRST."

(And, similarly, we have our own priorities . . .)

COMMENT: If you want to use the story as a lead-in about women, change the opening sentence to "In this situation we are going to have to yield to the women. We can't do as Winston Churchill when . . .)

Golden-Age Club

Dismiss the old horse in good times lest he fail
in the lists and the spectators laugh.
                                    —Horace

242   A lot of wonderful things have been said about me on this evening's occasion. And I'm here tonight to tell you that they are all true.

243   Really, though, I am very happy to be here. In fact, at my age, I'm very happy to be anywhere.

244   The only thing, though, is that I wish I had known I would live to be eighty. I would have taken better care of myself.

245   Of course, I have always believed in exercise—limited exercise. I get mine acting as pallbearer to my friends who do.

246   You see, I always followed the advice of Sir Winston Churchill, who said, "Never walk if you can drive, and of two cigars always choose the longest and strongest."

247   Yes, I suppose I do have some regrets on how I spent my life—particularly my money. A lot of it went for liquor, much of it went for women, and the rest I spent foolishly.

248   I guess the reason I have lived to such a ripe old age is that I never expended any energy resisting temptation.

249 The only thing I don't like about old age is when you feel like the morning after the night before—and you haven't even been anywhere.

250 When people ask me how I feel these days, I say what Somerset Maugham once said on his ninetieth birthday, "Not bad when you consider the alternative."

Action—*Lifeless*

251 *I am rather annoyed at the indifference and the insensitivity of some men to these problems.* It reminds me of a friend of my mother. The lady is a widow and is eighty-two years old. One night, just to get her out of the house, my mother arranged a date for her with a man who is eighty-five years old. She returned home from the date very late that evening and more than a little upset. "What happened?" my mother asked.

"Are you kidding?" she snapped. "I had to slap his face three times!"

"You mean," asked my mother, "he got fresh?"

"No," she replied. "I THOUGHT HE WAS DEAD!"

(And likewise, some of these people act as if they hadn't had a new or fresh idea . . .)

Action—*Talk*

252 *I wonder if we are going to take any action or whether we have only the capacity to talk.* I hope we aren't in the situation of an elderly gentleman who went into the office of a doctor acquaintance of mine to have a medical checkup. "My friend," the doctor said, "I can't find anything wrong with you. But you aren't getting any younger, so I would suggest you give up some of your love life."

After a long moment the patient said quietly, "DOCTOR, WHICH HALF DO YOU RECOMMEND I GIVE UP—THINKING ABOUT IT OR TALKING ABOUT IT?"

Age—*Birthday*

253 *Someone approached me earlier in the evening and told me that he hoped to be here next year when I celebrate my seventy-fifth birthday.* I told him what Winston Churchill said on his

eightieth birthday to a reporter who said he hoped to see him on his one hundredth birthday. Sir Winston replied, "I DON'T SEE WHY NOT. YOU LOOK HEALTHY ENOUGH TO ME."

Birthday—*Enjoyment*

254   *I was always told that as you get older you get treated with more respect.* When I told that to one of my father's friends, he said, "I'm told that doesn't come until you're a hundred." Well, I'm not sure I aspire to that magic number. I recently met a man who told me, "I don't drink, smoke, or chase women, and I just celebrated my one hundredth birthday."

And I asked, "HOW?"

(Seriously, with you I can still celebrate in some way . . .)

Birthday—*Fanfare*

255   *As I look at this cake, I am grateful that no one tried to put on the appropriate number of candles.* It recalls the remark that Ethel Barrymore once made when she invited friends over for her seventy-fifth birthday. Someone asked where the candles were for the cake. She replied, "MY FRIEND, THIS IS A BIRTHDAY PARTY, NOT A TORCHLIGHT PROCESSION."

Birthday—*Reminder*

256   *I didn't know people were going to honor me for my birthday tonight.* I must confess I have rather mixed feelings about it. I recall once at a White House news conference in 1960 a reporter asked President Eisenhower, "Sir, do you realize that on your upcoming birthday you will be the oldest President ever to serve?"

Ike smiled and said, "I BELIEVE IT'S A TRADITION IN BASEBALL THAT WHEN A PITCHER HAS A NO-HITTER GOING FOR HIM, NO-BODY REMINDS HIM OF IT."

(And similarly when you reach my age I am not sure you would want everyone to know about it. . . .)

Blame—*Flattery*

257   *I suppose I should be flattered by being singled out for all the blame.* To be the cause of all I'm accused of would take quite a man. In that sense I feel like the seventy-year-old man who met

a friend on the street one day and asked him what he'd been doing lately. The friend said he'd just spent six months in jail, after being convicted of rape. "Rape!" shouted the first man. "At your age? That's the most ridiculous thing I ever heard of!"

"I know," replied the other, "BUT I WAS SO FLATTERED I PLEADED GUILTY."

Cost—*Cheaper*

258   *It may be hard to believe, but actually it's cheaper for us to do it this way.* In that sense we are like the elderly couple who go to a doctor. The man says, "Doctor, we want to know if we're making love properly. Will you watch us?"

The doctor says, "Go ahead," so they make love.

The doctor says, "You're making love perfectly. That will be ten dollars."

They come back six weeks in a row and do the same thing.

On the seventh visit the doctor says, "What are you coming here like this for? I told you you're making love properly."

The old man says, "She can't come to my house, I can't go to her house. You charge us ten dollars, the motel would cost us twenty dollars, and this way we get eight dollars back from Medicare."

Friends—*Loyalty*

259   *Now there are those who want me to change my position, but I feel I would be turning my back on those who have worked with me.* I feel like that old man who had lived a full life, tasting deeply of all its manifold pleasures, and was dying. As the family gathered around the old unregenerate, the preacher asked him to repent his sins.

The impassioned parson urged, "Now is the time for you to turn your heart to God. Now is the time for you to renounce the devil."

"NO," said the old man, "AT THIS STAGE I CAN'T AFFORD TO ALIENATE OLD FRIENDS."

Longevity—*Enemies*

260   *Fortunately I have reached the age where I can be charitable toward just about everybody.* I'm like the old man my minister once told me about. It was during a sermon on brotherly love. The preacher asked the congregation whether anybody could honestly say that he didn't have a single enemy.

The old guy stood up and said, "Right here!" The preacher then went into a tribute to the old man and finally asked him to tell his secret—how he happened to be without enemies.

Said the old man, "I OUTLIVED THE S.O.B.'S."

Problem—*Awareness*

261   *It's one thing to have a problem but it's another not even to be aware you have a problem.* That's like the eighty-year-old I heard about in Miami. He was vacationing with another octogenarian in Florida. During their stay they both made the acquaintance of some ladies younger than themselves. They both fell in love and decided to get married in Florida in a double ceremony. Following the wedding night, they are both in their rocking chairs after breakfast.

The one says, "You know, I better see a doctor."

The other says, "Why?"

"Well," the first says, "I couldn't consummate the marriage."

"Oh," said the second. "I better see a psychiatrist."

"Why?" said the first.

"I DIDN'T EVEN GIVE IT A THOUGHT."

Theories—*Enjoyment*

262   *Sometimes we try to make our theories fit our facts.* I am reminded of the story of a prominent citizen who lived to be ninety-six years of age. On his ninety-sixth birthday the newspapers sent their reporters out to interview him. One of them asked, "To what do you attribute your long life?"

The old man replied, "I attribute it to the fact that I have never taken a sip of an alcoholic beverage or smoked a cigarette in all my days."

At that moment they heard a noise in an adjoining room that sounded like a combined earthquake and cyclone. One of the newspaper reporters said, "Good heavens, what is that?"

The old man said, "THAT IS MY OLD DADDY IN THERE ON ONE OF HIS PERIODIC DRUNKS."

ADVICE: This was one of Lyndon Johnson's favorite stories.

Timing—*Sickness*

263   *In everything there is a matter of timing—a right move at the right moment.* It recalls the time when Somerset Maugham,

the writer, who was nearly ninety, had a bout with influenza. One day a lady admirer phoned and asked if she might send fruits and flowers. "IT'S TOO LATE FOR FRUIT," Maugham replied, "AND TOO EARLY FOR FLOWERS."

Urgency—*Compelled*

264   *The urgent situation we find ourselves in reminds me of the explanation once given to a New York sports reporter.* Interviewing the sixty-year-old rodeo champion in Austin, Texas, the New York newspaperman remarked, "You're really an extraordinary man to be a rodeo champion at your age."

"Shucks," said the cowboy, "I'm not nearly the man my pa is. He's still place-kicking for a football team and he's eighty-six."

"Amazing!" gasped the journalist. "I'd like to meet your father."

"Can't right now. He's in El Paso standing up for Grandpa. Grandpa is getting married tomorrow. He's a hundred and fourteen."

"Your family is simply unbelievable," said the newspaperman. "Here you are, a rodeo champion at sixty. Your father's a football player at eighty-six. And now your grandfather wants to get married at a hundred and fourteen."

"Hell, mister, you got that wrong," said the Texan. "GRANDPA DOESN'T WANT TO GET MARRIED. HE HAS TO."

Venture—*Risk*

265   *We may get shot down for trying out this new endeavor, but we're going to have a lot of fun doing it.* It's like the three retired men in Miami who were passing the time of day discussing the ideal way to leave this world. The first, aged seventy, said, "I'd like to crash in one of those new supersonic transport planes." The second, aged seventy-five, agreed on a speedy end but thought he'd prefer a crash in a new Maserati sports car.

"I've got a better idea," mused the third, aged eighty. "I'D RATHER BE SHOT BY A JEALOUS HUSBAND."

Yearning—*Youth*

266   *Despite my advancing age, I am not ready to be counted out yet.* I take heart in some remarks made by the late Justice Oliver Wendell Holmes. The ninety-year old justice was walking

down Pennsylvania Avenue in Washington with a colleague and encountered two attractive young girls. Holmes turned to his fellow justice and said, "OH, TO BE SEVENTY AGAIN."

(And so by that standard I foresee quite a little action. . . .)

Halls of Ivy

A professor is one who talks in someone else's sleep.
                                          —W. H. Auden

267   When I first started college I was told that if you steal from one person, it's plagiarism; if you steal from ten people, it's research; and if you steal from hundreds, you're a scholar. Well, speaking as a scholar . . .

268   Seriously, the trouble with being a scholar is that the more you know, the less you understand.

269   I am a little nervous at being introduced as a professor and a scholar in my field. It reminds me of the essay a child wrote once about Socrates: "Socrates was a famous Greek teacher who went around giving people advice. They poisoned him."

270   Seriously, though, I don't like being called a scholar since all of you know what scholarship really signifies. It means the attempt to exhaust the subject by first exhausting the reader.

271   Thank you for your generous introduction—but if it's all the same, I'd rather not be called an intellectual. That just means a man educated beyond his intelligence.

272   And as one described the British social scientist Macaulay, "He not only overflows with learning, he wallows in the slop."

273   Thank you for your introduction. As the chairman mentioned, I am currently a professor. But that only makes me think of what John Kenneth Galbraith once said: "Professor is just another name for a pedagogue, and a pedagogue is just a demagogue with a Ph.D."

274   Or as Adlai Stevenson said, "The professor is just a man who takes more words than necessary to tell more than he knows."

275   It is always nice for someone in the education field to get such appreciative words. We like to think we have advice to give, warnings to make. The only problem is our warnings are like that of a foghorn—we call attention to the fog without doing anything to lift it.

276   Really, though, we professors like to believe we teach our students how to solve various social problems—what we of course avoid by becoming professors.

Book—*Creativity*

277   *Today on the campuses there is so much pressure on the faculty to write books, it is a wonder they devote any time to giving a good lecture or counseling their students.* It reminds me of what two citizens of ancient Athens said about Socrates.

The first asked, "Have you heard the news about Socrates? He's been sentenced to death."

"What a terrible shame!" said the other. "He's such a great teacher."

"Yes," said the first man, "HE IS. BUT YOU KNOW, HE NEVER PUBLISHED."

(And it's a shame, too, that we don't let teachers concentrate. . . .)

Facts—*Solution*

278   *First of all, I want to say that tonight I am not going to give you easy answers or simplistic solutions.* I was asked to outline the dimensions of the problem. In that way I feel like a fellow classmate of mine. The professor of our philosophy class was cross-examining a student. Every time the student would try to come up with an answer, the professor would show how stupid the answer was. Finally, the student said, "Sir, you have knocked holes in everything I ever believed in, and you have given me nothing to take its place."

"Young man," replied the professor, "you will recall that Hercules, among his labors, was required to clean out the Augean stables. He was not, I assure you, REQUIRED TO REFILL THEM."

Problems—*Change*

279   *Times change and old solutions are no longer the answers to new problems.* I remember a friend of mine went back to a big Princeton football weekend to visit his son. When he found out his son was taking the same philosophy course under the same professor he had thirty years ago, he decided to pay a visit to the class. To his dismay he found the same questions in a class test he had answered many years ago. On this he challenged the old professor.

"OH, YES, I GIVE THE SAME QUESTIONS, BUT AS THE YEARS GO ON I KEEP ASKING FOR DIFFERENT ANSWERS."

(And perhaps we need different answers. . . .)

COMMENT: You can substitute "economics" for "philosophy" or, for that matter, other subjects such as "sociology," "political science," "psychology," etc. It is a good opener for any talk.

Report—*Inspection*

280   *As I look at the agenda, I see now's the time to read our report.* Unfortunately we can't make such an account sound as titillating as an Irish Catholic priest once did. He heard that one of his parishioners—a wealthy old bachelor in the Morningside Heights area—wanted to write a will leaving all his estate to Columbia University. Most perturbed, the good Father called on the old gentleman. "Father," the old man said, "all my life I have lived in the shadow of Columbia University. Though I never went to college, I have come to think of this university as my own. I have seen it grow and develop and now I'd like to be part of it. I have no children or close relatives. So I would appreciate it if you would be a witness to the will."

The Father replied, "Well, naturally, I will accede to any of your wishes. Of course, as you know, Columbia isn't a Catholic school, although that shouldn't be your only criterion. But I am rather surprised you are in favor of the heterosexual carryings-on over there that go under the name of progressive education."

"What do you mean, Father?"

"I mean that at Columbia, boys and girls share the same curriculum."

"No!" said the old man.

"Yes, and as a matter of fact, boys and girls actually *matriculate* together."

"Father, I had no idea," replied the man.

"Yes, I have even heard some stories about young girls having to show their theses to their professors."

"FATHER, FATHER, STOP! I WANT TO LEAVE MY MONEY TO FORDHAM."

(Well, gentlemen, the thesis of the report we are going to show to you today . . .)

Shortage—*Delay*

281   *The temporary difficulty we face reminds me of the sociology professor I once knew who liked to weave in racy stories during class.* A group of coeds once decided that the next time he started to tell one, they would all rise and leave the room in protest. The professor, however, got wind of their scheme just before class the following day, so he bided his time. Then, halfway through the lecture, he began. "They say there is quite a shortage of prostitutes in France."

The girls looked at one another, arose and started for the door. "YOUNG LADIES," said the professor with a broad smile, "I'M AFRAID THE NEXT PLANE DOESN'T LEAVE UNTIL TOMORROW AFTERNOON."

(Similarly, I'm afraid we face a delay . . .)

Head Table

Say what you have to say and the first time you come to a sentence with a grammatical ending —sit down.

—Winston Churchill

282   Thank you for your kind introduction. Actually, the only thing that discomforted me a bit, Mr. Chairman, was what you said before you stood up to introduce me. You'll remember you said, "Shall we let them enjoy their dessert and coffee a little longer or had we better have your speech now?"

283   Thank you, thank you for your welcome. In accepting your invitation, I was reminded what the Tower of London said to the Tower of Pisa: "If you have the inclination, I have the time."

284   But just how far should I take that inclination? I went to your chairman and asked how long I should speak. He said, "Take as long as you want. We all leave at 1:45."

285   You know, in Japan the speech comes before the meal. That's so the serving of the luncheon will automatically stop the guy who goes on too long. No wonder the Japanese lead the world in production.

286   Thank you, thank you for this fine reception—a full audience complete with reporters and photographers. But as I look at the photographers I remember the sign I saw at a speech I gave the other month: "Do not photograph the speakers while they are addressing the audience. Shoot them as they approach the platform."

287   As the last speaker on the program tonight, I feel like an Egyptian mummy—pressed for time.

Chairman—*Leadership*

288   *Gentlemen, I think we all agree that we owe a great debt of thanks to the chairman who has presided so capably in the chair.* His unique abilities bring to mind an Irish fable told me many years ago by a kindly old cop on my neighborhood block. He told me that the Irish believe that a leprechaun kisses each baby when it is born. If the kiss is on the brow, the child is destined to be an intellectual; if on the eyes, a great beauty; if on the fingers, a great artist. NOW, I AM NOT IN A POSITION TO TELL YOU WHERE THE LEPRECHAUN KISSED OUR CHAIRMAN. BUT YOU'LL HAVE TO ADMIT HE MAKES A WONDERFUL PRESIDING OFFICER.

(Seriously, let us thank our chairman . . .)

ADVICE: This is a good story to close an evening. It is better if you give some semblance of realism by saying you learned it from a longtime maid, policeman, etc.

Conformity—*Conspicuous*

289   *Of course, it is most embarrassing for a speaker to forget an introduction or mispronounce a name.* But I always take comfort that I didn't fall into the embarrassment of one speaker I read about. This particular speaker had finally consented, with some trepidation, to address a banquet at a nudist colony. Upon his arrival at the extensive premises he was greeted by large numbers of men and women in their pristine natural state. He was shown into the headquarters building, and it was suggested that he might like to prepare for dinner.

Upstairs in the room they allotted him he felt that there was nothing he could do except face the fact that he was expected to divest himself of his garments. In extreme mental anguish he determined to be equal to the situation. At last, hearing the bell for dinner, he marched downstairs as bare as Adam to discover that the NUDISTS, IN DEFERENCE TO THE SPEAKER, HAD DONNED BLACK TIE AND FORMAL DRESS.

(Well, I don't feel quite that exposed. . . .)

Message—*Purpose*

290   *The question is, what is the message we want to give?* What is the issue we want to leave in the people's minds? I remember once coming in late to a conference. I asked a man who was coming out of the hotel ballroom, "Has the congressman begun speaking yet?"

"Yes," replied the man. "He has been speaking for half an hour."

"What is he talking about?" I asked.

"I DON'T KNOW," said the man. "HE HASN'T SAID YET."

Money—*Gratitude*

291   *There is nothing wrong with our situation that one thing wouldn't cure—money.* Clarence Darrow once expressed his feelings about the shallowness of plain good feelings at a women's club in the West where he had been delivering a lecture on ancient history, in the course of which he had touched upon the arts, customs, and achievements of the ancient Phoenicians. "Oh," said the portly and laudatory chairlady when Mr. Darrow had finished, "how can we thank Mr. Darrow for the fascinating lecture he has given us tonight?"

Darrow returned to the lectern and added, "I ENTIRELY FOR-
GOT TO TELL YOU THAT IT WAS THE PHOENICIANS WHO FIRST
INVENTED MONEY."

Nervousness—*Speech*

292   *We all get a little anxious as we make last-minute prepara-
tions in anticipation of the big moment.* I remember once my
wife telling me of the time she entered a room in the old Willard
Hotel in Washington and recognized a well-known government
official pacing up and down, and she asked what he was doing
there. He said, "I'm going to deliver a speech shortly."

"Do you always get so nervous before addressing a large audience?"

"Nervous?" he replied. "No, I never get nervous."

"IN THAT CASE," my wife said, "WHAT ARE YOU DOING IN THE
LADIES' ROOM?"

Speech—*Exchange*

293   *After that fine last speech you have just heard, I wish I
could say what Chauncey Depew once said on an occasion when
he and Mark Twain were both to speak at a banquet.* Twain spoke
first for some twenty minutes and was received with great enthusi-
asm. When Depew's turn came, immediately afterward, he said,
"Mr. Toastmaster, ladies and gentlemen. Before this dinner Mr.
Twain and I made an agreement to trade speeches. HE HAS JUST
DELIVERED MINE AND I'M GRATEFUL FOR THE RECEPTION YOU
HAVE ACCORDED IT. I REGRET THAT I HAVE LOST HIS SPEECH AND
CANNOT REMEMBER A THING HE HAD TO SAY."

(But I do have a speech here . . .)

Speech—*Nervousness*

294   *When I was invited to speak here tonight, I knew exactly
how Androcles felt.* Androcles, you know, was the fellow who
made quite a reputation fighting man-eating lions for the entertainment of the Caesars. One Roman emperor noted that the
gladiator's system seemed to consist of whispering in the lion's ear,
whereupon the beast would demonstrate a complete loss of appe-
tite and slink away spiritless and defeated. Androcles was summoned to the royal box, and the emperor asked, "Androcles, what
is your secret?"

Androcles answered, "It's this, Your Highness. I MERELY TELL HIM, 'AS SOON AS YOU'VE FINISHED YOUR DINNER YOU'LL BE ASKED TO SAY A FEW WORDS.'"

(Fortunately, it is only a few words that I am going to say about the . . .)

ADVICE: This is good to use if you are one of a group of people at the head table who is going to be called upon to say a few brief remarks.

Speech—*Subject*

295   *When I was first invited to give a speech I was asked to talk on multi-nationalism and the world market.* Before agreeing to speak on that subject I remembered the advice of a college classmate I had. We were enrolled in a popular elective—"A Survey of the New Testament." All the football players used to sign up for it. An old minister gave the course, and for years his final exam question was the same: "Trace and Discuss the Travels of the Apostle Paul." Every student carefully memorized the answer to this exam question. One year the professor crossed them up. The question was "Discuss the Sermon on the Mount." All but one dumb football player, Butch, left the classroom. The marks were announced. All failed except Butch, who barely passed. We were all curious as to his answer so we asked Butch what he wrote. He replied, "I started out by saying, 'WHO AM I TO CRITICIZE THE WORDS OF THE MASTER, BUT I WOULD LIKE TO RELATE THE TRAVELS OF THE APOSTLE PAUL.'"

(And similarly, who am I to expound on a subject that even confounds the leading economists, but I would like to talk about something I know about. . . .)

COMMENT: I have used this story repeatedly with unfailing success. It is a good ice-breaker—expecially when it can be used to explain why you chose your particular topic. Remember to tell it as if it happened to you.

Toastmaster—*Introduction*

296   *I am happy to introduce the toastmaster this evening.* Fortunately, he is not like the one who introduced the famous after-dinner speaker Senator Chauncey Depew. The talkative

toastmaster had made a long introduction of Depew, ending with the statement "Depew, then, is like an automatic machine. You put in a dinner and up comes a speech." Depew rose to respond.

"I'M HAPPY I DIFFER FROM THE TOASTMASTER. WITH HIM YOU PUT IN A SPEECH AND UP COMES YOUR DINNER."

(Luckily, tonight our toastmaster is one who lets you keep your dinner down while keeping your spirits up. . . .)

Home on the Grange

Some people tell us that there ain't no Hell, But they never farmed, so how can they tell?
—*Congressional Record,* 1940

297   I appreciate your welcome. As the cow said to the farmer one winter morning, "Thank you for a warm hand."

298   Really, we farmers need all the help we can get. As Pope John, whose own roots were in the soil, once said, "People go to ruin in three ways—women, gambling, and farming. My family chose the slowest one."

299   Actually, if you work hard and long enough on a farm, you can make a fortune—that is, if you strike oil.

300   My ambition, though, is to be one of those gentlemen farmers. That's one who has time to read all the government literature on farming.

301   The government does help out. In fact, there are those who say that the only thing you need to be a successful farmer these days is faith, hope, and parity.

302   Actually, you sometimes wonder if we do not have more employees in the Department of Agriculture in Washington than farmers. In fact some years ago a congressman offered an amendment to the farm bill to ensure that "the total number of employees in the Department of Agriculture at no time exceeds the number of farmers in America." It lost—only by 230 to 171.

Communication—*Simplicity*

303   *If we are going to succeed in communicating this problem, we can't talk in technical jargon.* We should remember the story Mark Twain once related to a young political candidate. Twain told the strange story of a farmer who aspired to serve in the Missouri state legislature.

This farmer was anxious to make a good impression and thought he could do this by using every big word in the dictionary. As a result, his speeches were almost impossible to follow, and his campaign made little progress.

One evening while the candidate was milking a cow and practicing one of his speeches at the same time, the cow, evidently fed up with his harangue, kicked him in the jaw, causing him to bite off the end of his tongue.

"Well," commented the young candidate, "I suppose that put an end to his career as a politician."

"Oh, no," replied Twain. "AFTER THAT HE COULD USE ONLY WORDS OF ONE SYLLABLE, AND IT MADE HIS SPEECHES SO SIMPLE AND APPEALING TO THE FARMERS THAT HE WAS RE-ELECTED EVERY TIME."

Diligence—*Patience*

304   *Some of us may get by for a while not working, not doing our very best.* But eventually there will be a reckoning. It reminds me of an old Quaker farmer back in Indiana who would never use the name of the Lord in vain. But one day his mule, who was hitched to a hay wagon, wouldn't budge an inch.

The farmer patiently tried every known bit of coaxing without any success. Finally he reached the end of his rope. "Mule," he said without raising his voice, "thee knows that because of my religion I cannot beat thee, or curse thee, or abuse thee in any way. BUT, MULE," he continued, "WHAT THEE DOESN'T KNOW IS THAT I CAN SELL THEE TO AN EPISCOPALIAN."

ADVICE: You may also tell this story to indicate impatience—that you have taken just about all you can. By the way, this was a favorite anecdote of Dwight David Eisenhower.

Example—*Family*

305   *Our honoree has been an outstanding example in more ways than one.* And for that he should be held up as a source of inspiration. One of the earliest experiences of witnessing that sort of thing was a state fair I attended when I was a boy. In the cattle exhibition hall in Harrisburg a prime attraction was a champion Aberdeen Angus bull named King Duncan. A poor farmer from Bedford had driven his family in his pickup truck to Harrisburg mainly to see this black Angus bull. But when he arrived at the entrance he was told he would have to pay fifty cents for each member of his family. With seven children that would come to $4.50.

The old farmer raised a fuss. "Me and the missus and the young ones have traveled quite a piece to see this, but I'll be hanged if I'm going to pay $4.50 to get in." The pavilion manager asked, "Are all those children yours?" "That's right," said the farmer. "Let them in free," said the manager to the ticket taker. Then, turning to the farmer, he said, "WE WANT OLD KING DUNCAN TO TAKE A LOOK AT YOU."

Facts—*Arrogance*

306   *Sometimes we aren't as smart as we think we are.* Often we fail to check our facts. We think we know the whole situation before we check it out. I remember hearing about a young attorney whose first job was with a large railroad company. It wasn't long until he had his first case to try. A farmer noticed that his prize cow was missing from the field through which the railroad passed. He promptly went down and filed suit in the justice of the peace's office against the railroad company for the value of his cow.

In due course the case came up for hearing before the local justice of the peace in the back room of the general store, and the smart young attorney came down from the big city to defend the railroad company. The first thing he did was to take the farmer, who had no attorney, over into a corner and begin talking to him about settling the case. Well, the young lawyer talked and talked and finally twisted the old farmer's arm so that the farmer, very reluctantly, agreed to accept half of what he was claiming to settle the case.

After the farmer had signed the release and taken the check, the young lawyer just couldn't resist gloating over the old farmer a little bit, and he said, "You know, I hate to tell you this, but actually I put one over on you this morning. I couldn't have won that case. The engineer was asleep, and the fireman was in the caboose when the train went through your farm that morning. I didn't have one witness to put on the stand."

The old farmer smiled a bit and went on chewing his tobacco. Then he said, "WELL, I'LL TELL YOU, YOUNG FELLER, I WAS A LITTLE WORRIED ABOUT WINNING THAT CASE MYSELF. YOU KNOW, THAT DURNED COW CAME HOME THIS MORNING."

Involvement—*Investment*

307   *It's very true that you get out of life what you put into it.* I recall one time a friend of mine wanted to board his horse for a short while.

The first farmer he approached said he would keep it at $25 a day, plus the manure.

Too high, my friend thought, and went to another farmer, whose price was $15 a day plus manure. Seeking yet a cheaper price, he went to a third, who offered to board the animal at $5 a day.

"How come you didn't ask for the manure, too?" my friend asked. The farmer replied, "FOR FIVE DOLLARS A DAY THERE WON'T BE ANY."

COMMENT: Senator Edmund Muskie told this story in his 1972 presidential campaign.

Misrepresentation—*Liar*

308   *There is only one word to characterize this type of misrepresentation, and it's a word the House of Commons as well as our House of Representatives bars from debate.* As you know, the Society of Friends also frowns on such name-calling. But I do recall the exchange between two Indiana farmers of the Quaker persuasion. Joshua felt that Ephraim had misrepresented the value of a horse he sold and said, "Ephraim, thee knows that I do not believe in calling anyone names; but, Ephraim, if the judge of the county should come to me and say to me, 'Joshua, I want thee to bring to

me the greatest liar in the county,' I would come to thee, Ephraim, and I would lay my hand on thy shoulder, and I would say to thee, 'EPHRAIM, THE JUDGE WANTS TO SEE THEE.' "

Neuroses—*Busy*

309   *You know our rich society ladies have so many more neuroses and mental disturbances than farmers' wives.* The answer might be in the case I heard of a wife of an upstate Pennsylvania farmer. She raised nine children on a large farm, fed them and the farmhands, did all her housework, and helped with outdoor chores. She's never been ill a day in her life. A doctor asked her to reveal her secret.

"I constantly see young women," the doctor said, "who have one or two children. They have maids and their homes are full of gadgets to lighten work, but they suffer from nervous exhaustion or psychosomatic aches and pains. How is it that you managed to go through all these years and never had a nervous breakdown?"

"You know, Doctor," said the hard-working woman wistfully, "I've always wanted to have a nervous breakdown and have the chance for a good rest. BUT EVERY TIME I WAS ABOUT TO GET AROUND TO IT, IT WAS TIME TO FIX A MEAL OR CLEAN UP."

News—*Unpleasantness*

310   *First, I suppose I should give you the bad news.* There is no way to break it to you gently the way an eastern Kentucky woman advised a motorist from up north. The driver, passing the cabin of a mountaineer, had the bad fortune to run over and kill a hound dog that happened to be the owner's favorite hunting dog. He went into the house and told the man's wife what had happened and how sorry he was. The owner of the dog was out in the fields, and the motorist decided he had better go out and tell him of the accident, too.

"BETTER BREAK IT TO HIM EASY LIKE," advised the wife. "FIRST TELL HIM IT WAS ONE OF THE KIDS."

Opportunity—*Repeat*

311   *We must act now. We can't expect to get a second chance.* A Yankee farmer in New Hampshire learned this when he found that his daughter had become involved with a Navy ensign sta-

tioned at Portsmouth. The father met the naval officer in the classic encounter.

"Will ye marry Hannah?"

"No, I can't do that."

"What can ye do?"

"My uncle died. I have a lot of money. I can take care of the hospital expenses."

"Is that all?"

"I can provide $2,000 yearly allowance for the child."

"Is that all?"

"If there is a boy, I'll provide $5,000 for education."

"What if she be a girl?"

"I'll provide $5,000 on her marriage to set up housekeeping."

"I can see, boy, ye are trying to do the right thing. I just have one question. IF THERE IS A MISCARRIAGE, WOULD YE GIVE HER A SECOND CHANCE?"

COMMENT: I have also heard this story told about an angry Scots-
   man whose young lass got involved with an American soldier.

Practicality—*Experience*

312   *What we need in government is not necessarily better educated but more experienced officials.* When young Jay Wilkinson, an alumnus of a Harvard graduate school, took on veteran Oklahoma Congressman Tom Steed, it promised to be quite a battle. Young, handsome and idealistic, Wilkinson had a good image for an agency to project on television. One forty-second slot showed Wilkinson walking through an Oklahoma pasture soulfully looking upward at the sky.

The spot made an opening for the veteran Steed: "I MAY NOT HAVE HAD A FANCY EDUCATION LIKE YOUNG WILKINSON. I DIDN'T GO TO HARVARD. BUT I KNOW ENOUGH TO LOOK AT THE GROUND WHEN I'M WALKING AROUND COWS."

COMMENT: This story can also be used to register disbelief in a
   great build-up. You could say, "I think all of us know when to
   watch out for a big load . . ."

Responsiveness—*Attention*

313   *I think once the people are aware of the problem they are going to respond.* It is like the mule one farmer sold to his neighbor. The beast was sold as a trained mule who would respond

directly to commands. But later when the buyer got it home and tried to make it pull the plow the mule would not even budge—not even to shrill and strident commands. In disgust he called back the farmer he bought it from. The old farmer got a 2′ × 4′ and whacked the mule on the nose and then gave it the command to pull the plow, which it did. "I thought you said it was a trained mule."

The old farmer answered, "IT IS, BUT FIRST YOU NEED TO GET ITS ATTENTION."

Unions—*Monopoly*

314   *Every day it seems like more and more employee groups are becoming unionized.* Now it's teachers and firemen, while the rest of the working population—the white-collar workers and the farmers—feel the squeeze. The other day I heard about a case in upstate Pennsylvania where a farmer was rushed to the hospital. It seems it was an emergency appendectomy. He was brought in and placed in a room with expectant mothers. One woman was in pain, and the nurse came in and gave her a shot that relieved her distress.

The farmer, also in pain, asked for a shot. The nurse explained that the woman was in labor. The farmer replied, "THAT'S THE PROBLEM WITH THIS COUNTRY—EVERYTHING FOR LABOR BUT NOTHING FOR THE FARMER."

Warning—*Message*

315   *I think we can look at the recent development as a fair warning.* In that sense we are not unlike the Texas bride. A taciturn but terrible-tempered rancher got married and, after the wedding, started out with his bride to his ranch, riding a buckboard with a mare in front. After a while the mare stumbled.

"That's once," the rancher said.

After they had ridden along a while the mare stumbled again. "That's twice," the rancher said.

When the mare stumbled for the third time, the rancher cried, "That's three times."

He stopped the buggy, got out his gun and shot the mare dead.

Angry at this shooting, his wife said, "Why did you shoot that good horse?"

The Texan waited until his wife had finished and said, "THAT'S ONCE!"

Home Town

There isn't much to be seen in a little town but what you hear makes up for it.

　　　　　　　　　　　　　　　　—Frank Hubbard

Administrator—*Supervisor*

316　*The only way to be a successful executive is to attend to details.* You can't expect things to take care of themselves without supervision. It's like a friend of mine who went through his closet and found an old sport jacket he hadn't worn for a long time. In one of the pockets he had a shoe-repair ticket—fourteen years old.

The man went to the shoe-repair place just on the chance that they might still have the shoes he forgot to pick up fourteen years ago.

The white-haired little shoemaker peered at the ticket and said, "Yep, that's our ticket. And yep, there are the shoes on the shelf."

"Great," said my friend. "How much do I owe you? I'll take them with me."

"Oh," said the shoemaker, "THEY WON'T BE READY TILL NEXT TUESDAY."

Bankruptcy—*Decline*

317　*Business has been pretty bad lately.* But it could be worse. It could be as bad as for a clothing-store merchant I ran into the other day.

When I asked how he was he answered, "Terrible, terrible. Business is just terrible. Monday we had only one customer. Tuesday we had none at all. And then Wednesday was even worse than Tuesday."

I said, "How could Wednesday be worse than Tuesday if you had no customers at all on that day?"

"OH, IT WAS WORSE. THE MAN WHO BOUGHT A SUIT ON MONDAY CAME IN AND WANTED A REFUND."

Conformity—*Tastes*

318   *Everyone wants to do his own thing.* We cannot prescribe a rule of conduct for others. I remember driving back to my old home town. There on the outskirts of the town was a huge revival tent. On the highway just where the road turned in was a big sign advertising a gospel assembly. It said: IF YOU'RE WEARY OF SIN, COME ON IN. Underneath someone had inked in IF NOT . . . CALL SYCAMORE 9–6520.

Consumerism—*Credibility*

319   *You can't believe everything you hear in sales promotion.* A very proper friend of my mother who is a schoolteacher bought a secondhand car. A day later she drove it back to the dealer's lot. "What's wrong?" asked the dealer anxiously.

"Nothing at all," said the teacher sweetly. "I just want to return these things for the dear little old lady you told me owned the car before you sold it to me. SHE LEFT THIS CASE OF CIGARS IN THE GLOVE COMPARTMENT AND THIS HALF-EMPTY BOTTLE OF RYE UNDER THE SEAT."

Consumerism—*Expedite*

320   *The fantastic claims we hear remind me of a friend of mine who went to a Fifth Avenue clothing store and was immediately asked his name, address, family history, favorite pastimes, political affiliation, and his wife's maiden name.*

"Why all these questions?" he demanded. "I only want to buy a suit." "Ah, my friend," said the salesman smoothly. "Before we sell you a suit here, we make sure that it fits your personality and position in life. We send to Australia for the proper blend of wool for you. From France we import just the right lining, from England the buttons you should have. Then five tailors in our shop make it fit you to perfection, regardless of the fittings that may prove necessary."

"Oh, that's too bad," said my friend. "I need this suit to be married in tomorrow morning."

"STOP WORRYING," said the salesman. "YOU'LL HAVE IT."

Contribution—*Cheapness*

321   *Well, I know you will find people are going to respond better to our cause than did the sons of a hard-working couple back in my home town.* This couple had struggled for thirty years, depriving themselves for their three sons, whom they put through college. Never once did they take a vacation. Now they wanted to take a trip to Florida and they asked their sons for some money.

The first son was a lawyer. "No, I can't do it. I'm just fitting out a new law office and sending my son to an expensive camp."

The second son, a doctor, said, "No, I can't. I've just bought a new house, and my wife is putting in a new kitchen."

The third son was an engineer. "It would just be impossible for me to do it. I have just bought a big boat for the family and am remodeling our summer home on the lake."

"You realize," said the old man, "that your mother and I were so busy working trying to save money that we never took the time out to get a marriage license?"

"But you know what that makes us?" said the sons.

"YES," replied the father, "AND CHEAP ONES TOO."

(But I know there is nothing cheap . . .)

COMMENT: Remember, let the audience think "bastards" to themselves.

Contribution—*Cheapness*

322   *Some of you might have heard the words on the tombstone of the Earl of Devon,* "What we gave we have/What we spent we had/What we left we lost."

This might have been good advice to a rich old crotchety man back in my home town. I was only a boy, but I remember how various town leaders went up the hill to his house to ask him to pledge a gift for the creation of a hospital so badly needed in the community. Finally in one last effort the Presbyterian minister made the journey to his mansion. Again the old man was obdurate. He wasn't going to give a penny. The minister, rebuffed, started to leave. As he got to the door he said, "Tell me, sir, why do you take so much care of your money? It can't be of much use to you in this world, and you can't take it with you to the next. EVEN IF YOU COULD, IT WOULD ONLY MELT."

Cost—*Consumerism*

323   *Some of the old attitudes of business are best exemplified by the practice I heard about in a neighborhood optical-goods store.* A new assistant was being instructed by the proprietor: "Now, son, we want to get a fair and honest price out of every customer. After you have fitted the glasses and the customer asks 'What's the charge?' you say, 'The charge is ten dollars.' Then you pause. If the customer doesn't flinch, you say, 'That's for the frames; the lenses will be another ten dollars.' Then you pause, and again you wait. And if the customer doesn't flinch, you say 'EACH.' "

(Of course, that is not very funny to the . . .)

Crime—*Degeneracy*

324   *I suppose in these degenerate times the reports we hear of people claiming to have seen the spirit of Diogenes stalking the streets is not so surprising.* The learned Greek was first spotted in Paris. Some gendarmes approached the lamp-bearing philosopher.

"Diogenes, what are you doing in Paris?" Said the toga-garbed Greek, "Messieurs, I am searching for truth."

And then not too much later I heard reports from London. Some bobbies found him again with his lamp.

"Diogenes, what are you doing in London?" The old man said, "Gentlemen, I am searching for truth."

Then inevitably he was reported to have been in New York. Two of the city's finest approached him and asked, "Diogenes, what are you doing in New York?"

"Patrolmen," he replied, "I AM SEARCHING FOR MY LAMP."

(And reading the recent crime statistics, it is no wonder . . .)

Criticism—*Press*

325   *When I was asked whether I minded the recent editorial attacking my role in the recent development, I recalled what my Uncle Zeke once said.* Zeke had gone down to visit the doctor about his poor hearing. The doctor examined him and then asked how much mountain dew he was drinking a day. Uncle Zeke said about a quart.

"Well," said the doctor, "at that rate you are going to become completely deaf."

"What do you recommend?" asked Zeke.

"Well, if you want to keep your hearing, you'd better stop drinking."

Uncle Zeke replied, "IF IT'S ALL THE SAME TO YOU, I LIKE WHAT I HAVE BEEN DRINKING BETTER THAN WHAT I'VE BEEN HEARING. SO I THINK I'LL JUST BECOME DEAF."

COMMENT: Franklin Delano Roosevelt told this story in response to queries about whether newspaper criticism was bothering him.

Dream—*Negativism*

326   *Tonight we celebrate the fruition of a dream.* Now there were those of little faith who thought this day would never come to pass. It brings to mind a friend of Italian ancestry who had one dream. That was to go to Italy and see the Pope. He saved his money and finally had enough to make the trip. Just before he was about to leave my friend went to the barbershop to get his hair cut, and the barber asked, "How are you going to get to Italy?" "I'm taking Alitalia airlines." The barber said, "Forget it. They've got a terrible reputation; you'll be sorry. Where are you gonna stay?" He said, "I'm gonna stay at the Hilton in Rome." The barber said, "Forget it. They've got terrible service. What are you going to do when you're there in Rome?" My friend answered, "I'm gonna see the Pope." "You'll never see the Pope," the barber said. "You're a nobody, you're a Mister Zero. The Pope only sees important people. Forget it!"

Well, about six weeks later the same man went back to the barbershop. The barber said, "Eh, you never got to Italy." My friend replied, "Yes, I did. I flew Alitalia and they were just wonderful to me. When I got to Rome I stayed at the Hilton and they treated me like a king." The barber asked, "What did you do when you got there?" "I went to see the Pope." "Well, what happened?" asked the barber anxiously. "Well, I bent down and kissed the Pope's ring." "Wow, you kissed the Pope's ring! What did he say?" "Well, the Pope looked down at me and said, 'SON, WHERE DID YOU GET THAT TERRIBLE HAIRCUT?'"

(And surely wouldn't we be in a terrible situation if we had listened . . .)

ADVICE: This story depends on the steady build-up of the barber's negative character. Unless you know some Italian don't try to imitate the Italian accent.

Finances—*Treasurer*

327   *When I think of our treasurer and the financial wizardry he has performed over the years, I think of a sideshow strongman back in my childhood.* The strongman was exhibiting his prowess and as a final trick he squeezed the juice from a lemon between his hands and then offered ten dollars to anyone in the audience who could squeeze another drop out of it. After a pause a slight bespectacled man came forward and tried it. After straining, he managed to get one drop from the lemon, to the delight of the audience.

As the strongman turned over the ten dollars, he asked the man, "What is the secret of your strength? How did you do it?"

"OH," the man replied, "I WAS TREASURER OF THE METHODIST CHURCH FOR THIRTY YEARS."

(And our friend here . . .)

ADVICE: I have also heard this story used about an IRS agent, a banker, and a chairman of a United Fund campaign.

Optimist—*Worse*

328   *Sometimes speakers seem to think they have to talk about the dreadful state of affairs.* I, for one, like to look on the bright side. Perhaps you will accuse me of being like a guy I heard about in my home town. Bill would constantly irritate his friends with his eternal optimism. No matter how bad the situation, he would always say, "It could have been worse." So to cure him of his annoying habit, his friends decided to invent a situation so completely black, so dreadful, that even Bill could find no hope in it. Approaching him at the club bar one day, one of them said, "Bill, did you hear what happened to Tom? He came home last night, found his wife in bed with another man, shot them both, then turned the gun on himself."

"Terrible," said Bill, "but it could have been worse."

"How in hell," asked his dumfounded friend, "could it possibly have been worse?"

"WELL," said Bill, "IF IT HAD HAPPENED THE NIGHT BEFORE, I'D BE DEAD NOW."

(Well, seriously, I like to believe that things could be much worse. . . .)

Pledge—*Contribution*

329   *I hope you think our work merits your support—though perhaps not in the way of a woman I heard about in the apartment house nearby.* A wealthy old woman, she caught a burglar ransacking her things. "Listen, lady, keep quiet if you don't want to be hurt. Just tell me where your jewels are."

She said, "I don't keep them there. They're in the bank in the safe-deposit vault."

"Where's all your silver, then?"

"I'm sorry, but it's all out being cleaned and polished."

"Give me your money, then."

"I tell you," she said, "I don't keep any cash on hand."

"Listen, lady, I'm warning you—give me your money or I'll rip it off you." And he started feeling her up and down.

"I keep telling you," she said, "I don't have any money. BUT IF YOU DO THAT AGAIN, I'LL WRITE YOU A CHECK."

Progress—*Status Quo*

330   *In the last few months it seems that every time we get over one crisis, another pops up.* It reminds me of the town my grandfather used to live in. A government census-taker was questioning him about the town. "How many people live in this town?" he wanted to know.

"About four thousand, two hundred and ten people, and it's been that way for twenty-five years" was the reply.

"You mean to tell me," said the census-taker, "that there were four thousand, two hundred and ten people here twenty-five years ago and the same amount today? Haven't any people moved in— any babies been born here?"

"There sure have been babies born," said my grandfather. "TROUBLE IS, EVERY TIME A BABY IS BORN, SOMEBODY LEAVES TOWN."

Salesman—*Aggressiveness*

331   *Our speaker tonight is one of the great salesmen.* His energy, enthusiasm and drive overwhelms listeners. He reminds me

of a young man who came into one of our downtown men's clothing stores and told the manager he wanted a job as a salesman. "I don't need any salesman," said the manager. "Oh, but I'm not just any salesman," said the young man. "I'm the world's greatest salesman. You've got to hire me."

Again the manager refused, but the man was so insistent and persuasive that he said, "Okay, I'll tell you what. See that suit over there on the rack? It's sort of green and mauve plaid with padded shoulders, has pointed lapels and a belt in the back. I don't know how I ever got stuck with it. Now I'm going to lunch. I'll leave you here. If you sell that suit while I'm gone, you're hired."

In an hour the manager returned. The store was in shambles— showcases turned over, carpeting ripped, chandeliers hanging from frayed wires, merchandise strewn all over. But the suit was gone.

"I see you've sold the suit."

"Yep."

"But you seem to have had quite a bit of trouble with the customer."

"Nope. No trouble at all with the customer. BUT, OH, THAT SEEING-EYE DOG!"

(Seriously, while our speaker wouldn't do that, he might . . .)

Hotel Lobby

*The great advantage of a hotel is that it's a
refuge from home life.*
—George Barnard Shaw

Cost—*Economy*

332   *I know the price seems less, but I think we should be aware of some hidden costs in this proposal.* It reminds me of the young man-about-town who enjoyed luxury but didn't always have the means to buy it. He walked out of a Miami Beach hotel when he found out the charges for room, meals and golf privileges were fifty dollars a day. He registered across the street at an equally elegant hotel where the rates were only fifteen dollars. The follow-

ing morning he went down to the hotel's golf course and asked
Scotty, the pro, to sell him a couple of golf balls. "Sure," said
Scotty. "That'll be fifteen dollars apiece."

"What?" screamed the bachelor. "In the hotel across the street
they charge only a dollar a ball!"

"Naturally," replied the pro. "OVER THERE THEY GET YOU BY
THE ROOMS. HERE WE GET YOU BY . . ."

Cure—*Problem*

333   *I question the solution proposed. Not only is it more trouble than it's worth, but it won't solve the problem.* It recalls the
time W. C. Fields came into the dining room of the Manhattan
hotel he was staying at. Fields was suffering from one of his many
hangovers. "May I fix you a Bromo-Seltzer?" suggested the waiter.

"Oh, no!" replied Fields, "I COULDN'T STAND THE NOISE."

Emergency—*Impossibility*

334   *I cannot believe that it is impossible—that there is no way
it can be done.* Somewhere there must be provisions for emergen-
cies like this. It is like the situation a friend of mine encountered
at a hotel desk. He had made a hotel reservation for his stay in
Chicago. But unfortunately his plane to O'Hare was held up in a
landing pattern. So when he got to the hotel at midnight he found
his room had been assigned to someone else. At length he pleaded
with the hotel clerk, saying, "At this late hour it is impossible to
find room in another hotel."

The manager shook his head. "Look," said my friend, "isn't
there a reserve conference suite that has a day bed in it that can
be pulled out?" "No," said the manager. "We had one but that has
been taken."

"Look," said my friend, "you must have at least one room held
back for emergency occasions." The manager shook his head
firmly. "You mean," said my friend, "if Queen Elizabeth came
here right now and asked for a room, you couldn't accommodate
her?"

"Well, yes, I think we could," the manager replied.

"Well good," said my friend. "The queen isn't coming. LET ME
HAVE HER ROOM."

Excellence—*Effort*

335   *We owe a vote of thanks to the many who have done much of the planning to make this conference a success.* It has all been so smoothly done that it seems effortless, yet we know the amount of preparation that has gone into it. Such preparation reminds me of the reply of Cesar Ritz, then the manager of London's Savoy Hotel, to one of the city's most celebrated courtesans. As Ritz passed by her table, she stopped the Swiss hotel genius to pay him a compliment.

"You know, Monsieur Ritz, both of us have achieved the ultimate in our respective professions."

"Yes," replied Ritz, "BUT I HAVE ATTAINED IT WITH MUCH MORE TROUBLE AND MUCH LESS PLEASURE."

Excellence—*Standards*

336   *When I am asked what standards I expect, I can only cite what the British embassy official in Washington said to the manager of the Plaza Hotel in New York who was awaiting a visit from Winston Churchill.*

The hotel manager asked about Churchill's taste in food and drink.

"Mr. Churchill's tastes are very simple," the embassy aide replied quickly. "HE IS EASILY PLEASED WITH THE BEST OF EVERYTHING."

Harassment—*Marriage*

337   *There has been much talk from Washington recently about New Federalism, revenue-sharing, equal partnerships between the federal government and the states.* Well, this is all very fine, but I wish they would start acting like an equal partnership. It is like a couple of people I heard about. A man and a single woman were attending a large convention. They found themselves, through an accidental oversight of the hotel, assigned to the same room. Since both were mature individuals and knew how difficult it would be to get the matter straightened out in such crowded conditions, it seemed the wiser course to accept the situation.

Each chose a bed and a dresser and proceeded to ignore the

other with a kind of tactful politeness.

But on the second night it turned out that the woman didn't know how cold it was going to get. She was freezing. Hesitantly, she called out, "Would you be so good as to get me one of the blankets from the chest?"

The man, who had been nearly asleep, thought that over and said, "Listen, if you're going to be this friendly and as long as we are in the same room, how about acting as though we were man and wife?"

The girl thought that over, giggled and said, "Well, I think— perhaps I might be willing."

The man said, "GOOD! IN THAT CASE, AS MY WIFE, GET YOUR OWN DARNED BLANKET AND LEAVE ME ALONE."

(And similarly I would say if we are going to be in equal partnership with the government, they might start becoming as close . . .)

Nostalgia—*Homesick*

338   *I know we had our own type of problems and crises, but somehow I'm homesick for those days.* I understand now the feelings of a man a hotel waitress told me about the other week. She said the man came down to the hotel coffee shop looking so sad. He said to the waitress, "Bring me two eggs fried hard, a slice of burned toast and a cup of weak coffee."

The waitress said, "What did you say?" He repeated his order and she got it. As she set it down in front of him she said, "Anything else?"

"Yes," he said. "Now sit down and nag me about my being overweight and my clothes. JUST NAG ME—I'M HOMESICK."

Specifications—*Perfection*

339   *It is hard to get everything exactly as you ordered—to have everything letter-perfect.* I remember a friend of mine and his wife were in Washington for a convention. They walked in for breakfast. The waiter came over. My friend said, "I want my fried eggs cold, my toast soggy, my orange juice warm, and my coffee bitter."

"But, sir," the waiter said, "that's impossible."

"Why not? That's what I want."

The startled waiter said, "Why, no amount of money could make us bring that kind of breakfast to you."

"I don't see why. THAT'S JUST WHAT WE BOTH GOT YESTERDAY."

Viewpoint—*Fairness*

340　*As all of you know, I represent the opposing view.* But there is another side to this story that from your vantage point you might not see. It is like the attractive blond wife of a friend of mine. He was attending a convention in Las Vegas. Since she had nothing to do, she went up to the terrace to get some sun.

Armed with a towel, she disrobed, lay down and took her sunbath. Some moments later the manager rushed up.

"You must get down off there right away."

"Why, that's ridiculous. Only planes could see me here, and anyway I have a towel to cover me."

"YES, BUT YOU'RE LYING ACROSS THE DINING-ROOM SKYLIGHT."

(And similarly, I hope to show you another side . . .)

Locker Room

Games are for people who can neither read nor think.
　　　　　　　　　—George Bernard Shaw

341　As the chairman said, there is something special about baseball. It's more than a game; it's a way of life. And the way I figure, if at first you don't succeed, try playing . . . second.

342　Really, though, there is something unique in baseball, in its ideals. It's the only place in life where a sacrifice is really appreciated.

343　Of course you can carry sacrifice too far. In the Emancipation Proclamation Lincoln signed the document that abolished conditional servitude. As I read it, it covered everybody but us professional ball players.

344   You know in certain uncivilized countries, native tribes beat the ground with clubs and utter blood-curdling screams. Anthropologists call this "primitive self-expression." In America we call it golf.

345   Well, people make fun of us golf enthusiasts. But the way I figure it, there must be time for both work and play. And if you watch a game, it's fun. If you play it, it's recreation. If you work at it, it's golf.

346   Really, though, if you want to be good at golf you have to be serious about it. I know some men who play golf religiously—every Sunday.

347   You know why spectators find pro football so fascinating. It's the speed, the action pace. Even if you can follow the movement of the ball, you can hardly keep up with the shifts in rules.

348   Seriously, however, they revised the rules. Spectators shouldn't worry. The one thing they won't take away in the touchdown score is your extra pint.

349   And you fans will also still have the whole four quarters to finish that fifth.

Advice—*Interference*

350   *We don't need their advice on how to run our affairs.* One of these days I would like to do what Frankie Frisch once did when he was manager of the Pittsburgh Pirates. All through a particular game one obnoxious heckler keep screaming to him how he should run the game. In the ninth inning he walked over to the stands and politely asked the heckler his name and business address.

Flattered, the man told Frankie and then asked him why he wanted to know.

"Because," replied Frisch, "I'M GOING TO BE AT YOUR OFFICE BRIGHT AND EARLY TOMORROW MORNING TO TELL YOU HOW TO RUN YOUR BUSINESS."

Advice—*Late*

351   *What I am warning you about is all very true, but advice is of no purpose unless it is received in time.* I recall the case of

a fine businessman who gave his business to his employees and decided to retire. In recognition of this his employees chipped in and got him a membership in a lovely club close to his home and a beautiful set of matched golf clubs. He'd never played the game before; it was all a complete mystery to him. So the first day out he called the caddy and asked, "What am I supposed to do?" The caddy said, "Well, you see that flag down there? You hit the ball toward that flag." Either the man had untold power or the winds were in his favor, but, believe it or not, the ball landed three inches from the hole. He walked all the way to the green and said to the caddy, "What am I supposed to do now?" The caddy said, "You're supposed to hit that ball into that cup." He said, "NOW HE TELLS ME."

(Well, I hope this advice is in time . . .)

Appreciation—*Gesture*

352   *It is always nice when people take the time to show their appreciation.* I remember hearing about a golfing pair at the country club the other day. They were on the fourteenth green ready to tee off. Now, in our club this green happens to run parallel to a highway. Just as the first golfer was in the middle of his back swing a funeral entourage passed by. The golfer stopped his swing, removed his hat, and placed it over his heart. His golfing partner, quite impressed, complimented him. "That's a nice thing to do— to show your respect that way."

And his partner replied, "WHY NOT? SHE WAS A GREAT WIFE FOR TWENTY-EIGHT YEARS."

(And while this presentation is a very small gesture . . .)

COMMENT: You might try to act out the gestures, particularly if you play golf yourself. Don't overdo it. Be deliberate and deadpan.

Commitment—*Thorough*

353   *Once you start something, you can't do it halfway.* You have to throw all of yourself into it. With all your heart, mind and body. That's what a golf pro was trying to tell Supreme Court Justice McKenna, who took up golf late in his life.

One day while practicing on a golf course near Washington he missed teeing off. He tried three or four times, but each time his club hit several inches behind the ball. His instructor watched silently. Finally the justice, becoming disgusted, glared at the still stationary ball and muttered, "Tut-tut, tut-tut!"

Gravely the instructor walked toward him. "Sir," he said, "YOU'LL NEVER LEARN TO PLAY GOLF WITH THEM WORDS."

Critics—*Insensitivity*

354   *These critics are about as dense as the umpire the Dodgers' Fresco Thompson once described.* One day in a mix-up involving the infield-fly rule, Thompson challenged the umpire's decision. The angry umpire waved a rule book in Fresco's face, shouting, "I got my rule book right here."

"IF IT'S YOURS," Fresco said, "I'LL BET IT'S WRITTEN IN BRAILLE."

(And similarly, any critic who writes such statements must be just as blind . . .)

Diplomacy—*Tact*

355   *The best definition of a diplomat came from the author John Steinbeck,* who wrote about two men meeting in a bar when the subject of Green Bay, Wisconsin, came up.

The first man said, "It's a real nice place."

The second responded, "What's nice about it? Only things ever come out of Green Bay are the Packers and ugly whores."

"Now, wait just one minute, you sonofabitch," said the first man. "My wife is from Green Bay."

"Oh," the other replied. "She is? WHAT POSITION DOES SHE PLAY?"

(Such finesse and ingenuity distinguishes our speaker . . .)

Enthusiasm—*Apathy*

356   *A lot of us seem to be standing around oblivious to what is happening.* It reminds me of the time Frankie Frisch was manager of the Pirates. He was mad at the umpire's decision. As he came striding toward home plate, the umpire braced himself against the impending storm. Instead of tearing into the arbiter in his usual heated way Frisch merely smiled a sweet smile. "Have you a cigar in your pocket?" he asked in the friendliest way.

"A cigar? Why?" asked the surprised umpire.

"IT SEEMS LOGICAL," answered Frisch, "BECAUSE ON THAT

LAST PLAY YOU LOOKED LIKE A CIGAR-STORE INDIAN."

(We have too many cigar-store Indians . . .)

Habit—*Reflex*

357 *Like so much of life, it becomes a habit—a matter of reflex.*
It's like an insomniac boxer who went to the doctor for some
medical help. The ex-pugilist had tried mild sedation, but it didn't
seem to work. The doctor, hesitating to prescribe a more addictive
kind, said, "Look, before I prescribe this heavier injection, I want
you to try the old-fashioned remedy. You may laugh, but it actually
works. Try getting yourself completely relaxed and then start
counting to a hundred."

A few days later the old fighter came back and said, "Doctor, I
can't do it. EVERY TIME I START COUNTING, I JUMP UP AT THE
COUNT OF NINE."

Intentions—*Mistake*

358 *As I apologize for the error, I want to say that at least my
heart was in the right place—that I meant well.* It reminds me of
the occasion at the turn of the century when that respected name
in Massachusetts politics, Senator George Hoar (H-o-a-r), decided
to invite John L. Sullivan to dinner. Sullivan was, of course, a hero
to most of Hoar's Irish constituents; and Hoar viewed the invitation as a good political gesture. Sullivan and his wife came to
Hoar's Beacon Street house, and the dinner between the Boston
Strongboy and the Boston Brahmin was a greater success than
could have been anticipated.

As they were leaving, at the doorstep the senator was telling the
Sullivans how much he enjoyed their company. Sullivan replied,
"ME AND THE MISSUS HAD A FINE TIME TOO. AND WE CERTAINLY
WISH THE FINEST TO BOTH YOU AND MRS. W."

Misstatement—*Exaggeration*

359 *I guess I have the unfortunate task in this case of having
to eat my own words.* I know how Mark Twain once felt. He had
spent a very pleasant three weeks in the Maine woods one year
and was making himself comfortable in the smoking car on the
way back to New York. A sour-faced New Englander sat down
next to him, and the two struck up a conversation.

"Been in the woods, have ye?" asked the stranger.

"I have indeed," replied Twain. "And let me tell you something. It may be closed season for fishing up here in Maine, but I have a couple hundred pounds of the finest rock bass you ever saw iced down in the baggage car. By the way, who are you, sir?"

"I'm the state game warden. Who are you?" was the reply.

Said Twain, "I'M THE BIGGEST DAMNED LIAR IN THESE WHOLE UNITED STATES!"

(Well, I won't say I'm a liar, but I will say with Ron Ziegler, "I misspoke.")

Mistake—*Briefing*

360   *I always think that in situations like this a little briefing is necessary if we are going to avoid the mistakes a lover-of-the-ponies once made.* This compulsive race-track bettor promised to attend church each Sunday with his wife if she would agree not to nag him about the nags the rest of the week. The wife agreed, hoping that this contact with religion might cure her husband of his habit. On the very next Sunday the couple were seated side by side in the center of the church. The husband joined in singing the final hymn with such enthusiasm that several parishioners in the nearby pews were visibly impressed. As the couple emerged from the church, the husband acknowledged the smiles with which they were greeted, remarking in a whispered aside to his wife, "I'll bet you didn't expect me to make such an impression! It wouldn't surprise me if they wanted my bar-room baritone in the church choir."

"You did very well, dear," his wife remarked, "EXCEPT FOR ONE SMALL THING. IT'S HALLELUJAH, NOT HIALEAH!"

Mistake—*Enthusiasm*

361   *It was a mistake. But I hope it will be forgiven as a mistake made out of enthusiasm.* I recall a story about Dublin Hospital's rugby football final against the College of St. Vincent. A back for St. Vincent scored the winning touchdown even though he was far offside, as he well knew. For the rest of his life the way he won that touchdown for St. Vincent worried him, but not enough to prevent him from becoming one of the most distinguished surgeons of Dublin.

In the fullness of time he passed on and made his way to the golden gates, where a kind old gentleman smiled benevolently at him.

"I think I should confess," said the surgeon, "something that has been bothering me for over fifty years."

"Certainly," replied the gentleman, "you can't mean that incident in the rugby final. We all know and laugh about it. It was one of those things that happen in the enthusiasm of a match."

"By the way," the gatekeeper whispered, "I'm not the usual keeper. I'm standing in for St. Peter today. MY NAME IS ST. VINCENT."

(And I hope you too will overlook . . .)

Patience—*Change*

362   *I think we've had just about enough.* We need relief the way Casey Stengel once did with his hopeless Mets. His pitcher was getting shelled. Casey walked to the mound, but his pitcher assured him he wasn't tired. Casey let him stay on and walked back to the dugout. The next thing the pitcher was in trouble again. So Casey walked out to have a chat. Again he decided to leave him in. Hands jammed into his back pockets, he trudged back to the dugout.

A few innings later the pitcher was knocked for a single, then a triple. This time as Casey plodded out to the mound he signaled to the bullpen for a replacement.

"But, Casey," said the pitcher, "I tell you I'm not tired."

"MAYBE YOU'RE NOT," said Casey, wiping his brow, "BUT I AM."

Perspective—*Reform*

363   *The Administration just doesn't get the message.* They have their own way of reckoning that they are doing all right. They remind me of a young man in the 1960 Mets who thought he was hot stuff as he pitched his first game, but he walked the first seven batters, so Casey Stengel took him out of the game.

The rookie stormed into the dugout mumbling, "How do you like that dumb Stengel? HE TAKES ME OUT OF A GAME JUST WHEN I HAD A NO-HITTER GOING."

Politics—*Appointment*

364   *I thank you for the very kind introduction and the nice words you said about my present position.* It is nice to hear how

qualified I am, but the real truth is best explained by a remark of Leo Durocher, who was managing the New York Giants when they were playing an exhibition game at West Point. One cadet bench jock yelled out at Leo, "How did a runt like you ever make it to the big leagues?"

And Leo replied, "I GOT APPOINTED BY MY CONGRESSMAN."

(And similarly, it was my backing by . . .)

Priority—*Basics*

365   *It is all very well to talk out loud on all the things we could do to make our facilities better.* But first we have to look at the basics. It is like the time the veteran Charlie Grimm was managing the Chicago Cubs one year when they couldn't hit the size of their hats and thus had sunk deep into the National League cellar. One evening a Chicago Cub scout phoned excitedly from some tank town in Nebraska and said, "Boss, I've just stumbled onto a great pitching find. This afternoon the kid pitched a perfect game. Twenty-seven strike-outs in a row! Nobody even touched the ball till a guy hit a foul in the last inning. Listen, Boss, the kid's with me right now. Shall I sign him up?

"NO," Grimm said, "SIGN UP THE GUY WHO GOT THE FOUL. WE NEED HITTERS."

Priority—*Basics*

366   *Everything has its priorities—the basics that have to be taken care of first.* I remember an interview with a skiing sensation who was uncovered in the tryouts for the winter Olympics some years ago. At the tryouts this local-grown Coloradan skied for the qualifying tests. Amazingly enough this young man, who had never skied in college because he didn't go to college, made the Olympic team. The Colorado press made much over this simple-living youth who lived with his wife in a cabin on top of one of the mountains. There was a celebration in the nearby town at the foot of the valley. One of the local reporters said, "Tell me, what was the first thing you did to greet your wife when you came home in triumph as a member of the U. S. Olympic team." The boy blushed and stammered, "Why don't you ask me what the second thing I did was?" "Very well, what was the second thing you did?" said the reporter. The lad replied, "I TOOK OFF MY SKIS."

(Seriously, the first thing we have to do . . .)

Problem—*Diagnosis*

367   *I don't think we are really diagnosing the problem in the right way.* It reminds me of the time Babe Ruth had a big tummy ache. Once, minutes before a game was to start, Babe sneaked in a couple of liverwurst-and-onion sandwiches, ate a dozen hot dogs, gulped down six bottles of cherry soda pop, and then he topped off that hurried snack with an apple. Before the ninth inning he caved in with a stomachache heard round the world. As they carted him off to a hospital the very sick and unhappy Babe moaned, ˙

"I KNEW I SHOULDNA ATE THAT APPLE."

(And we shouldn't blame . . .)

Problem—*Technique*

368   *There are some people who always look for the difficult side of the problem.* To them the easy solution never appears. They always have to think of the most complicated way. I recall a young man who was applying for admission to one of the most exclusive country clubs in Newport. The rather reserved, unimpressive-looking young man was notified that he must play a round of golf with the club officers as a prerequisite to his acceptance.

On the appointed afternoon he met them on the first tee equipped with a hockey stick, a croquet mallet and a billiard cue. The officers looked him over incredulously but nevertheless proceeded to tee off. To their dismay the young man coolly drove off 275 yards with the hockey stick, gracefully arched his second shot to the green with the croquet mallet and sank a twenty-foot putt with the billiard cue.

After soundly drubbing the baffled officers with a subpar 68, the applicant retired with them to the club bar. There he ordered a Scotch and soda, and when it arrived he mixed the drink himself by tossing the contents of the shot glass over his shoulder into the waiting soda behind him on the bar. This further display of the young man's incredible physical coordination was too much for the officers of the club. "You're miraculous!" they exclaimed. "What's the story behind these fantastic talents of yours?" "All my life," the man explained, "physical activity of any sort has been child's play for me. To overcome the boredom that has resulted from my monotonous mastery of everything, I try to do almost everything in the most difficult way possible. Thus I play tennis with a Ping-Pong paddle, Ping-Pong with a tennis racket, and so on."

"Wait a minute," interrupted one of the club officers. "If it's true, as you say, that you do everything physical in the most difficult manner possible, I have one question."

"I KNOW," said the young man, smiling. "EVERYONE ASKS ME THE SAME THING, AND I DON'T MIND TELLING YOU. STANDING UP —IN A HAMMOCK."

(Well, while some might like to look for a difficult way, I think the solution here is so simple . . .)

COMMENT: This is a good story for an all-male audience. Do not try to shorten the story. A good mental picture must be painted of all the feats.

Reform—*Practice*

369   *I think this is the time to reassess our situation and see where we can improve our performance.* In that sense we are like the weekend golfer who, having four-putted the last hole, threw his clubs into the golf cart and drove toward the clubhouse. Arriving there, he saw a squad car parked by the entrance. As he walked toward the locker room a policeman stopped him. "Did you drive from the fifteenth tee about half an hour ago?" the officer asked.

"Yes."

"Did you hook your ball over those trees and off the course?"

"Yes, as a matter of fact, I did," replied the puzzled golfer.

With anger in his voice the policeman continued, "Your ball sailed out on the highway and cracked the windshield of a woman's car. She couldn't see where she was going and ran into a fire truck. The fire truck couldn't get to the fire, and a house burned down. What are you going to do about it?"

The golfer pondered a moment, picked up his driver and said, "WELL, I THINK I'M GOING TO OPEN MY STANCE A LITTLE AND MOVE MY LEFT THUMB AROUND FARTHER TOWARD MY RIGHT SIDE."

(Well, the first thing we should do . . .)

COMMENT: If you are a golfer, you might try demonstrating the golf stance.

Rules—*Scrutiny*

370   *It has been suggested that we make an exception here and break the rules a bit.* I disagree. I feel like old Brooklyn Dodger first baseman Gil Hodges when the team was flying back from St. Louis one Friday. The club secretary, Harold Parrott, kidded the Catholic Rex Barney for eating the steak dinner. "My bishop told me it was okay to eat meat on Friday," said pitcher Barney, "in extraordinary circumstances where nothing else is available."

Parrott passed the news along to Gil Hodges, who was disinterestedly toying with a fruit salad. "How high up is this plane?" asked Hodges.

"Twenty-one thousand feet," answered Parrott.

Hodges shook his head. "No steak for me then," he said. "WE'RE TOO CLOSE TO HEADQUARTERS."

(And similarly I think we are too closely observed . . .)

Responsibility—*Blame*

371   *When a great operation is managed to a successful conclusion, everybody likes to get his share of the credit.* But when there is a failure no one answers for the responsibility. It is somewhat like the time I was in our golf-club locker room one Saturday afternoon and the locker-room boy answered the phone and heard a female voice say, "Is my husband there?" The boy answered immediately, "No, ma'am." The woman yelled, "How can you say he isn't there before I even tell you who I am?" "Don't make no difference, lady," the boy said. "THERE AIN'T NEVER NOBODY'S HUSBAND HERE."

(And there's no one also who wants to . . .)

Sacrifice—*Commitment*

372   *Gentlemen, we want your help in this endeavor.* We need your commitment. By that I don't mean we want you to overextend yourselves. We aren't like the pro-football coach who finally called on the rookie end who had been longing to get into a game week after week, but was left sitting on the bench.

Finally, his big chance came. It was the last quarter of the game, the team was way behind, and suddenly the coach called his name. He threw off his warm-up coat and ran to the coach for instructions. "WE'VE RUN OUT OF TIME-OUTS," barked the coach. "GO IN THERE AND GET HURT!"

Schedule—*Timing*

373   *We have run into a little problem in program planning.* For that reason we might have to take the advice a football referee once gave in a somewhat different situation. It was a game some decades ago between the fighting Irish of Notre Dame and the University of Pennsylvania. It was a spirited match. A Catholic priest would even lead the Notre Dame team in prayer before the beginning of each quarter. Sometimes the Notre Dame players would go too far in the desire to win. After a particularly bruising scrimmage play the Penn captain called time and sought out the referee.

"Sir, I want to protest the unnecessary roughness of Notre Dame. Their big center bites my leg everytime he gets the chance in a pile-up. What can be done about his taking a bite out of me?"

Said the referee, "I WOULD SUGGEST RESCHEDULING TO PLAY THEM ONLY ON FRIDAY."

Single-mindedness—*Responsiveness*

374   *The problem with too many businessmen is that they are so wound up in their own affairs that they fail to see the needs of the community.* It is like the way old Notre Dame football players said Frank Leahy used to greet them. The old coach used to ask former players three questions—How do you feel? How is your mother? What is your weight?

An old player, when asked how he felt, said, "I'm getting around a little better since my major operation."

Leahy said, "Great."

When the player was asked about his mother, he replied, "My mother passed away two months ago."

"Great," said Leahy.

Then Leahy asked him his weight.

The player said, "I weigh 242 pounds."

"What's the problem?" said Leahy. "YOU'RE FOUR POUNDS OVERWEIGHT."

Success—*Comparison*

375   *While our record is not an unmixed record of success, it will stand up to comparison.* It recalls the time in the spring of 1932 when Babe Ruth of the Yankees was told by club president Jacob Rupert that he had to take a cutback to $80,000. The shrewd Colonel Rupert informed the gay-living Babe that there was a depression throughout the country. Babe was shocked. It was news to him. But when the wise millionaire club owner tried to win that salary dispute by pointing out that even with his salary cut Ruth would be receiving more than Herbert Hoover, the President of the United States, the Babe said, "WHAT THE HELL HAS HOOVER GOT TO DO WITH IT? BESIDES, I HAD A BETTER YEAR THAN HE DID."

(And similarly, we had a better year . . .)

Madison Avenue

*An advertising agency is 85 percent confusion
and 15 percent commission.*
                                        —Fred Allen

376   As an advertising man let me say that that was a fine introduction. You turned a kernel of fact into a field of corn.

377   Seriously, though, imagination is what makes a great copywriter. If you don't believe me just read my write-up of my monthly expense account.

378   It doesn't bother me, though; I know that my ulcers react only when I begin to get inhibited by the facts.

379   Really, though, I am proud of my profession. Advertising has made America great, but then you might say advertising makes everything look great.

380   Seriously, advertising is to business like horse is to carriage or love is to marriage. I know critics say we encourage people to live beyond their means—but doesn't marriage?

381 Actually, getting married is very much like marketing in advertising—trading reach for frequency.

382 Of course I know we advertising men get accused of drinking our meals. But as a matter of fact, I work for a very old-fashioned company. There is a strict policy against any drinking —before breakfast.

383 Really, though, we advertising men do have some constraints about drinking. We make it a rule never to dine on an empty stomach.

384 After all, a lot of overweight people are now trying the drinking man's diet. I don't know about the rest of your body, but it sure makes your head feel lighter.

385 Well, at least I can say as Winston Churchill did, "I have taken more out of alcohol than it has taken out of me."

Advertising—*Image*

386 *I am glad to say the image of advertising is getting better.* The other day I saw three children playing in the yard. The first said, "Let's play cops and robbers." "All right," the oldest said to the next biggest. "I'll be the good guy and you be the robber." And the tag-along little brother said eagerly, "CAN I BE THE COMMERCIAL?"

Advertising—*Rumor*

387 *The ingenuity of American advertising men is a never-ending source of amazement.* For example, one ad man died and went to the pearly gates, but St. Peter stopped him and said, "Sorry, the quota for your profession is filled. You can get in only if you persuade another man to leave."

"Fair enough," our man said. "Just give me twenty-four hours."

Before a day went by there wasn't an ad man-angel left in heaven.

"How did you do it?" St. Peter asked.

"Easy," said the ad man. "I JUST STARTED A RUMOR THAT THE DEVIL WAS LOOKING FOR A NEW AGENCY."

(Incidentally, I'm not staying either. You never can tell about those rumors. . . .)

COMMENT: This story can also be told as a warning against relying on every rumor.

Communication—*Revenge*

388   *They say old speechwriters never die; they just give up the ghost.* But seriously, the job of writing for others is an emotional drain as well as a physical one. There is not only the problem of adjusting to the speaker's temperament—there's also having to take the responsibility for failure but no credit for the success. I remember one acquaintance of mine was assigned by his advertising and public-relations company to write speeches and articles for this self-made millionaire egomaniac, who not only underpaid but continually subjected my friend to a continuous shower of abuse. The ghostwriter finally had his revenge. He provided his employer with a long speech to read at a very important convention. The employer read the first eight pages of the speech typed in big printer's type, but when he turned to page nine in the middle of a sentence he found only these words, printed in red: "FROM HERE ON, YOU POMPOUS ASS, YOU'RE ON YOUR OWN."

Obsession—*Compassion*

389   *Businessmen are often so obsessed with their own jobs that they become insensitive to the concerns of others.* Some advertising types were sipping their lunch in a bar off Madison Avenue.

"Where," asked Harry, lifting his lunch and sipping it, "has Bill Williamson been hanging out?"

"Haven't you heard? Bill went to the Great Agency in the Sky."

"You're kidding!"

"No. He died last month."

"Good Lord. What did he have?"

"NOTHING MUCH," Joe said reflectively. "A SMALL TOOTHPASTE ACCOUNT AND A COUPLE OF HOTELS BUT NOTHING WORTH GOING AFTER."

(There are things worth going after in life, and they count more than new business. . . .)

Opinion—*Press*

390   *The fickleness of public opinion is shown by the apocryphal items of news which appeared in the forerunner of the Paris newspaper* Le Monde.

When Napoleon returned from Elba, the newspaper screamed, "The Corsican Ogre Invades France at Antibes."

Ten days later the same paper said, "General Bonaparte Reaches Lyons."

Fifteen days later there appeared the next headline, "HIS MAJESTY, THE EMPEROR, ENTERS HIS PALACE OF THE TUILERIES."

(And similarly I have detected a change of attitude . . .)

Profession—*Criticism*

391   *With the recent publicity of my profession, I am somewhat hesitant about talking about the problems in my field.* I recall the time a man gave a speech at a Rotary Club in my city on the subject of advertising and advertising people. It is one of the tenets of the Rotarians that they may not swear or use cuss words. But the speaker, not being a Rotarian himself, didn't know this, and in his talk he used a profanity he shouldn't have used in that particular hall to that particular audience.

At the end of the meeting a local minister in the audience approached the speaker and dressed him down for having used the language he did. The speaker apologized profusely, and the minister went on about how Rotarians, to say nothing of the church, strongly disapproved of bad language. He then walked away.

He got about ten feet down the corridor, then turned around and approached the speaker again.

"OFF THE RECORD", he said, "AND JUST BETWEEN US, ANYTIME YOU WANT TO CALL AN ADVERTISING MAN A SONOFABITCH, IT'S OKAY WITH ME."

(Now many people want to use the same language to describe . . .)

ADVICE: You can substitute almost any profession instead of advertising—law, medicine, etc.

Publicity—*Solution*

392   *We are getting tired of being offered slogans instead of solutions, public relations instead of programs.* It reminds me of the tale about Moses when he and his troops reached the Red Sea in the flight from the Egyptians. With the Egyptian soldiers in hot pursuit, Moses had a real problem in how to cross the Red Sea. Moses called a staff meeting and asked for solutions. He turned to the head of his army and said, "General, what do you suggest?" The general replied, "Moses, we might be able to lay pontoons, but it would take at least two years." Moses then turned to his admiral. "Admiral, what do you say?" "Well, Moses, if we had landing barges, we could do it, but it would take six months to build them." Then Moses looked over at his chief of engineers and asked him for suggestions. He replied, "Moses, we could erect a bridge, but that would take at least three years." At that point the public-relations man at the table raised his hand. Moses looked down at him, "Okay, what's your solution?" "OH, I DON'T HAVE A SOLUTION, MOSES, BUT I PROMISE YOU THIS. IF YOU FIND A WAY TO DO IT, I CAN GET YOU TWO PAGES IN THE OLD TESTAMENT."

Public Relations—*Advertising*

393   *The best argument I ever heard for hiring a public-relations agency was the pitch given by a young man trying to sell a manufacturer his services.* Said the manufacturer, "Our company dominates the field. Anything we do is reported."

But the young man was not to be put off. "Ever hear of Napoleon?"

"Of course, but what has that to do—"

"How about Wellington? Who was he?"

"Well, didn't he have something to do with Waterloo?"

"Yes, he did. He wiped the floor with Napoleon at Waterloo—yet it's Napoleon you always hear about. THAT'S BECAUSE HE HAD PUBLIC RELATIONS."

Salesmanship—*Publicity*

394   *I like being with advertising men; they are so enthusiastic and so full of ideas.* The only thing is that sometimes they let their imagination run away with them. They forget the real purpose of

the promotion. I recall the case of a single lady who had been married three times but had never been divorced. The reason she gave is that all of her marriages had been annulled because they hadn't been consummated.

"My first husband was a charming alcoholic, but he'd get drunk every night, and by bedtime he'd be dead to the world. My second husband was quite handsome, but on our wedding night I discovered he was more attracted to my brother than to me. My third husband, the advertising executive, was a persuasive fellow, but he turned out to be a complete captive of his craft."

"What do you mean?" asked her friend.

"Well," she said, "HE WOULD SPEND THE WHOLE NIGHT SITTING ON THE EDGE OF THE BED TELLING ME HOW GREAT IT WAS GOING TO BE."

Work—*Extracurricular*

395   *In this new assignment there will be no time for fun and games.* We won't be able to relax until the job is done. We are going to become what a Chicago advertising agency became. Once it was known as the type of agency where all the executives played around with the secretaries. A new secretary came in one day and didn't go for the game. She decided to stop it once and for all. One morning she got to the office at 7:30 and put on each executive's desk an envelope marked confidential. Inside was a typewritten note that read, "I'm pregnant." From that day on it was like a monastery.

(And from now on we are going to . . .)

Main Line

In Boston they ask, How much does he know?
In New York, How much is he worth?
In Philadelphia, Who were his parents?
                              —Mark Twain

Anticipation—*Revenge*

396   *As toastmaster tonight I have the responsibility of introducing the head table.* The great thing about this is that I can say

anything I want to about these distinguished gentlemen arranged on my right and left, and they can do nothing about it. With this opportunity I feel like the maid at one of our better homes on the Main Line. This maid's mistress is particularly renowned for her elaborate dinners. Unfortunately this lady discovered just before the guests were expected that her butler was ill and therefore unable to perform his usual duty. So in the emergency she summoned from her staff of servants Mrs. O'Brien, a trusted employee in the family for many years, and she said to her, "Now, Nora, you stand at the drawing-room door and call the guests' names as they arrive."

Nora's face lit up at the very prospect of such a privilege, and she said, "THANK YOU, MA'AM. I HAVE BEEN WANTING TO DO JUST THAT TO SOME OF YOUR FRIENDS FOR THE LAST TWENTY YEARS."

Communication—*Intentions*

397   *So many of our problems arise out of lack of communication, because we don't tell others what we really want to do or what our intentions really are.* We can sympathize with the English duchess whose husband had come over to Philadelphia to open the Devon Horse Show. The head of the arrangements committee was asked to entertain the duke and duchess. Not knowing quite what to do with the distinguished couple, the Main Line hostess asked if they wanted to play some bridge. The husband paired with the duchess and the wife with the duke. Continually the poor-playing husband frustrated the duchess with his bidding. On one occasion the husband excused himself. The door of the downstairs powder room was not fully closed, and the purpose of the husband's mission was clearly audible.

The wife, visibly upset, hastily got up to close the door. "Excuse me, Your Grace. This is so embarrassing."

"REALLY," said the duchess, "I'D RATHER YOU DIDN'T. THIS IS THE FIRST TIME THIS EVENING I ACTUALLY KNOW WHAT HE HAS IN HIS HAND."

COMMENT: Obviously this is not the story to tell to a mixed audience.

Conservatism—*Progress*

398   *When I am accused of being a reactionary in expressing my opposition to some of the recent highly ballyhooed programs,*

I am always reminded of what an old member of Philadelphia's Union League said. He was an old Penn grad and had rowed on one of the University of Pennsylvania's championship crew teams back before World War I. Accordingly, he never missed any of Penn's races on the Schuylkill River.

At one of the meets a reporter asked him, "Rowing must mean more to you than just exercise. It must be a sort of ritual of symbolic significance."

"Yes," he said. "I HAD RATHER BE A MEMBER OF A SOCIETY OF EIGHT MEN FACING BACKWARD AND GOING FORWARD THAN A MEMBER OF A CROWD FACING FORWARD AND GOING NOWHERE."

Excellence—*Dilution*

399   *What we have is excellent, and I would oppose any move that would weaken the effectiveness of this very successful operation we have going.* It is like a friend of mine, owner of a handsomely manicured estate in Philadelphia on the Main Line, who noted that appreciable inroads were being made into the supply of twenty-year-old Scotch that he kept in the library. Very carefully, he made a small pencil mark on the label of the bottle on his side table opposite the current level of the liquid.

Returning home that night, he found this note from the chambermaid, "Please don't put any more pencil marks on this bottle, BECAUSE I DON'T WANT TO HAVE TO PUT WATER IN SUCH WONDERFUL WHISKEY."

(And I don't want to water down this operation . . .)

Gloom—*Enthusiasm*

400   *I hope I haven't presented too black a picture.* Things, of course, could be worse. It's like a friend of mine who was walking with me down Broad Street, the main thoroughfare of Philadelphia. We went past the Union League Club, the huge mausoleum structure that has been the citadel of Philadelphia's old-line Republicans for over a century. My companion noted that there was black crepe on the big windows that faced the street and asked why.

"Probably someone died," I said.

He replied, "WELL, IT DOES SORT OF LIVEN UP THE PLACE."

Instructions—*Mix-up*

401   *There will be no problem if we all follow the list of instructions.* If you don't, you may find yourself in a mix-up like a man I heard about in Philadelphia. He had been complaining to an acquaintance in his office that he was not lucky in finding attractive women to take out. His friend said, "You ought to try my ploy. Drive up late one afternoon to the station at Devon and wait at the station for the train to pull in. The wives will be waiting to drive their husbands home, and there are always one or two husbands who miss the train. Ask one of the girls for a date and she'll be so mad at her husband for missing the train that she'll jump at the invitation."

The man thought this a great idea and set out the very next evening. Impatient when he got to Bryn Mawr, he thought, "Why should I go any farther? There's a station here. I'll try my luck." So he waited for the next train, and sure enough the men got off and drove away with their wives, and one lovely girl was left over. He asked her to have dinner with him and she accepted. They dined and wined and danced and went back to her house for another drink or two. Just as things were getting exciting, the husband entered unexpectedly and started shouting abuse at his wife. Suddenly he noticed the man, who was attempting to sneak out the door.

"So it's you, you bastard," he yelled. "I TOLD YOU DEVON, NOT BRYN MAWR."

Knowledge—*Ignorant*

402   *If there is one thing worse than being ignorant and knowing it, it's being ignorant and not knowing it.* I once had a friend in Philadelphia who, widowed at the age of sixty, had married a woman he had met in business twenty years his junior. Although now bearer of one of Philadelphia's oldest names, she had relinquished none of her masterful career-success tactics. At the first dinner party she gave, she antagonized the women guests by pointing out ostentatiously the improvements she had made since moving into her husband's old Victorian mansion. After proudly showing guests around the house, she remarked, "Since our marriage, I've taught my husband the art of good taste."

"I see," remarked one of the guests, an old friend of the groom. "HOW FORTUNATE FOR YOU THAT YOU DIDN'T TEACH HIM BEFORE YOU MARRIED HIM."

Prejudice—*Mistake*

403   *Prejudice is a very ugly thing, but I am convinced that bigots usually end up being more damaged than those they try to hurt.* I recall during World War II a woman on the Main Line who decided to celebrate Thanksgiving by having several soldiers in as guests. She called the neighboring army base, was connected with one of the first sergeants and asked that three soldiers be sent to her house the following Thursday.

"And, Sergeant," she added, "I do not wish any of them to be Jewish."

"I understand, ma'am," said the sergeant.

Came Thursday and on the doorstep of her Main Line manor stood three fine-looking black soldiers in spotless uniforms. "We're here for Thanksgiving, ma'am," said one of the soldiers politely.

Eyes wide, she sputtered, "But . . . but . . . but . . . your sergeant must have made a mistake."

"No, ma'am," said the black positively. "SERGEANT COHEN DOESN'T MAKE MISTAKES."

COMMENT: I have also heard this story told about Lyndon Johnson. He was trying to round up some escorts at his ranch from a nearby army base. But in this case he specified no Mexican-Americans. It is naturally a Colonel Gonzales who never makes a mistake. Frankly, this is one of the few ethnic stories you can tell because the story ridicules bigotry, not an ethnic group.

Records—*Lost*

404   *Unfortunately, we seem to have no record of the incident.* In that way we have much the same problem as Mrs. Schwartz, whose husband had just been assigned to Philadelphia and who was being shown around Philadelphia by a Main Line matron whose husband was in the same company. When Mrs. Schwartz noted a brooch her guide was wearing, the lady replied, "Actually, it's an emblem of the Daughters of the Barons of Runnymede. It has to do with the signers of the Magna Carta in the days of King

John. Are you interested in family genealogy?"

"Well," said my friend, "I CAN'T REALLY SAY. ALL OUR FAMILY RECORDS WERE LOST EARLIER, IN THE GREAT FLOOD."

Repeat—*Invitation*

405   *I am really very pleased to be invited back a second time to address your group.* It shows some real enthusiasm on your part. It is not like the experience an acquaintance of mine had in Philadelphia. He was alone on a dreary night in the lounge of the Union League. Hoping to strike up a conversation with a distinguished-looking Philadelphian sitting nearby, he said, "May I buy you a drink?" "No," said the Main Liner coolly. "Don't drink. Tried it once and didn't like it."

Nothing daunted my friend, so he offered him a cigar, saying he had just picked up a good one. "No, don't smoke. Tried it once and didn't like it." "Then how 'bout a little game of rummy?" "No. Don't play cards. Tried it once, didn't like it. But my son will be dropping by after a bit. He might want to play."

My friend settled back in his chair and said, "YOUR ONLY CHILD, I PRESUME."

Responsibility—*Inflation*

406   *The main cause of inflation is excessive government spending—deficit spending.* Yet collectively the same people who demand more federal help for a wide range of public needs object to the inflation that follows. It reminds me of a maid I heard about in a suburban Philadelphia household.

Lizette, the upstairs maid in the Morris household, came to her mistress with a sad story to tell. Lizette, it seemed, was going to have a baby—out of wedlock—and she would have to quit. Mrs. Morris, though stunned, came back with a game offer, for good servants are hard to find, and Lizette was good.

"You'll do no such thing, my dear," she said. "You'll have your child here, and we'll adopt it and raise it as our own." And so it was arranged, and everybody was happy.

But the following year it was the same story. Once again Mrs. Morris insisted that the family adopt the child, and Lizette stay on. The third year was a repeat performance.

When Lizette came to her for the fourth time, Mrs. Morris shook her head from side to side. "Lizette, Lizette," she said, "whatever are we to do with you?"

"There's nothing to be done, madam," said Lizette. "THIS TIME I'M TRULY LEAVING. I REFUSE TO WORK FOR SUCH A LARGE FAMILY."

Similarity—*Coincidence*

407   *I don't regard this as a mere coincidence.* A further examination might show why this was a probable likelihood. It is like the exchange that two distinguished members of Philadelphia's Union League Club had on one occasion.

Standing up from his leather chair, one gentleman looked up Broad Street, which the grandiose structure faces, and cried out, "Look at that! What a coincidence! There is my wife and my mistress walking arm in arm up Broad Street." His friend, also looking out, said, "INCREDIBLE. I WAS JUST ABOUT TO SAY THE SAME THING."

Military Ball

Soldiers win battles; but generals get the credit.
        —Napoleon

408   First, I want to thank you for your kind introduction. You obviously don't agree with General Omar Bradley, who said, "The best service a retired general can perform is to turn in his tongue along with his uniform."

409   I guess Bradley agrees with MacArthur that old generals should just fade away. But he is wrong. Last night I tried getting into my old uniform.

410   If you want to know why I agreed to speak on this sensitive subject, you only have to look to the old Army saying that there are three types of fools—"fools, damned fools, and volunteers."

411   Actually there's another reason. As General Bradley said of Patton, "He'd move his army twenty miles for a headline or fly a thousand miles for a speech."

412   You know, Clemenceau might have said, "War is too important to be left to generals," but Patton and the rest of us generals seem to think that "generals are too important to lecture only on war."

413   Seriously, we generals respect the separation of military from civilian. We revere the Constitution, especially the Preamble—the part that reads "to promote the generals' welfare."

Assumption—*Planning*

414   *We cannot make our decision on an assumption.* We have no way of knowing how the thing will actually turn out. It reminds me of the time in the Army when an excited Army recruit asked our company commander for an immediate furlough, explaining that his wife was going to have a baby. Permission was granted, and the soldier was leaving, when his CO asked exactly when the baby was due. The soldier replied, "ABOUT NINE MONTHS AFTER I GET HOME, SIR."

Communication—*Love*

415   *We all express our feelings in different ways—love, for example.* I remember at a dance at the officers' club my eyes were attracted to a brooch worn by an attractive young lady. It depicted a cluster of naval signaling flags and the girl explained, "This brooch was a present from my bridegroom. The flags mean, 'I love you.'" I held my peace because I knew full well there was no such word as "love" in the naval signal manual. But when I got back home I dug out my own copy of the manual. What the flags actually signaled, I found out, was "PERMISSION GRANTED TO LAY ALONGSIDE."

Complaint—*Illogical*

416   *The logic of such a complaint reminds me of a letter a congressman once told me he had received.* A soldier, barely into his basic training, had written a furious letter to his congressman, detailing all the various indignities and evils to which he was being subjected. At one point he became quite eloquent. "And the food, sir, I can describe only as slop. I wouldn't feed it to pigs for fear

they would get sick to their stomachs and die of it. It would be rejected by any decent garbage man. AND TO MAKE MATTERS STILL WORSE, THEY SERVE SUCH SMALL PORTIONS."

Curiosity—*Evidence*

417   *The reassurances from Washington are acceptable at first, but then one begins to wonder if we aren't missing something.* There is something missing in the explanation. An Army lieutenant whom I heard about recently received from his fiancée a snapshot taken on the beach showing two couples smiling contentedly while his girl sat alone at one side, forlorn and lonely. The accompanying letter explained that this was how she was fretting away the time until he returned.

At first the lieutenant was delighted, displaying it proudly to several fellow officers. That night, however, after studying it a long time in silence, he turned to his roommate. "Hey, Buddy," he said. "YOU KNOW, I'M BEGINNING TO WONDER WHO TOOK THAT PICTURE."

Defense—*Preparedness*

418   *I am all for cutting waste in the defense budget, but I think the main factor in such budget discussions ought to be our basic defense.* It recalls the time in the Constitutional Convention when one of the delegates moved "that the standing army be restricted to 5,000 men at any one time." George Washington, as presiding officer, could not offer a motion. So he turned to another delegate and whispered, "AMEND THE MOTION TO PROVIDE THAT NO FOREIGN ENEMY SHALL INVADE THE UNITED STATES AT ANY TIME WITH MORE THAN 3,000 TROOPS."

Distortion—*Truth*

419   *The distortions and half-truths that attend this controversy remind me of the words once written in a ship log.* There was a New England shipmaster who had a first mate who was at times addicted to the use of strong drink. Once when the ship was lying in a China port the mate indulged in some of those vile Oriental compounds. He came on board outrageously drunk. One of the duties of the first mate is to write up the "log" each day, but as that officer was not able to do it, the captain made the proper

entry, but added: "The mate was drunk all day." The ship left port the next day and the mate got sobered up. He attended to his writing at the proper time but was appalled when he read what the captain had written.

The next day the captain was examining the book, and he found at the bottom of the mate's entry of observation, course, winds, and tides: "THE CAPTAIN TODAY WAS SOBER."

Flattery—*Exaggeration*

420   *Thank you for that introduction.* It was not, however, completely accurate. But I am not one to criticize particularly exaggerations made in my behalf. The best example of that I recall was how a British naval officer took a remark from a young Annapolis graduate. The ensign, a Southern boy, had met an English girl on his first cruise. Eventually he was invited to a Sunday dinner at her home in Southampton, England. On hand was the girl's favorite uncle. Uncle Derek, who came in his gold-braided uniform, got along swimmingly with the young officer. Suddenly the uncle turned to the young Southerner and asked casually who, in his opinion, were the three greatest sailors in British history. "I'm sorry, sir," the lad replied. "I DIDN'T QUITE GET YOUR NAME —BUT THE OTHER TWO ARE NELSON AND DRAKE."

Favoritism—*Speed*

421   *These laws should apply to everybody, with no exception being made for anyone.* All of us have known someone like the Navy commander I heard about recently. At one of the larger naval installations in San Diego there was a crackdown on excessive speed. A Marine private stopped a military jeep for exceeding the speed limit and politely asked the driver, a Navy commander, for his operator's permit. The Marine proceeded to make out the traffic-violation certificate.

"Private," the commander yelled, "do you know who I am? I'm the executive officer at this base and I'm en route to a golf engagement with your commanding officer, and this will undoubtedly make me late."

"I'M SORRY, SIR," the Marine replied. "BUT I'M WRITING AS FAST AS I CAN."

Fear—*Snub*

422   *Soon we will be put to the test. We cannot show our doubts and fears.* No matter what we do we are going to be remembered in the future for how we handled this situation. I remember the story of the Duke of Wellington after the battle of Waterloo. The victorious general was appointed the new Ambassador to France. At a reception given by the newly throned Louis XVIII some French generals made a point of snubbing the British general. When King Louis tried to make amends for their rudeness the Iron Duke shrugged and replied, "YOUR MAJESTY, IT IS NOT IM-PORTANT. YOU SEE, IT IS NOT THE FIRST TIME I HAVE SEEN THE BACKS OF FRENCH OFFICERS."

Mistake—*Next Time*

423   *Next time, gentlemen, I assure you I won't make the same mistake.* All you need is one lesson like that of the French aide-de-camp. During World War I this aide to Marshal Joffre was approached by a pretty American girl at a Washington reception who said, "Sir, did you really kill a German soldier in battle?"

"Yes."

"With what hand did you do it?"

"With this right hand."

At that point the pretty American girl seized his right hand and kissed it. A French colonel beside him said, "HEAVENS, MAN, NEXT TIME WHY DON'T YOU TELL A GIRL THAT YOU BIT THE GERMAN TO DEATH?"

Oversell—*Overqualified*

424   *Sometimes one can oversell his case or tell too much about himself.* A friend of mine who is a colonel told me about a recruit being inducted into the Army. The young man was being questioned by a sergeant. "Did you have six years of grade-school education?"

"Oh yes, sir," said the recruit. "I also graduated from high school. I went to Yale for my college degree. And then I did graduate work at Columbia University and then got my Ph. D. at Harvard."

The sergent then yelled over to the stenographer and said, "CHECK THIS ONE IN THE SPACE MARKED 'LITERATE.' "

Regulations—*Reason*

425 *Knowing the rules is good, but knowing the reasons behind the rules is even better.* I remember in basic training a sergeant was asking some of us recruits why walnut was used for the butt of a rifle.

"Because it has more resistance," volunteered one man.

"Wrong!"

"Because it is more elastic."

"Wrong!"

"Perhaps it's because it looks better than any other kind of wood," volunteered another.

"Don't be a fool," snapped the sergeant. "IT'S SIMPLY BECAUSE IT WAS LAID DOWN IN REGULATIONS."

Responsibility—*Care*

426 *The chairman was very kind in his introduction, but I think it's only fair to add that my efforts were not solely altruistic.* It reminds me of an officer's remark to General Eisenhower in the last war. On an inspection trip in North Africa General Eisenhower stopped at a forward position held by British troops.

Accompanied by the officer in command, he toured the area by jeep. Suddenly an enemy plane made a sweep with guns blazing. Jamming on the brakes, the officer hustled Eisenhower out of the jeep and pushed him into a ditch. Then, when the danger had passed, he anxiously inquired, "Are you all right, sir?"

Eisenhower was touched by the other's solicitude. "I want to thank you for taking such an interest in my welfare," he said. "Not at all," replied the other. "I DIDN'T WANT ANYTHING TO HAPPEN TO YOU IN MY SECTOR."

Secret—*Leadership*

427 *Gentlemen, while I can't say that I have ever been offended by the attention given to me because of my position, I do think that if the full story of how I got here came out, it might put things in better perspective.* It reminds me of the time in World War II when Admiral Nimitz and General MacArthur found themselves fishing together off the Philippines. In a sudden squall the boat capsized, and the eminent fighting men were floundering helplessly in the water.

The admiral was first to reach the boat. With the aid of an oar he finally got the general aboard. "Now, Mac," he cautioned, "don't mention this to anyone. You see, I'd be disgraced if the men of the Navy learned I can't swim."

"Don't worry," MacArthur replied. "YOUR SECRET IS SAFE. YOU SEE, I'D HATE TO HAVE MY MEN FIND OUT I CAN'T WALK ON WATER."

(And, gentlemen, tonight I'd hate to have people find out . . .)

ADVICE: This is a good anecdote to use in replying to a toast or beginning a speech after a flattering introduction.

Strange—*Unfamiliar*

428   *As the chairman indicated in his introduction, this is a new role I find myself in.* It reminds me of some remarks made at a wedding reception a friend of mine attended in Hawaii. This officer fell in love with an officer patient, and they planned to marry the day he was released from the hospital. Not wishing to be married in her khaki uniform, she got permission to wear a wedding gown.

After the ceremony the overwhelmed groom announced to all, "Isn't she lovely? This is the first time I've ever seen her with a dress on!"

"Isn't he handsome?" the excited bride exclaimed. "IT'S THE FIRST TIME I'VE SEEN HIM WHEN HE WASN'T IN PAJAMAS!"

Suspicious—*Misimpression*

429   *I know some of the things that have happened recently might give one a contrary impression, but actually it is not the case.* It recalls that unusual case in World War II when an RAF pilot was shot down over Germany and wound up in a German hospital.

The doctor fixed the British flyer up but told him he would have to amputate his right leg to save his life.

After the flyer recovered from the shock of the bad news, he asked the doctor if he would do him one favor. The doctor, being a compassionate man, said that he would try. The flyer said, "Would you give the leg to one of your friends in the Luftwaffe on the next run and have him drop it over England with a note, 'In service of my King.'?"

The doctor agreed, and it was done.

A week later the doctor came in with the sad news that the other leg would have to be amputated also.

The flyer naturally was upset but requested that the doctor please have one of the German flyers drop it over England with the label, "In service of my King."

The doctor agreed, and it was done. A month later the doctor came in again and told the flyer he was sorry, but to save his life he would have to amputate his right hand. The patriotic English flyer started to make his usual request, but the doctor interrupted him and said, "I'm very sorry but I can't grant your request this time."

The pilot asked, "Why not?" The doctor replied, "THE S.S. THINKS YOU'RE TRYING TO ESCAPE!"

Neighborhood Pub

Ale, man, ale's the stuff to drink
For fellows whom it hurts to think.
                                    —A. E. Housman

430   My friends, I know you too well to call you gentlemen.

431   You know, the obvious duty of a toastmaster is to be so infernally dull that the succeeding speakers will appear brilliant by contrast. I've looked over this list, however, and I don't believe I can do it.

432   There are a lot of things I don't like about our honoree tonight. After all, it was Mark Twain who said, "Fewer things are harder to put up with than the annoyance of a good example."

433   Good evening, ladies and gentlemen—and those of you who are neither.

434   I want you to know that everything I say in this little speech is true—only the facts have been changed.

435   First of all, I want to toast the program chairman for the fine job he did in not being able to obtain a speaker.

436   Then I want to say the party tonight is going to be a memorable occasion. It is either going to be one you'll never be able to forget or one you'll never be able to remember.

437   At this time I think it appropriate to recall what Robert Benchley once told his valet! "Let's get out of these wet clothes and into a dry martini."

438   And then remember what James Thurber said about martinis: "One is all right, two is too many, three is not enough."

439   As I look around at this group and reflect on their character and virtue, I think of Shaw's play when the devil says, "Heaven suits some people, but as for me I prefer the company of gentlemen."

440   Seriously, though, over the years I have learned to value your friendship and companionship, for as Winston Churchill once said, "Never can a man be trusted who has not a single redeeming vice."

441   At this time I think it only fitting to recall that French ambassador's words just before the fall of France: "The only thing to do in the time between the crisis and the catastrophe is to raise our glasses with wine."

442   And if you don't believe in drinking wine, remember what Bobbie Burns wrote: "Freedom and whiskey gang together."

443   Seriously, whatever your views, Republican or Democratic, I think we can all agree on what Henry Clay once said: "What makes this country strong is the two-party system—a party on Friday night and another on Saturday."

Character—*Enjoyment*

444   *We have heard so many fine things about our honoree tonight that I think I shall tell this story, which gives another dimension about his character.* Some time back he and I were walking over to the hotel when a panhandler stopped us. I pretended I didn't see him, but he buttonholed our guest and asked him for a couple of bucks to get something to eat, and our friend

said, "As a matter of principle, I don't give money to beggars. But since it is cold and rainy and we're heading for a quick one in the bar before lunch, suppose I buy you a drink. That will warm you up at least."

"No, thank you, sir, I don't drink." "Well," our friend said, "here's a couple of cigarettes anyway." "No, thank you," the bum said. "I don't smoke."

I was wondering what our friend was going to say to that, and he said, "Look, I don't give money out. I don't believe in it. But since you are so persistent, I'll tell you what I'll do. Right after lunch I'm putting a couple of bucks on a horse that is running at the raceway. To show you I'm a good sport, I'll put two dollars on him for you. How's that?" "I appreciate your thoughtfulness, mister, but I don't gamble. All I want is some money for something to eat."

That moved our friend. He said, "Okay, you win. I'll buy you a steak dinner, but only on one condition. AS SOON AS THIS DINNER IS OVER, I WANT TO DRIVE YOU OUT TO MY HOUSE TO MEET MY WIFE. I WANT HER TO TAKE ONE LOOK TO SEE WHAT HAPPENS TO A MAN WHO DOESN'T DRINK, SMOKE, OR GAMBLE."

Confused—*Hectic*

445   *In the last weeks things have been so hectic that sometimes I find myself in sympathy with the intoxicated young man who was apprehended after gunning his Mercedes the wrong way down a one-way street.* He was asked where he thought he was going by an inquisitive police officer.

"I'm not really sure," he confessed, "BUT WHEREVER IT IS, I MUST BE LATE, BECAUSE EVERYBODY SEEMS TO BE COMING BACK ALREADY."

(And similarly in these last few weeks I don't know whether I'm coming or going.)

Criticism—*Advice*

446   *I guess we can expect a lot of second-guessing in this type of work.* Sometimes it is even supposed to be helpful. At least I have heard that the Royal Mounted Police of Canada rely on it at times. A newly commissioned Mountie was being shown his new locker by a senior officer. There was the famous red uniform, the

black boots, and the Mountie travel kit. The new Mountie looked
in the case. There were the trusted compass, a map of the Yukon,
a jackknife, a small rope, and, beside those, the Mountie to his
surprise found a small aluminum shaker, a miniature bottle of gin
and a vial of vermouth.

"What is that there for?" asked the young Mountie.

"WELL, IF YOU ARE EVER LOST IN THE SNOWY NORTH WOODS,
ALL YOU HAVE TO DO IS START TO MAKE THE DRINK AND SOMEONE
IS BOUND TO TURN UP AND TELL YOU HOW TO MIX YOUR MAR-
TINI."

(And similarly, all we have to do . . .)

COMMENT: The build-up is important in this story. Remember to
describe what was in the locker and then what was in the
travel kit.

Fellowship—*Congenial*

447   *As I look around this crowd assembled here tonight, I see
some hale and hearty spirits.* At least they aren't ailing in just the
way a man I heard about recently. This rather stuffed shirt walked
into a doctor's office and said, "Doctor, I feel terrible. Give me a
complete examination and tell me what's wrong with me."

"Fine," said the doctor, "but first let me ask you a few questions.
Do you drink much?"

"You mean alcohol? I am a teetotaler—never touched a drop in
my life."

"Do you smoke at all?"

"Never—not a cigarette, cigar, or pipe. I'm against tobacco on
principle."

"Well, do you run around much at night?"

"You mean carousing with women? Of course not. I'm home in
bed at ten o'clock every night."

"Tell me," the doctor continued, "do you have sharp pains in
your head?"

"That's just it," the man replied. "I have acute pains in my
head."

"That's your trouble, my dear man," the doctor said. "YOUR
HALO IS ON TOO TIGHT."

(And as I look around this room, I see no one suffering from a
headache. Tomorrow morning that is another thing.)

Fuel—*Rationing*

448   *I didn't realize how bad the energy crisis was until I saw my friendly service-station manager filling up five-gallon containers from his own tanks.* It reminds me of the time they had a big fire in a Midwestern brewery that caused a temporary beer shortage in those parts, and every bar and grill had to go on a quota. The proprietor of one roadside retreat called to plead for an additional shipment "urgently." "It's an emergency," he declared. "But you've had your quota for the week," the brewery superintendent pointed out. "I KNOW I HAVE," answered the caller, "BUT WHAT ABOUT MY CUSTOMERS?"

Gratitude—*Woman*

449   *It may seem that W. C. Fields had little in common with our guest of honor tonight.* But what our big-nosed friend once said might apply in a different sense to the situation tonight.

Fields said, "It was a woman who drove me to drink. AND I NEVER GOT A CHANCE TO THANK HER."

(But we have a chance to thank tonight . . .)

Preference—*Technique*

450   *As we all know there is a right way to do everything, and the success of an operation depends upon the perfect execution.* I remember hearing a story about John Barrymore, who was a connoisseur of martinis, when he was ordering his favorite drink. "Very dry," he told the bartender. "Twenty parts gin to one part vermouth."

"All right, Mr. Barrymore," said the bartender. "Shall I twist a bit of lemon peel over it?"

"MY GOOD MAN, WHEN I WANT LEMONADE I'LL ASK FOR IT."

(And similarly, if we want an operation that is. . . .)

Progress—*Criticism*

451   *To those who have criticized some of our past policies, I would like to answer in the same way Abraham Lincoln did once when he was criticized by Stephen Douglas for once having been a bartender.* "What Mr. Douglas has said, gentlemen, is true enough. I did keep a grocery, and I did sell cotton, candles and

cigars, and sometimes whiskey; and I remember in those days that Mr. Douglas was one of my best customers. Many a time have I stood on one side of the counter and sold whiskey to Mr. Douglas on the other side, but the difference between us now is this. I HAVE LEFT MY SIDE OF THE COUNTER, BUT MR. DOUGLAS STILL STICKS TO HIS AS TENACIOUSLY AS EVER."

(And similarly, we have come a long way in the last few years . . .)

Quality—*Choice*

452   *In this choice before us we must examine the comparative assets and liabilities inherent in each course.* Perhaps we need the same discriminating taste an old roué showed. He was relaxing over an after-dinner drink following an especially enjoyable meal when his dining companion, knowing of his friend's true appreciation for the finer things, asked him, "As a lover of wine, women, and song you would, no doubt, have no difficulty in eliminating song from your life, but what would you forgo if you were forced to choose between women and wine?"

The suave gentleman paused to inhale the bouquet of his cognac, then replied, "THAT WOULD DEPEND ON THEIR RESPECTIVE VINTAGES."

Realism—*Superficial*

453   *You can't expect to come up with a solid answer by a quick superficial appraisal.* It is like the case of a young bride I heard about recently.

The bride of three months complained to her relatives about her husband's continued drinking habits.

"If you knew he drank, why did you ever marry him in the first place?" she was asked by a friend.

"I didn't know he drank," the girl replied, "UNTIL ONE NIGHT HE CAME HOME SOBER!"

(Just as in marriage, it takes living with a problem day in and day out to gain a real understanding . . .)

Regret—*Nostalgia*

454   *As much as we would like to return to the way things were, we can't.* We are in the position of the drunk an executive friend of mine noticed sitting on the edge of a potted palm in the lobby,

crying like a baby. Because my friend had a couple himself that night and was feeling rather sorry for his fellow man, he asked the inebriated one what the trouble was. "I did a terrible thing tonight," sniffed the drunk. "I sold my wife to a guy for a bottle of Scotch."

"That is terrible," said my friend, too much under the weather to muster any real indignation. "And now that she's gone, you wish you had her back."

"That's right," said the drunk, still sniffling.

"You're sorry you sold her because you realize too late that you love her," sympathized my friend.

"NO, NO," said the drunk. "I WISH I HAD HER BACK BECAUSE I'M THIRSTY AGAIN."

(And we would like to have back . . .)

Technique—*Difficulty*

455   *Some people can find the hard way to do anything.* Of course, sometimes there is a method to their madness, as Shakespeare said.

A fellow came into a bar, ordered a martini, and put the olive in a jar. Then he ordered another martini and did the same thing. After an hour, when he was full of martinis and the jar was full of olives, he stumbled out.

"Well," said a customer, "I never saw anything quite so strange as that."

"What's so strange about it?" the bartender said. "HIS WIFE SENT HIM OUT FOR A JAR OF OLIVES."

Viewpoint—*Interpretation*

456   *It is interesting to hear the way they interpret the facts.* But there is always another point of view. It reminds me of the time my grandfather told me about when a lecturer on the evils of alcohol came to town. The temperance speaker ended his pitch with this peroration.

"Who lives in the finest house in town? The tavern keeper. Who drives the most expensive car? The tavern keeper. Whose wife wears the mink coat? The tavern keeper's wife. Now, friends, who pays for this finery? You, who drink alcoholic beverages, pay the bills!"

After the lecture a happy-looking couple came to the speaker and shook his hand. "We want to thank you," said the man, "for making up our minds for us."

"That's fine," said the speaker. "So you two have decided to become teetotalers."

"HECK, NO," the man answered. "WE'VE DECIDED TO BUY A TAVERN!"

Old Plantation

There have been too many [times when] some Southern youth is being chased through the magnolia bushes by his aunt.
—Bennett Cerf

Ambition—*Change*

457   *Some people have no ambition, no desire to get out of the rut and change their status-quo way of doing things.* I remember a black-tie dinner I went to in Charleston. It was sponsored by an organization called Sons of the Confederacy. A very proper Bostonian had been invited as a guest. As the dinner progressed, the tributes to Robert E. Lee and the virtues of the South wore the Bostonian's patience rather thin. Finally, when he could take it no longer, he got up and said, "I was born a Yankee. I have lived as a Yankee. I shall die as a Yankee."

That rather quieted the audience, until one old colonel called out, "SON, WHAT'S THE MATTER WITH YOU? HAVE YOU NO AMBITION?"

Character—*Adoption*

458   *Our honoree is no stranger to our association.* In fact, over the years we have just about adopted him. We feel about him much the way an old Southern lady I once knew felt about her kind. She was an aged woman, born and nurtured in the South. She was always endeavoring to impress upon her nephews and nieces the beauties of the South and its people. One day one of the young men spoke up.

"Auntie," he asked, "do you think that all of the virtues originated and have been preserved by the Southern people?"

"No, not all, but most of them," she replied.

"Do you think that Jesus Christ was a Southerner?" asked the young man.

The old lady hesitated a moment and then said, "HE WAS GOOD ENOUGH TO BE A SOUTHERNER."

Condition—*Mess*

459   *I admit that we face a few problems, but I will not take complete responsibility for the situation.* I sympathize with what old Senator Cotton "Ed" Smith of South Carolina said in reply to Olin Johnston during one senatorial primary. Johnston, challenging Smith, opened a campaign debate, saying, "My friends, Senator Smith is chairman of the Agricultural Committee in the United States Senate. How can he explain to the people of South Carolina why he has let his farm go to weeds, his fences break down and his buildings lay in disrepair? It's a disgrace to the people and a dishonor to the state."

Smith got up and said, "It is true, my friends, that the fields have gone to weeds, that the fences are broken down, and the buildings are in disrepair. BUT THEY'RE THERE JUST THE WAY GENERAL SHERMAN LEFT THEM."

(Of course, I don't have to tell you who won that debate, and I don't have to tell you who is responsible for the present condition. . . .)

Defeat—*Friends*

460   *One thing about defeat is that you find out who your real friends are.* In my case I am happy to say that I didn't have the same problem as a man in Selma, Alabama, who not long ago ran for sheriff and managed to get only fifty-five votes out of a total of 3,500. The next day he walked down Main Street with a gun hanging from his belt. Two townspeople approached him and said, "Hey, you weren't elected. You have no right to carry a gun." "LISTEN, FOLKS," he replied, "A MAN WITH NO MORE FRIENDS THAN I'VE GOT IN THIS COUNTY NEEDS TO CARRY A GUN."

(But I am happy to say that looking out among this audience, I have a lot of friends. . . .)

ADVICE: This story may also be used to thank a group of friends when there is no defeat involved.

Elitism—*People*

461   *I am quite content to let it be decided by the people.* There are always more soldiers than generals, more Indians than chiefs, and more consumers than captains of industry. A good example of that fact was a Southern congressman who always went by the name of Private John Allen of Tupelo, Mississippi. He always carried the title "Private" because of the way he was elected in 1884. His principal opponent was General Tucker of the Army of the Confederacy, in which Allen had served as a private. In one memorable debate the General contrasted his high rank with John Allen's.

"Yes, sir," said Allen, "I admit I was only a private. In fact, I was a sentry who stood guard over the general when he slept. And now all you fellows who were generals and had privates standing guard over you vote for General Tucker. BUT ALL YOU BOYS WHO WERE PRIVATES AND STOOD GUARD OVER THE GENERALS, VOTE FOR PRIVATE JOHN ALLEN."

They did, and he served for the next sixteen years.

Euphemism—*Introduction*

462   *The only way I can describe such an introduction is pure euphemism—you know, perfumed language.* The best way to define that is to tell you what an Alabama girl once did when she was sent to a fashionable Eastern boarding school. Now she was very self-conscious about her father being an undertaker. One day one of the girls asked her what business her father was in and, fearing the truth would damage her fashionable image, she casually answered, "OH, MY FATHER'S AN OLD SOUTHERN PLANTER."

Opportunity—*Location*

463   *There is no reason to look elsewhere.* We have the opportunity right in front of us. It recalls the words of a telegram I heard about once.

A young gentleman from an old Mississippi family was stationed outside Hartford before being sent abroad. While there, he became intensely involved with a young Hartford girl. The soldier was suddenly called to Japan and left.

The girl found out she was pregnant. Thus she wired: "Am

pregnant. Leaving immediately for your ancestral home. Please wire your family."

The Mississippi soldier wired back: STAY WHERE YOU ARE. A BASTARD HAS A BETTER CHANCE IN HARTFORD THAN A YANKEE IN MISSISSIPPI.

Practical—*Problem*

464   *I think we should treat not the symptoms but the real problem.* This was the approach of the Southern planter just after the Civil War. This gentleman of the old school found his wife in the arms of her lover and, mad with rage, killed her with his revolver. A jury of his Southern peers had brought in a verdict of justifiable homicide, and he was about to leave the courtroom a free man when the judge stopped him.

"Just a point of personal curiosity, suh, if you're willing to clear it up."

In reply the gentleman bowed.

"Why did you shoot your wife instead of her lover?"

"Suh," he replied, "I DECIDED IT WAS BETTER TO SHOOT A WOMAN ONCE THAN A DIFFERENT MAN EACH WEEK."

Preparedness—*Competition*

465   *If we don't make the necessary investments now, we are not going to be able to survive the competition.* It reminds me of the time former Governor Happy Chandler was speaking at a political rally. An admirer came over and said, "My daddy always said he'd whip anyone who spoke against the name of Happy Chandler."

Chandler replied, "Well, my granddaddy was a sergeant in Morgan's Cavalry. He always said we could have whipped those Yankees with cornstalks. TROUBLE WAS, THOSE DAMN YANKEES WOULD NEVER FIGHT WITH CORNSTALKS."

(And similarly, our good name and high sentiments are not going to be enough . . .)

Proper—*Irregular*

466   *I have been asked if we should go through outside channels to get this done.* In other words, should we try to put some hard pressure on someone? I am not quite yet prepared to do so.

It reminds me of what I heard an Episcopal rector say once. You know that in the South the aristocratic church is generally the Episcopal Church. In a Charleston church the rector was once stopped by a communicant after a sermon.

"Father, is it possible for a man to achieve salvation outside of the Episcopal church?"

The rector replied, "IT IS CONCEIVABLE THAT SUCH A POSSIBILITY MIGHT EXIST. HOWEVER, NO GENTLEMAN WOULD AVAIL HIMSELF OF IT."

(And I don't think it is proper for us yet . . .)

Self-Reliance—*Help*

467   *If we are going to succeed in this venture it will be by our own efforts.* No one is going to give us a grant or finance our activities. It reminds me of a Bostonian down in a Washington hotel nursing his own drink. He could hear at the other end of the bar a loud Texan bragging about Jim Bowie, Sam Houston, Davy Crockett and their heroic contributions to America. Finally the Bostonian had enough and went over to the bar and said, "By the way, have you ever heard of Paul Revere?" "Yes," said the Texan, "ISN'T HE THE MAN WHO RAN FOR HELP?"

COMMENT: If you are speaking in Texas, you might try telling the story as if it happened to you.

Oval and Other Offices

> *If I were forced to choose between the penitentiary and the White House for four years, I would say the penitentiary, thank you!*
> —General W. T. Sherman

Association—*Introduction*

468   *As I am supposed to respond to the head-table introduction, my thoughts are not unlike those of the alderman from the Bronx who rode in an open car down Fifth Avenue with FDR during his 1940 campaign tour.* While the onlookers cheered lustily, the old politician begged, "Mr. President, won't you tell the

driver he's going too fast?" "It's all right," Roosevelt assured him. "They all know who I am."

"I KNOW," said the hanger-on, "BUT I'D LIKE TO GIVE THEM A CHANCE TO SEE WHO'S RIDING WITH YOU."

(And similarly, I want everybody in the audience to see who I am sitting with tonight. . . .)

Action—*Delay*

469   *I, for one, am anxious to start.* I know the feeling of restlessness Winston Churchill often had. One particular time during World War II he worked far into the night without maintaining even a pretense of a schedule. In sharp contrast, General Bernard Montgomery, Britain's top army commander, retired early and kept regular hours.

Once when the two were conferring in Montgomery's headquarters, the general glanced at his watch at 10:00 P.M. and observed, with a suggestion of weariness, "It's past my bedtime. Why don't we call a halt?"

Reluctantly, Churchill agreed. In the morning when they met again the Prime Minister inquired, "Do you feel rested now?"

"No," answered Montgomery. "I have a headache. I didn't sleep enough."

"I HAVE A HEADACHE, TOO," declared Churchill. "I SLEPT TOO MUCH."

Advice—*Chief*

470   *We are beset by too many advisers telling us what we should or shouldn't do.* I am beginning to feel the way Abraham Lincoln did. He once regaled his Cabinet with the story of the king who wanted the weather foretold. He found a stable boy who could. Each day after a request the lad would directly leave the palace for a time and come back with the correct prognostication after a short while. Being curious, the king had the boy followed. He learned that the boy went to a stable and asked a donkey if the weather was to be fair. If it was, the donkey's ears would go forward. If not, they would point backward. The king, upon this discovery, made the donkey Prime Minister. But the problem was, the first thing you knew, EVERY JACKASS WANTED TO BE PRIME MINISTER.

(And sometimes it seems as if everybody thinks he knows how . . .)

Advice—*Unresponsive*

471   *The problem often is that we are so interested in making an impression on others that we fail to listen to them.* I recall the story about President Theodore Roosevelt, who, before leaving the White House in 1909, was making detailed plans for an African big-game hunt. Hearing that a famous British big-game hunter was in the country, he invited him to the White House to gain some pointers for his trip.

After a two-hour conference, during which the two were not disturbed, the Englishman came out.

"What did you tell the President?" a reporter asked.

The visitor replied, "I TOLD HIM MY NAME."

Concern—*Hypocrisy*

472   *The concern shown by some of my opponents reminds me of the remark of Woodrow Wilson at the time of his valiant fight for the League of Nations which ruined his health to a point where rumors hinted that his mind had been affected.* Senator Albert Fall, a bitter Republican foe of Wilson, called at the White House to see what truth there might be in these rumors. "Well, Mr. President" was Fall's greeting, "we all have been praying for you." Wilson answered, "WHICH WAY, SENATOR?"

(And I might question the concern . . .)

Conversion—*Recruit*

473   *We are happy to gain any new recruits to our cause.* We don't feel the way a Whig felt about the conversion of Andrew Jackson.

Andrew Jackson was as hated by Whigs as Franklin Delano Roosevelt was detested by Republicans during the New Deal days. One Whig, Tom Marshall of Nashville, described Jackson thus: "What a career has been that of Andrew Jackson! A career of success by brutal self-will. No impediment stood in his way. If he saw and fancied a pretty woman, even though she be another man's wife, he took possession of her. If he entered a horse race, he frightened or jockeyed his competitor. If he was opposed by an independent man, he crushed him. He saw the country prosperous under the Bank of the United States and shattered it from turret to foundation stone. His rule has been ruin to the people, his counsel full of calamity.

"AND NOW, WHEN HE IS APPROACHING HIS LAST HOURS, WHEN GOOD MEN ARE PRAYING THAT HE BE PUNISHED FOR HIS MISDEEDS, HE TURNS PRESBYTERIAN AND CHEATS THE DEVIL HIMSELF."

COMMENT: This historical anecdote depends on the right build-up.

Cost—*Inflation*

474   *Frankly, the rise of costs is imperiling our operation.* I now know what Lincoln meant at the church bazaar he attended once as president. Buying a bunch of violets, he gave the lady at the booth a twenty-dollar bill. She made no attempt to make change and gushed, "Oh, thank you, Mr. President."

At this Lincoln reached down from his great height and gently touched the woman's wrist and asked, "What do you call this?"

"Why, Mr. President, that is my wrist. What did you think it was?"

Replied Lincoln, "WELL, I THOUGHT IT MIGHT BE YOUR ANKLE. EVERYTHING ELSE IS SO HIGH AROUND HERE."

Criticism—*Mediocrity*

475   *All criticism has to be judged by its source.* In this case I think a detailed answer to the charges is no more called for than the time a Socialist named Denis Palings attacked Winston Churchill in the House of Commons. Palings, whose name means the high spiked fence around the House of Commons or the White House on which you can literally be "impaled," called Churchill "an exponent of dirty-dog capitalism"—"dirty dog" being a term much like "yellow dog," which we use to describe certain types of contracts or journalism.

Now Palings, who had served as a deputy Postmaster General in the Socialist government, was really not a worthy foe for the great Churchill. But Sir Winston replied in this fashion: "I will not answer the gentleman's attack. IT IS ALREADY TOO GRAPHICALLY CLEAR WHAT A DIRTY DOG DOES TO PALINGS."

Difficulty—*Progress*

476   *After the recent decline I tend to view any success, however small, as a measure of progress.* It's like the time Churchill as leader of the opposition took sick. During the illness his trained nurse heard him chuckling as she left the room bearing a bedpan. She said, "Mr. Churchill, I don't see anything funny about taking out a bedpan." Replied Churchill, "It's not you. It's myself. IT'S THE FIRST TIME A MOVEMENT I'VE BACKED HAS BEEN CARRIED OUT SINCE THE LABOUR GOVERNMENT CAME IN."

Expensive—*Temporary*

477   *As we consider the cost of such an undertaking, it might be well to recall the story of Charles de Gaulle.* The former President of France in his last years instructed an aide to purchase a monument or burial crypt suitable to the majesty of the Great Charles. After much study the aide brought back a plan for a magnificent mausoleum. de Gaulle studied it, then rejected it. "Impossible—much too costly." The aide want back to the architects. After some months the aide showed a plan for an elegant obelisk. It was brought to the attention of the president. Again de Gaulle objected. So the aide consulted the architects once more. Another plan was presented. This design showed a simple tall memorial shaft with an entombment place. de Gaulle was apparently satisfied until he asked the aide for the price. "Mr. President, it will be five hundred thousand francs."

"ISN'T THAT A BIT EXPENSIVE? I ONLY NEED IT FOR THREE DAYS."

(And similarly, I would say it is much too expensive for a project that . . .)

ADVICE: You will note the "rule of three" in the build-up.

Freedom—*Restriction*

478   *We are told we have freedom to do what we want to do in this area.* But the more I look at it, the more strings I see attached. What they give with one hand they take away with another. In other words, we are free to do what they choose. It reminds me of the American who got into an argument with a visiting Russian.

"In the United States," said the American, "I can walk right up to the gates of the White House and yell at the top of my lungs,

'To hell with Jerry Ford' and I won't be arrested."

"Well," said the Russian, "that's not so different from me. IN THE SOVIET UNION I COULD WALK RIGHT UP TO THE GATES OF THE KREMLIN AND YELL AT THE TOP OF MY LUNGS, 'TO HELL WITH JERRY FORD.' "

Gratitude—*Desperate*

479   *These days we have to be thankful for any help we get.* When you are starving you take anything you get. It's like the time George Reedy, the press secretary for LBJ, was sent to the hospital for a strict diet reduction. When his office staff sent him a big basket of flowers, Reedy acknowledged the gift with this telegram: "THANKS FOR THE FLOWERS. THEY WERE DELICIOUS."

Hybrid—*Mixture*

480   *I find the proposal an unsatisfactory compromise that satisfies none of the principals.* It recalls the comment of Sir Winston Churchill about a new member of the House of Commons by the name of Bussom. The young member was introduced to the Prime Minister.

The old man, not quite sure which of nature's more beautiful fruits was being mentioned, said, "What did you say, young man?"

"Bussom, sir. B-u-s-s-o-m."

"Curious name," replied Churchill. "NEITHER ONE THING NOR THE OTHER."

Ingratitude—*Enemy*

481   *The strange silence of our friend is all the more puzzling considering our broken record of support.* It recalls the time Franklin D. Roosevelt was asked by his secretary whether he had heard that one of his old friends was saying very nasty things about him. Roosevelt said, "Is that so? When did this happen?"

His secretary said, "Oh, the past few weeks."

Roosevelt leaned back in his chair, took a puff from the long cigarette holder, blew out a thoughtful ring or two and said, "THAT IS STRANGE. I DON'T RECALL EVER DOING HIM ANY FAVOR."

Name—*Lineage*

482   *I am sure our honoree would admit his name was no hindrance to his career.* In fact he takes pride in his family. Neverthe-

less, there are some drawbacks when you start trying to build your own record. I recall when Teddy Kennedy first ran for the Senate. His brother Jack was President. His other brother Bobby was Attorney General.

Ted told his brother he thought it best to change his name. It was too well known politically.

"But," said the President, "when you go in front of the judge to petition a name change, what name are you going to ask for?"

"Well, I think I'll keep my first name. After all, I'm used to responding to that," said Teddy. "BUT FOR THE LAST NAME I'D LIKE ROOSEVELT."

Opposition—*Criticism*

483   *Recently we have heard some pretty irrational criticism of the project.* Of course, they are perfectly free to say what they want to, even though in my opinion they look ridiculous. It reminds me of the time Prime Minister Lloyd George put forth his policy of Home Rule All Round—a federal solution for the running of Britain. In one speech Lloyd George declared, "Home rule for Ireland! Home rule for Wales! Home rule for Scotland! Yes, and home rule for England too!"

And one heckler yelled, "Aw, home rule for Hell!"

"Quite right," said Lloyd George. "LET EVERY MAN SPEAK UP FOR HIS OWN COUNTRY."

(And similarly, if these critics want to argue . . .)

Outlook—*Criticism*

484   *Whenever I hear such doom and gloom criticism I am reminded of what Abraham Lincoln once replied to Senator Wade of Ohio.* Wade, who came to the White House to see Lincoln, told the President, "You are the father of every military blunder that has been made during the war. You are on your road to hell, sir, with this government, by your obstinacy, and you are not a mile away this minute."

The President responsed, "SENATOR, THAT IS JUST ABOUT THE DISTANCE FROM THE WHITE HOUSE TO THE CAPITOL, IS IT NOT?"

Planning—*Delay*

485   *Before we count too heavily on the success of this new project, it is important to realize the preparation for it cannot be*

done overnight. I recall Winston Churchill replying to FDR when the American President thought the establishment of the UN should take at most five or six days.

In a memo to FDR Churchill wrote, "I DO NOT SEE ANY WAY OF REALIZING OUR HOPES ABOUT A WORLD ORGANIZATION IN FIVE OR SIX DAYS. AFTER ALL, EVEN THE ALMIGHTY TOOK SEVEN."

Practical—*Politician*

486   *Although I differ with the honored guest on more than a few points, I would like to say that not only do I respect him but also that I find him a man whom you can sit down and discuss things with.* I remember an occasion when Winston Churchill was flying to Cyprus to meet Archbishop Makarios for the first time. Prime Minister Churchill turned to his defense minister, Harold Macmillan, and said, "What type of man is this Makarios? Is he one of those ascetic, priestly men of the cloth concerned more with spiritual rewards or is he one of those crafty, scheming prelates concerned rather with temporal gain?"

"Regrettably, Winston," said Macmillan, "The archbishop seems to be one of the latter."

"Good," said Churchill. "THEN HE IS ONE OF MY KIND AND I CAN WORK WITH HIM."

Preference—*Team*

487   *Sometimes leadership means the choice between two difficult alternatives.* I remember President Johnson was once approached by his attorney general, Nicholas Katzenbach, on a delicate matter. "Mr. President," Katzenbach supposedly said, "I think the time has come for you to give public testimonial to J. Edgar Hoover's many years of service to his country as director of the Federal Bureau of Investigation."

Johnson looked at Katzenbach and barked, "Well, Nick, what if J. Edgar Hoover doesn't want to retire?"

"Mr. President," Katzenbach allegedly stated, "The time has come to bite the bullet and if necessary request the resignation of the director."

"Well," said LBJ, "I'D JUST AS SOON HAVE J. EDGAR INSIDE THE TENT PISSING OUT THAN OUTSIDE THE TENT PISSING IN."

(And in the situation facing us, we'd just as soon . . .)

COMMENT: Unless you're a Southerner, don't try to imitate LBJ.

The story is obviously appropriate for some audiences. You might try the story as a humorous toast to someone you have worked with. Your lead-in would mention how one in leadership position should know the individual talents of his colleagues. The bridge after the punch line should run, "Well, whatever our friend is doing we are certainly glad . . ."

Profession—*Politician*

488   *Our speaker today by his own admission is a politician.* Now I know that that has become a pretty unrespectable word lately in the wake of Watergate and other public scandals. But we must remember that Lincoln, by his own admission, was a politician and proud of it. And so was Thomas Jefferson. In fact, we may paraphrase the words of a Vatican official to former Prime Minister Golda Meir. She was on a visit in Rome to see Pope Paul. Being somewhat overwhelmed by the prospect of a Jew visiting the Pontiff of the Catholic Church, she said to a monsignor as she waited to go in for an audience, "Just think, Golda Meir, daughter of a poor Milwaukee carpenter, going in to talk with the head of Rome."

"WATCH YOUR LANGUAGE," said the papal aide. "CARPENTRY IS CONSIDERED A VERY ESTEEMED PROFESSION AROUND HERE."

Region—*Home town*

489   *When the chairman mentioned the various things this community is known for, I couldn't help but remember a story Lyndon Johnson told on himself.* In the time of his deepest unpopularity, LBJ told of an Easterner, a Republican, who was doing some business near Johnson City, Texas. One day after he finished work for the day he wandered out of his motel into the town tavern. He ordered a double martini on the rocks. When he finished it, he had enough liquid courage to express what he always wanted to. So in loud tones he stood up and yelled "Lyndon Johnson is a horse's ass!" He had no sooner sat down when a big mean hombre at the end of the bar marched down, picked him up and threw him out of the swinging doors. The next day when he was through with his business he got to wondering about the way he was treated. He knew this was the area Johnson was from, but after all it is a free country. So, teeth clenched, he went back

into the same saloon. This time he ordered two double martinis one right after the other. Thus fortified, he slowly got to his feet, looked down the length of the bar and yelled again, "Lyndon Johnson is a horse's ass!" Right away another big hombre stalked down the floor. "Wait a minute," said the Easterner. "Why can't I say the President is a horse's ass? After all, this is a free country, isn't it?"

"You don't understand, mister," said the hombre. "THIS IS HORSE COUNTRY."

Religion—*Controversy*

490   *I did not want to talk on abortion.* Anything that touches religious beliefs is too sensitive an issue. In doing this I feel that I am following Jack Kennedy's advice. You will recall that in the 1960 campaign Nixon raised as an issue Harry Truman's profanity and Kennedy wrote the former President: "Dear Mr. President, I have noted your suggestion as to where those who vote for my opponent shall go. While I understand and sympathize with your deep motivation, I think it's IMPORTANT THAT OUR SIDE REFRAIN FROM RAISING THE RELIGIOUS QUESTION."

Rhetoric—*Emptiness*

491   *There is so much empty rhetoric spilling forth out of Washington these days—empty promises, empty statements of assurance.* It reminds me of the time Senator Chauncey Depew was seated next to President William Howard Taft when the great after-dinner wit took note of Taft's obese girth in his way. Looking at his ample stomach, he said, "I hope if it's a girl Mr. Taft will name it for his charming wife."

To which Taft replied, "If it's a girl, I shall of course name it for my lovely helpmate of many years. And if it's a boy, I shall claim the father's prerogative and name it Junior. BUT IF, AS I SUSPECT, IT IS ONLY A BAG OF WIND, I SHALL NAME IT CHAUNCEY DEPEW."

Savings—*Budget*

492   *Gentlemen, I see no compelling reason to start a new project just because we have reaped an unexpected savings.* It reminds me of the time Secretary of the Treasury Henry Morgenthau was paid a visit by an old friend. His friend found him,

normally a shy and diffident man, radiating joy. "You must have struck gold, Henry," said the friend. "I did," grinned Morgenthau. "I've just figured a way to save the government three million dollars."

"Wonderful!" said his friend. "That should make FDR very happy."

"Oh," cried Morgenthau, "I can't tell FDR. ON THE STRENGTH OF THAT SAVINGS OF THREE MILLION DOLLARS, HE'D GO OUT AND SPEND SIX MILLION DOLLARS."

(And I see no reason why we have to spend . . .)

Specialists—*Common Sense*

493   *What we need in government are officials who understand people as people and not as units or statistics.* We need the type of people old Sam Rayburn was talking about when the newly installed Vice President Lyndon Johnson happened to hear talk about President Kennedy's bunch of academic experts he had assembled around him. Johnson said, "Mr. Sam, you know I never felt so inadequate as when I sit around that Cabinet table. Why, everyone seems to be a Harvard man or a Ph.D."

The Speaker replied, "LYNDON, I'D FEEL A LITTLE BETTER IF SOME OF THOSE MEN HAD RUN FOR SHERIFF IN THEIR HOME COUNTY."

Wife—*Beauty*

494   *I would like to propose a toast to our honoree's wife.* Her beauty, grace and charm need no embellishment from me. The sentiment that comes to mind is the story about the beautiful Jenny Jerome, mother of Sir Winston Churchill. Her husband, Lord Randolph Churchill, then Chancellor of the Exchequer, was standing for re-election in his borough.

Lady Churchill, canvassing for her husband, encountered a working man. She asked him for his support.

"No, certainly not," he replied. "I should never think of voting for a lazy fellow who I hear never leaves his bed until dinner time."

Lady Churchill assured him that he was wrongly informed, adding, "As I happen to be his wife, my evidence ought to be conclusive.

"Blimey, ma'am," he replied, "IF YOU WERE MY WIFE, I SHOULD NEVER WANT TO GET UP."

Parish and Pulpit

As the French say, there are three sexes—men, women and clergymen.

—Sidney Smith

495   First let me thank the chairman for the nice things he said about my various activities in the community. Sometimes we clergymen have the reputation of being "other-worldly"—of being so heavenly minded that we are of no earthly use.

496   Or as a member of my parish told me, "Father, for six days of the week you're just about invisible and then on the seventh incomprehensible."

497   Seriously, I find that most people are interested in theology. They don't mind if a sermon goes over their head—and hits someone else.

498   Actually, that's our job as ministers. When we're not comforting the afflicted, we should be afflicting the comfortable.

499   On Sunday noon, though, I can always tell if a sermon's not quite hitting any hearts, so I try a little longer; at least then I'm hitting some stomachs.

500   Thank you, thank you for such a nice turnout. It is always nice to see a hall filled. You don't have to do what I had to have inserted in the outside church sign the other week—"Come early if you want a back seat."

501   Seriously, attendance some Sundays is so low that some of my families must think that going to church is like going to a convention—they only send one delegate.

502   Really, things get so desperate that one time last year I put in the bulletin, "Come to worship; avoid the Easter rush."

Action—*Politics*

503   *I think it is about time to stop talking about the politics of the situation and get down to business.* I remember reading about the bloody "home rule" fighting some decades ago. An Irishman who had killed two policemen approached his weekly confessional with some trepidation. Summoning up his courage, he recounted in the box his dark deeds. When there was no response, he repeated his tale. Still there was no reply from the priest. So he raised his voice a little higher and asked, "Father, are ye dead?"

"DEAD I'M NOT" was the prompt reply. "I'M WAITING FOR YOU TO STOP TALKING POLITICS AND START CONFESSING YOUR SINS."

(And similarly it is time to stop talking politics and begin . . .)

Ancestry—*Heritage*

504   *As Franklin Delano Roosevelt once said, "We are all immigrants. We all have our own unique heritage."* We recall what Rabbi Stephen Wise once said when he was seated at a dinner next to a man of old New England extraction.

"One of my ancestors," said the man, "signed the Declaration of Independence."

"Yes, indeed," said the rabbi. "AND ONE OF MINE SIGNED THE TEN COMMANDMENTS."

Awareness—*Finance*

505   *I am not saying pressure should be applied, but sometimes people change their mind once the facts are fully explained.* It reminds me of a man I heard about whose dog died. Now he was a real dog lover. He missed him like a son. In his brokenheartedness he felt the only comfort he could get would be to see that the dog had a burial ceremony as elaborate and as solemn as a human being would get. He was not a churchgoer, but there was a Methodist church on his street and it was there he applied. The Methodist minister heard him out politely but could offer no hope. He said, "I am sorry, sir, but it would be blasphemy to bestow upon an animal lacking a soul the ritual we offer a human being made in the image of God. This, however, may not be the view that all men take. There is a synagogue two blocks down. Their attitude may be different."

The rabbi listened but was even more discouraging. "You must understand," he said, "that a dog is ritually unclean. While many Jews these days keep dogs as pets, I am afraid I could not lend this temple to such a ceremony. It may be different elsewhere, however. There is a Catholic church a few blocks from here, and perhaps they can help you."

Father Riley listened and shook his head. "I appreciate the sensitivity of your feeling and sympathize with you in your sorrow. A dog can be a wonderful companion. Still, it cannot be done, I'm afraid."

By now the poor man was in despair. He said, "Well, Father, if it can't be, it can't be; but it grieves me. Why, to show you how much this meant to me, I was prepared to donate three thousand dollars to any house of worship that would have taken care of my little dog for me." And as he rose to go, Father Riley lifted a hand and said, "One moment, my son. Perhaps I was hasty and did not understand all the facts of the case. DID I UNDERSTAND YOU TO SAY THAT THE DOG WAS CATHOLIC?"

COMMENT: The build-up in this story employs the familiar rule of three—Protestant, Jewish and Catholic.

Awareness—*Interference*

506   *Sometimes we are not quite aware of the effect we have on other people's lives.* I remember a certain Episcopal archbishop, getting along in years, who had been worried for some time that he would fall victim to a paralytic stroke. One evening, while playing chess with a very charming young lady, he suddenly became very agitated, and feeling that his presentiment had been fulfilled, he fell back in his chair, murmuring, "Your move."

Alarmed, his partner hurried to his side. "Are you ill?" she asked.

"It has come," the archbishop replied. "At last it has come. My right side is paralyzed."

"How can you be so sure?"

"I have been pinching my leg," said the archbishop weakly, "and there is absolutely no feeling."

"Oh," said the charming young lady, blushing profusely, "YOUR GRACE, I DO BEG YOUR PARDON, BUT IT WAS MY LEG YOU WERE PINCHING."

(And it is our lives that are being affected . . .)

Awkward—*Embarrassment*

507   *Considering my background, I find it a bit funny as well as awkward to be talking to this group at this time.* It is not as embarrassing as a Boston priest I happen to know who had volunteered to work part time in a peace group protesting the war in Vietnam. Doing some writing as well as organizing, he would scurry in and out the storefront headquarters among the motley assembly of bearded students, jean-clad coeds and young mothers with babies in papoose sacks or strollers. Once when he had to make an important phone call, he found all the phones taken. Knowing there was a pay phone in the basement, he rushed downstairs. There at a table was a bare-breasted mother who had just finished giving lunch to her baby. In great embarrassment, the girl crossed her arms over her chest and said, "I beg your pardon, Father." The priest smiled. "Don't be embarrassed, young lady. We priests may be celibate, but in our work we grow accustomed to a great many things. I assure you your condition does not trouble me in the least. In fact, you can perhaps do me a favor. COULD YOU GIVE ME A DIME FOR TWO NIPPLES?"

COMMENT: Remember the key word is "nipples." Be sure to end the punch line on it.

Bigotry—*Opposition*

508   *Some of the opposition we are encountering these days reminds me of the time a prejudiced minister one day met the great abolitionist Wendell Phillips.* It was during the time of the great abolition furor, and Wendell Phillips was accosted on a lecture tour by this minister, who hailed from the state of Kentucky, a place with very different views concerning the ideas of the abolitionists. The clergyman, who was more militant on behalf of his prejudices than on behalf of his creed, said, "You're Wendell Phillips, I believe."

"Yes, I am."

"You want to free the colored, don't you?"

"Yes, I do."

"Well, why do you preach your doctrines up north? Why don't you try coming down to Kentucky?"

Phillips replied, "You're a preacher, are you not?"

"Yes, I am, sir."

"Are you trying to save souls from hell?"

"Why, yes, sir. That is my business."

And Phillips replied, "WHY DON'T YOU GO THERE THEN?"

(And I might suggest a similar destination for those who would try to block . . .)

ADVICE: Try to use two different tones of voice for the two speakers, one of them Southern.

Communication—*Loser*

509   *Some people just don't know how to read the signs and know what spells the inevitable defeat and disaster.* An acquaintance of mine has a friend who likes to go to the races. He was having some bad luck, but below him he spied a priest giving some sort of blessing to a horse. Lo and behold in the next race the horse won. Again he saw the priest administer to another. Again the nag won. When the priest was spied giving a ritual to another horse by the name "Sureshot" the fellow raced to the window, putting his last dollar on him. Sadly the nag came in last. The fellow approached the priest and asked him what happened. "Son, are you a Catholic?"

"No."

"I THOUGHT NOT. YOU DON'T UNDERSTAND THE DIFFERENCE BETWEEN GIVING A BLESSING AND ADMINISTERING THE LAST RITES."

(And people don't understand . . .)

Contribution—*Appeal*

510   *Gentlemen, I am now going to ask for contributions.* For those of you who prefer, we are also going to circulate pledge cards. I assume we are not going to embarrass anyone by reading them or publishing them. I for one don't want to arouse the fears of some I heard about in a Pentecostal church. The pastor was concerned about one of the brothers who was carrying on with another woman. Just at collection time he announced to the congregation, "Brethren, I know that one of you has been carrying on with another man's wife. If he doesn't give twenty dollars in the collection box, I will announce his name to the congregation next Sunday." After the service he looked at the plate and saw four

twenty-dollar bills and one five-dollar bill pinned to a note which read, "IF YOU DON'T ANNOUNCE MY NAME, I'LL HAVE THE BALANCE NEXT WEEK."

Contribution—*Message*

511   *In introducing tonight's speaker, I can't help but recall a conversation I overheard from some neighborhood boys.* One boy, whose father was a salesman, was bragging that all his father had to do was to sell a car and he made fifty dollars. A second boy, whose father was a lawyer, said, "That's nothing. My father merely gives advice and he collects five hundred dollars." And the third boy, whose father was a minister, was not to be outdone and he boasted, "MY FATHER GIVES A TALK AND IT TAKES EIGHT MEN TO TAKE UP THE COLLECTION."

(Let's hope that we equally respond to his message . . .)

Contribution—*Possible*

512   *There is some way each of you can help—even if there are limits to your time and your money.* Even if you are a member of the opposite party there is some way you can play a role. I remember a popular Episcopal minister in my town who urgently needed funds to erect a new church. He sent appeal circulars far and wide, and one found its way to the study of the parish priest. He and the minister had been good friends for years, but it was unthinkable that he should subscribe to a Protestant church-building fund. However, after some thought, he wrote: "DEAR RECTOR: YOU WILL APPRECIATE THE FACT THAT I CANNOT ASSIST IN BUILDING YOUR NEW CHURCH, FINANCIALLY OR OTHERWISE. BUT I HAVE GREAT PLEASURE IN ENCLOSING MY CHECK FOR TEN DOLLARS TOWARD PULLING DOWN THE OLD ONE."

Credibility—*Cheated*

513   *There's an old saying, "Fool me once, shame on you! Fool me twice, shame on me!"* And today I find incredible what I am hearing in Washington. It reminds me of a church a friend of mine went to which runs raffles. Once a year they get three automobiles, and they put them up in front of the church, and they sell the chances. Last year they raffled off a Cadillac, a Mercury and a Plymouth. Three days after the raffle the pastor was walking down

the street, and he bumped into my friend coming out of a thirst parlor. My friend looked at him and he said, "Can you tell me who won the automobiles? Who won the Cadillac?" And the priest said, "Why, the Cardinal did; wasn't he lucky?" And my friend said, "Who won the Mercury?" "Why, the monsignor did; wasn't he lucky?" And my friend said, "Well, tell me, who won the Plymouth?" And the priest said, "Why, Father Murphy; wasn't he lucky?" And at that moment my friend started to go back in and get another drink. The priest grabbed him and said, "By the way, how many tickets did you buy?" And my friend said, "I DIDN'T BUY A DAMN ONE. WASN'T I LUCKY?"

(And I don't buy what I am hearing . . .)

Defection—*Membership*

514   *I am not unhappy with some of the defections from our midst.* In fact, it reminds me of what happened to a Presbyterian minister in my home town. One summer the Baptists and Methodists agreed to stage an evangelical revival week. The Presbyterians reluctantly agreed to go along with it. At the end of the week the ministers got together to discuss the results of the camp Bible session.

The Methodist said, "We won four new members."

The Baptist said, "We did even better. Six people became converts to the Baptist faith."

They both turned to the Presbyterian and asked him how he did.

The parson answered, "WE DID THE BEST OF ALL. WE DIDN'T ADD ANY BUT WE GOT RID OF TEN."

Dissension—*Complaining*

515   *We are calling this meeting today to clear the air and resolve some of the problems that have been dividing the membership.* We don't want to get into the position of that religious order —you know, one of those monastic orders where absolute silence is required. In this particular order speech was allowed on the feast day of the order's patron saint.

One year a monk said, "The potatoes are too lumpy."

The next year another monk said, "The peas are always overcooked."

The following year the Abbé Superior began the feast proceedings with an announcement: "BROTHERS, I'M GOING TO ASK YOU TO STOP THIS CONSTANT BICKERING."

Exclusiveness—*Cold*

516   *I'm all for maintaining our organization's traditions, but we aren't going to gain by being exclusive.* It reminds me of two dreams I heard between an Episcopalian vicar and a rabbi. The minister said to his friend, "Rabbi, I dreamed of a Jewish heaven the other night. It was very lifelike, and it seemed to me to just suit the Jewish ideal. It was a crowded tenement district with Jewish people everywhere. There were clothes on lines from every window, women on every stoop, pushcart peddlers on every corner, children playing stick ball on every street. The noise and confusion were so great that I woke up."

The rabbi said, "By a strange coincidence, Father Williams, I dreamed the other night of an Episcopalian heaven. It was very lifelike, and it seemed to me to just suit the ideal of Episcopalians. It was a neat suburb, with well-spaced English Tudor and manor houses, with beautiful lawns, each with its flower bed, with clean, wide, tree-lined streets and all was suffused in warm sunshine."

The vicar smiled. "And the people?"

"Oh," murmured the rabbi, "THERE WERE NO PEOPLE."

Experience—*Experts*

517   *I would rather leave that recommendation to those who have some experience in the field.* I like what the archbishop once said when he was visiting a small Catholic parish in a mining district of my state for the purpose of administering confirmation. During the course of the exercises he asked one nervous little girl what matrimony was.

"It is a state of terrible torment which those who enter are compelled to undergo for a time to prepare them for a brighter and better world," she said.

"No, no," remonstrated her rector. "That isn't matrimony. That's the definition of purgatory."

"LEAVE HER ALONE," said the archbishop. "MAYBE SHE IS RIGHT. WHAT DO YOU AND I KNOW ABOUT IT?"

Inevitability—*Involvement*

518   *There are those who counsel that a decline is inevitable—
that there is nothing we can do about it.* That kind of attitude
reminds me of a story about a chaplain in the Confederate Army
under Stonewall Jackson. This Reverend Mr. Dabney—a Presbyterian parson—used to preach repeatedly to the troops about
predestination. The chaplain told the soldiers not to worry about
their future or fate on the battlefield because if they were predestined to be killed, a bullet would find its mark, no matter where
they were; but on the other hand, if they were to be spared, no
bullet would hit them.

Some time later in the heat of battle, with bullets everywhere,
the parson hotfooted it over to the nearest and biggest tree. A
soldier who was behind him asked, "Father, you told us all about
predestination. Why should you be seeking shelter behind this
tree?"

"YOU DO NOT FULLY UNDERSTAND THE PRINCIPLES AND THEO-
RIES OF PREDESTINATION," the chaplain replied. "I WAS PREDES-
TINED TO RUN BEHIND THIS TREE."

(And I don't think a decline is predestined unless we . . .)
COMMENT: The source of this story is that master raconteur, Sam
    Ervin of North Carolina.

Investment—*Return*

519   *You only get as much return as you put in.* The moral of
that maxim was struck home some weeks ago when I was walking
out of church. A mother was complaining after church service that
the church was hot, the choir sang off-key, and the sermon was
terrible, whereupon her six-year-old daughter said, "MAMA, WHAT
DO YOU EXPECT FOR THE DIME YOU PUT IN THE COLLECTION
PLATE?"

Membership—*Snobbery*

520   *Our association will only thrive if we launch a campaign
to get new members and broaden our base of support.* We can't
afford to be like that fashionable city church. When a Negro tried
to join it the congregation turned him down. So he appealed to the

minister, who, in turn, suggested he take his troubles directly to the Almighty in prayer.

Some time after he received this advice, the Negro and the clergyman met on the street, and the Negro was asked how he had made out. The Negro replied, "I told the Lord I was afraid I wasn't going to be a member of this church, and He said to me, 'DON'T WORRY ABOUT THAT. I'VE BEEN TRYING FOR TWENTY YEARS TO GET INTO THAT CHURCH AND I HAVEN'T MADE IT YET.' "

Opportunities—*Prospects*

521   *I think this thing almost sells itself.* It is attractive, inexpensive, and something that everyone can find to his immense advantage. If you think about it, you'll think of as many prospects as the time Mike Ryan went to confession. Mike was asked to go to the horse races with his friend Joe Murphy, but Mike insisted he had to go to confession. "All right," said Murphy, "I'll go along and wait for you outside."

In the booth Mike said, "Father, I have committed the worst of sins." "What is it, my son?" asked the priest. "I have committed adultery," said Mike.

"Was it Mrs. Flanigan?" asked the voice.

"No, Father," said Mike.

"Was it Mrs. McGraw?"

"No, Father."

"Mrs. O'Neill?"

"No."

When Mike finally came out of the confessional, Murphy asked, "Well, did you get forgiveness for your sins?"

"NO, BUT I GOT A LOT OF GOOD LEADS."

(And if you think about it you know a lot of leads . . .)

Opportunity—*Risk*

522   *Although I am well aware of the risks involved in this undertaking, I can't help but be impressed at the great potential that can be realized.* The situation recalls an incident around the turn of the century in a Baptist church in my home town. A young soprano in the choir loft got so carried away with her solo that she fell out. Breaking her fall, the singer caught herself in the chandelier—and there she was suspended upside down. The fiery Baptist

minister was equal to the occasion. He said, "Speaking on my very sermon subject of 'Hell and Damnation,' I tell you that he who looks with lust in his heart shall be blinded."

An old codger in the front pew said, "REVEREND, WITH SUCH A GREAT OPPORTUNITY, IS IT ALL RIGHT TO RISK ONE EYE?"

Prejudice—*Sensitivity*

523   *To be without prejudice is more than just the absence of hate.* It means sensitivity to feelings. I recall the famous encounter at a London luncheon when Cardinal Vaughan, the ranking Catholic prelate, was seated next to Rabbi Adler, the late chief rabbi of England. "Now, Dr. Adler," said the Cardinal, "when may I have the pleasure of helping you to some ham?"

The rabbi replied without a pause, "AT YOUR EMINENCE'S WEDDING."

(Now this was all done in a sense of kidding, although there is a time when kidding can be very insensitive . . .)

Presentation—*Spirit*

524   *As I present this token gift to our speaker, I ask him to bear in mind the words a minister I know once said.*

The minister had gone to see an elderly parishioner and she had presented him with a jar of peaches saturated in brandy. The minister opened the jar, took a whiff, and said, "Oh, my dear, you don't know how grateful I am for this."

"Really," said the old lady? "It's only a small present."

"Yes, but it's not the present that counts," said my minister friend. "IT'S THE SPIRIT IN WHICH IT'S GIVEN."

(And similarly, it is the spirit in which . . .)

Press—*Distortion*

525   *We all know that members of the press are apt to turn the casual statement into a front-page story.* A good example was the experience of the head of the Swedish Luthern Church who came to America for a religious conference. The Swedish bishop had been warned that when he arrived in the United States he would have to watch what he said to reporters, as they were notorious for their ability to twist statements around to give them different meanings.

Vowing to be careful, the bishop was not alarmed when a sizable group of newsmen met him at the dock and one of them asked, "Do you intend to visit any nightclubs in New York?"

The bishop smiled benignly and asked, "Are there any nightclubs in New York?"

But the next morning when he opened his paper he realized what the warnings had meant, for the headlines read: "BISHOP ASKS: 'ARE THERE NIGHTCLUBS IN NEW YORK?' "

Problem—*Condition*

526   *The situation we find ourselves in reminds me in a way of how an old British admiral characterized a fat Anglican bishop.* They had been rivals at Eton. One had been captain of the cricket team, the other had been head prefect. Both hated each other, and over the years the enmity never abated despite the fact that they took separate paths in different professions. Many years later the bishop sighted his old rival, resplendent in the gold-braided navy-blue uniform of an admiral, in a London train station.

He approached the admiral and said, "I say, Conductor, when is the next train to Liverpool?"

The admiral recognized his old enemy, now rotund in his belted cassock robes.

"I DON'T KNOW, MADAM, BUT IN YOUR CONDITION I WOULDN'T THINK YOU WOULD BE TRAVELING ANYWHERE."

Provincialism—*Tolerance*

527   *Real tolerance means having the courage and imagination to look beyond our background and respect the way another would look at it.* We can't be like the Irish policeman who was a little groggy and went into a convenient church, where he soon fell asleep. The sexton aroused him and told him he was closing up.

"What do you mean?" asked the member of New York's finest. "The cathedral never closes."

"This is not the cathedral," said the sexton. "This is a Presbyterian church."

The Irish cop looked around him. On the walls were paintings of the apostles. "Isn't that Saint Luke over there?" he inquired.

"It is," said the sexton.

"And Saint Mark just beyond him?"

"Yes."

"And Saint Thomas farther on?"

"Yes."

"Tell me," he said, "SINCE WHEN DID THEY ALL BECOME PRES-
BYTERIANS?"

Question—*Role*

528   *When I was told by the chairman that I would be asked
to submit to a few questions after the talk, I hesitated.* He assured
me, however, they wouldn't be embarrassing. That is not so easy
to predict. I recall hearing about a distinguished rabbi who was
constantly asked to speak throughout New York State. His chauffeur always envied his boss for the admiration and esteem he
received when he answered what he thought were simple problems on marriage, love, and life. One day he asked to exchange
roles with the rabbi. The rabbi agreed. At the dinner, he fielded
faultlessly a few questions about raising children and young marriage. Then a young student asked, "Rabbi, do you think the onto-
logical argument for the existence of God is non-empirical?" "I am
ashamed at you for asking such a simple question of moral law,"
he answered. "WHY, THAT'S SO EASY, MY DRIVER COULD ANSWER,
AND I'M GOING TO LET HIM DO JUST THAT."

Responsibility—*Blame*

529   *I admit that we should share part of the blame for what
happened, but I am not willing for others to duck their own
responsibility.* It reminds me of the occasion of an ecumenical
conference for clergymen of various faiths. There three of the
delegates were relaxing one evening in a friendly game of poker.

Unfortunately, in their excitement they grew a little noisy, and
the hotel detective entered the room, confiscated the chips and
cards, and held them for arrest under the strict anti-gambling
statutes of the town in which the conference was being held.

The magistrate before whom they appeared was very embarrassed. "Gentlemen," he said, "I would rather this had not happened, but there seems to be evidence of a misdemeanor, and
since you have been arrested, I cannot dismiss the case without
some investigation. Nevertheless, in view of your profession, I feel

I can trust you to tell the truth. I will ask for no evidence other than your bare words. If each of you can tell me that you were not gambling, that would be sufficient for me and I will release you."
Father Flanagan replied, "Your Honor, surely it is important to be certain that we define what we mean by gambling. In a narrow but entirely valid sense what we describe as gambling is only truly so if there is a desire to win money, rather than merely to enjoy the suspense of the fall of cards. In addition we might define gambling as the situation where the loss of money would be harmful, as otherwise such loss might merely be viewed as a variable admission fee."

"I understand," interrupted the magistrate. "I will take it, then, that you, Father Flanagan, were not gambling by your definition of the word. And you, Dr. Osborne?"

The minister said, "I entirely agree with my colleague, Your Honor. Further, I might add that gambling is gambling only if there are stakes involved. Admittedly, there was money on the table, but it remains to be determined whether this money would would eventually have found its way into the possession of an individual not its owner at the start of the game, or if, in fact, it was merely being used as a convenient marker that would indicate the progress and direction of successive—"

"Yes, yes," interrupted the magistrate again. "I will accept that as satisfactory indication that you were not gambling, Dr. Osborne. And now you, Rabbi Greenberg. Were you gambling?"

The pious rabbi's eyebrows shot upward. "WITH WHOM, YOUR HONOR?"

Sales—*Responsibility*

530   *In response to your question, let me say that I do not make policy.* I am like the minister who was sitting next to a little old lady who was taking her first airplane ride, and she was a little jittery, as anybody is under those circumstances. As luck would have it, they got into a violent storm. The plane just tossed around. Finally she got a little panicked and she turned to the clergyman and said, "Father, you are a man of God. Can't you do something about this?" He said, "MADAM, I AM IN SALES, NOT MANAGEMENT."

(And similarly, I am not in management . . .)

Salesmanship—*Message*

531 *Gentlemen, our problem is a simple one—get our message to the people.* The commitment and drive we need is best exemplified by a young Catholic friend of mine, a Mary Flaherty.

Mary was in love with John and he in love with her, but Mary confided to her mother, "John is a Baptist and very much against marrying a Catholic." Mary was all in tears.

"No, Mary," said her mother, "let's use some salesmanship about this. John's an intelligent lad. You just sit down and talk to him about our great church. Explain to him about its long history, about its being the first among the Christian religions. Tell him about the great beliefs and the great martyrs and the noble saints and the wonderful cathedrals and the beauty of the service. Now, go out and give him a good selling job."

Mary dried her eyes and went out to see him. After the next date Mary could be heard sobbing. Mother, comforting her, asked, "What's the matter? Didn't you sell him?"

"SELL HIM," sobbed Mary. "I OVERSOLD HIM. HE WANTS TO BECOME A PRIEST."

(Well, we won't mind if we can make some true believers . . .)

ADVICE: The build-up is important—martyrs, saints, cathedrals, etc. This is good as a pep talk at a convention meeting.

Speculation—*Gossip*

532 *I hope you will indulge me in a little speculation—based as it often is on a combination of projected facts, hearsay, and rumor.* Discussions like this remind me of the three chaplains during the hours before D-Day when they sat together and solemnly discussed the possibility of dying. "It makes one feel the need to confess," said the Catholic chaplain. "I must admit to a terrible impulse to drink. Oh, I fight it, but it is my besetting sin and too often I imbibe too much."

"Well," said the Protestant chaplain, "I don't have a problem with liquor, but I must own up to a terrible impulse toward women. I fight it desperately, but every once in a while I am tempted and I fall."

After that, there was a pause, and finally both turned to the Jewish chaplain and one said, "And you, Chaplain Cohen, are you troubled with a besetting sin, too?"

The Jewish chaplain sighed and said, "I'M AFRAID SO. I HAVE THIS TERRIBLE, IRRESISTIBLE IMPULSE TO GOSSIP."

COMMENT: Note the rule of three in the build-up.

Speech—*Plagiarism*

533   *I can't claim that this idea is original with me.* In fact, I feel somewhat like the minister I once knew who so thoroughly bored the members of his congregation that they finally asked him to leave.

"Give me one more chance," he pleaded.

The congregation turned out in force the next Sunday and heard him deliver, to their surprise and delight, the most inspired sermon heard for years.

After the service, everyone shook his hand warmly. One man, an elder of the church, said, "You must stay, with an increase in salary, of course."

The minister accepted. Then the elder said, "That was the greatest sermon I have ever heard. But tell me one thing. As you began to speak you raised two fingers of your left hand, at the end two fingers of your right hand. What was the significance of those gestures?"

"THOSE," answered the minister, "WERE THE QUOTATION MARKS."

Subject—*Knowledge*

534   *We have been hearing some beautiful rhetoric on the problem.* But my reaction is not unlike that of the two ladies in Boston who heard the bishop give a rousing sermon on the beauties of married life. The ladies left the church feeling uplifted and contented. "'Twas a fine sermon His Reverence gave us this morning," observed one. "That it was," agreed the other, "AND I WISH I KNEW AS LITTLE ABOUT THE MATTER AS HE DOES."

Substitute—*Speech*

535   *I don't mind being a substitute for someone else as long as I don't have to worry about being someone else.* There is sometimes doubt about a substitute role. It reminds me of the vicar out

in a remote corner of England. One Friday he telephoned his bishop, "MY WIFE JUST PASSED AWAY. PLEASE DISPATCH A SUBSTI-TUTE FOR THE WEEKEND."

Support—*Attendance*

536   *Recently when I had just finished a speech, I was asked by someone in the audience what difference did it make if she wrote a letter expressing support.* The answer is, of course, that it does make a difference—that a few letters are representative of a lot of sentiment. But there is another reason for writing. That reason is best expressed by an old man I once knew in my home town. Every Sunday morning he used to walk to the church of his choice. He was deaf, so he could not hear a word of the sermon, or the music of the choir, or the hymns sung by the congregation. One day his nephew asked him, "Why do you spend your Sundays in that church when you can't hear a word?" He replied, "I WANT MY NEIGHBORS TO KNOW WHICH SIDE I'M ON."

(So it's up to you to let everyone know which side . . .)

Unpersuadable—*Insensitive*

537   *Our problem is not the merit of our case but getting people to listen, particularly when they are not really interested.* It re-minds me of our agnostic in my town who often got into discus-sions with our minister. After much urging, the agnostic finally agreed to attend a church service the following Sunday. The min-ister prepared a masterly discourse to appeal especially to his friend's appreciation of logic.

When the two met the next day the agnostic conceded, "I'll say this for your Sunday sermon, it kept me awake until the early hours of the morning."

The clergyman beamed. "I am happy that I succeeded in mak-ing you doubt the wisdom of your convictions."

"OH," said the other, "IT WASN'T THAT. YOU SEE, WHEN I NAP IN THE DAYTIME I CAN'T SLEEP AT NIGHT."

Press Gallery

*In the old days men had the rack. Now they
have the press.*

—Oscar Wilde

538   As I heard my introduction as a member of the press, I
thought of Oscar Wilde's distinction between a writer and a reporter. He said the former is unread and the latter unreadable.

539   Seriously, though, the problem with too many reporters is
that they don't follow the guidelines handed down by that great
publisher, James Gordon Bennett. He said, "So many a good story
is ruined by overreliance on truth."

540   Really, that's the great thing about being a reporter instead of a novelist or a poet. When you feel lost for words or
lacking in imagination you can always write the facts.

541   Of course, I know that some complain that we don't always
get our facts straight. We make our share of mistakes—just like any
other profession—but where doctors bury their mistakes, lawyers
hang theirs, ours go on the front page.

542   One advantage about being on the front page is that our
contributions do not go unrecognized. The great men of our time
recognize the role we reporters play in society. As Oscar Wilde
once wrote, "In the old days men had the rack. Now they have the
press." Or as the theologian Kierkegaard said, "If Christ came
back, he wouldn't attack the high priests but the low journalists."
Or as Winston Churchill said, "The problem with America is that
their toilet paper is too thin and their newspapers too fat."

Apology—*Retraction*

543   *Some of you might have caught the story about me in the
recent papers.* The headline was a little misleading. When I called
the paper on it, they were most sympathetic and promised the
next time they would call me directly before they published any
more articles about me. My feelings reminded me of the time a

British MP had read an insulting editorial about himself published in Lord Beaverbrook's *Daily Express*. A few days later he met Beaverbrook in the men's room of a London club. "Dear fellow," said Beaverbrook as he rinsed his hands, "I've been thinking things over, and I feel that the editorial was unjustified. I apologize."

The MP replied, "Beaverbrook, I accept your apology. BUT NEXT TIME WHY DON'T YOU INSULT ME IN THE MEN'S ROOM AND THEN APOLOGIZE IN THE NEWSPAPER?"

Exaggeration—*Truth*

544   *Sometimes I think the attitude of the press covering a story is like the telegram the New York tabloid editor sent to his correspondent in Havana covering the Spanish-American War.* It was the time of a great rivalry in sensationalism between the New York *World* and the *Morning Journal*. After the battle of San Juan, the editor of the *World* sent a telegram to his on-the-spot reporter. It read: "SEND ALL THE DETAILS. NEVER MIND THE FACTS."

(Similarly, I hope I won't bore the audience if I review the actual facts . . .)

Observation—*Stupidity*

545   *Some people can't even take notice of a significant development when it's right in front of them.* It recalls to me the time Charles S. Dana, editor of the New York *Sun*, tried out a new man on his staff as a reporter. Dana said, "Young man, the way you handle the next assignment will tell me whether you have it in you to become a reporter."

The young man listened, then sat in the outer office waiting. When a notice came in for a wedding, he was sent to cover it. Three hours later, as the paper was going to press, Dana called for his report.

The young chap said, "SIR, I HAVE NO REPORT. I WENT TO THE CHURCH, BUT THERE WAS NO WEDDING. THE GROOM DIDN'T SHOW UP."

(Similarly, most people can't see . . .)

Occasion—*Timeliness*

546   *The saying goes that there is a time "to fish or cut bait."* You can't keep waiting forever for that ideal moment. I recall the

experience of an editor of an upstate small-town newspaper. For years he had cherished a set of old-fashioned wooden scarhead type of some sixty-point size. On more than one occasion his assistants had tried to induce him to use it, but he always firmly vetoed the idea.

One summer the old man went away for a short fishing trip. In his absence a cyclone struck the town, tore the steeple off the church, unroofed several houses, sucked a couple of wells dry, and scattered a few barns around. No bigger catastrophe had hit the town in years. So, figuring "Now's our chance," his assistants got down the sixty-point type from the shelf and set up a sensational front-page headline with it.

Two days later the editor came storming into the office. "Great Jehosaphat!" he shouted. "What d'ye mean by taking down that type for a cyclone? ALL THESE YEARS I'VE BEEN SAVIN' THAT TYPE FOR THE SECOND COMING OF CHRIST."

(And today I don't think it's necessary to wait any longer . . .)

Quote—*Interview*

547   *As I look out in the audience, I see many of my friends in the Fourth Estate poised with pencil and notebook.* I suppose I should do what Calvin Coolidge did in one of his rare press conferences. The first reporter asked him, "Do you have any comment about tariffs, Mr. President?"

"No," Coolidge replied.

And the second reporter asked, "Do you have any comment about the farm bill?"

"No," Coolidge replied.

A third reporter asked, "Do you have any comment about the naval appropriation?"

"No," Coolidge replied.

As the reporters were leaving, Coolidge shouted to them, "AND DON'T QUOTE ME!"

Relationship—*Message*

548   *As I note the attendance of some of my good friends of the Fourth Estate in the audience, I want to say that my relationship with them has always been good—based on mutual respect.* I can say that I never had the opportunity for a relationship that a state

senator from Philadelphia once tried to establish. Herb McGlinchey, a Philadelphia ward leader, was once followed around by a reporter who was trying to write a feature story on how a busy politician spends his day. Now McGlinchey's drinking abilities were legendary. By the end of the day McGlinchey was still fresh and dapper, but the reporter who followed McGlinchey back to the bar at the forty-second ward clubhouse was soaked to the gills and was taking a nap sitting at the bar with his head resting on his folded arms.

McGlinchey was whispering into his ear, "McGlinchey's the greatest. McGlinchey's terrific."

"What are you doing, Herb?" an aide asked.

"Shut up," McGlinchey is reported to have said. "I'M TALKING TO HIS SUBCONSCIOUS. WE'RE GOING TO OWN THIS GUY."

Salary—*Discontinuance*

549   *Unless these conditions are changed, we will be forced to discontinue operations.* It is becoming a situation which John Kiernan once described when he was the sports columnist of the New York *Times.* Feeling the need for more money but wanting to be tactful about it, Kiernan went to his employer, Adolph Ochs, and said respectfully, "Mr. Ochs, WORKING FOR THE TIMES IS A LUXURY I CAN NO LONGER AFFORD."

He got the raise.

Publisher's Row

An editor is one who separates the wheat from the chaff and prints the chaff.
—Adlai Stevenson

550   As an author it is nice to hear such critical acclaim in your own backyard. I can assure you that's not the case in my own household, where I work most of the time. My wife says, "I married you for better or for worse—but not for lunch."

551 Really, my wife is most sympathetic. If I could only get her to understand that an author is working when he is staring out the window.

552 As I listened to your chairman's generous appraisal of my recent book I thought of the review given my first real literary effort. It was a thesis in college, and my professor handed it back with a note quoting Samuel Johnson. "This paper is both good and original, but the part that is good is not original and the part that is original is not good."

553 Then after that I had to put up with a run of rejection slips from publishers. In fact one publisher was so negative that I finally wrote back, "Your rejection slip does not meet our editorial needs."

554 I suppose I really should appreciate the introduction. The chairman is an old friend and he did give me a warm appraisal of my recent work. The only thing is, I can't help but remember what Dorothy Parker once wrote—that an author hasn't really made it until he no longer shows his books to his friends.

555 Well, I do show my books to those of my friends who have insight and sensitivity. Let me just quote from a letter I recently received. "You are the finest young writer in America today. You combine the power of Hemingway and the style of Updike with the wit of Roth. Furthermore, you are the most sensitive and appreciative man I've ever known." Signed "Mother."

556 Since this is my first novel, perhaps some of you missed some of the critics' reviews of my book. Several, for example, questioned my treatment of the character they considered the hero. They didn't understand that in a first novel the real hero is always the publisher.

557 Seriously, I know that particulary in a first novel biblio-philes want a first edition. But I'm more interested in the tenth.

558 You know, I didn't think I would enjoy speaking, but then I learned the great advantage it has over writing. As an author, you can always be shut up by closing the book.

559 But then I remember what Robert Benchley said of an editor trying to speak: "You're better sitting on your ass than being an ass on your feet."

560   As Anatole France once said, "A writer is rarely so well inspired as when he talks about himself."

561   Earlier someone asked me the secret of making a successful novel. I replied, "I always start writing with clean paper and a dirty mind."

562   Actually, like every other writer, I can't just sit down and type away. I can run hot and cold. But like someone wrote of John Updike, "When I'm good, I'm very very good, and when I'm bad, I'm lurid."

563   Seriously, to be really compelled to write I have to be inspired by the muse, which, as Cole Porter once said, means a telephone call from a producer or publisher.

564   When you made some kind comparisons in your introduction, I began to think that nearly all the literary giants are dead —Hemingway, Faulkner, O'Hara, Steinbeck—and I'm not feeling so well myself.

565   Really, you know writing is a great profession. I really like my work. I can sit and gaze at it for hours.

Assessment—*Mediocrity*

566   *I don't think we have to wait until the end of this whole operation before giving our assessment.* The record so far is indication enough. It is like the reply the famous editor, George Horace Lorimer, was said to have given when he sent back a manuscript to an author-hopeful.

She had written, "Last week you rejected my story. I know you did not read it, for, as a test, I pasted together pages 15, 16, 17 and 18 and the manuscript came back with the pages still fastened. You are a fraud. You reject stories you haven't even read."

Lorimer wrote, "DEAR MADAM: AT BREAKFAST WHEN I OPEN AN EGG, I DON'T HAVE TO EAT THE WHOLE EGG TO DISCOVER IT IS BAD."

Incredible—*Fiction*

567   *The situation, I know, sounds incredible.* I am reminded of the story my college bookstore owner, Ray Washburne, told me.

A very dignified lady entered his bookshop in Williamstown,

Massachusetts, and announced that she was looking for something "new and good" to read. Washburne suggested Pat Frank's *Mr. Adam.* "What's it about?" she asked. "Well," said Washburne, "an atomic bomb suddenly renders every male in the world completely sterile—every one but a single fortunate chap, that is, who was working deep in a mine shaft at the time of the explosion and who emerges with his powers unimpaired. You can imagine the spot in which he finds himself then!" "It sounds very interesting," agreed the dignified lady. "TELL ME, IS IT FICTION OR NON-FICTION?"

(Well, it is not fiction that . . .)

Mistake—*Repeat*

568   *You would think we would learn.* But sometimes we seem not to profit from our mistakes but to proliferate them. It reminds me of the wife of a successful novelist who got a divorce after ten years of marriage, saying writers were too temperamental and unpredictable and she just could not put up any longer with his moods and strange ways. Of course, what did she do next but fall in love with still another famous author.

The ex-husband read of the wedding and sent his former bride this cable: "HEARTIEST CONGRATULATIONS AND BEST WISHES. (SIGNED) FRYING PAN."

Rejection—*Talent*

569   *When I think of natural talent I recall the time a woman submitted several chapters and an outline of a romantic novel to a publisher and awaited word in vain from the editor for several weeks.* Finally she wired, "Please report on my story immediately as I have other irons in the fire." An answering wire—collect—read, "WE HAVE CONSIDERED YOUR STORY AND ADVISE YOU TO PUT IT IN WITH THE OTHER IRONS."

(Well, fortunately, in this case we are dealing with unusual talent . . .)

Service—*Patience*

570   *Anyone in that kind of position has to like people and hearing their complaints and handling their problems.* Not ev-

eryone is up to that type of dedication. I recall hearing about William Faulkner quitting his job as postmaster in Oxford, Mississippi.

Said Faulkner, "I COULDN'T STAND FOR ONE MINUTE LONGER BEING AT THE BECK AND CALL OF EVERY SONOFA-BITCH JUST BECAUSE HE HAD THREE CENTS IN HIS POCKET."

Titles—*Packaging*

571   *Of course, so much depends on how we package this idea.* It's like marketing a book these days where more creativity seems to go in developing the title than the story. Publishers follow the Maugham rule, which comes from the time a young writer who had just completed his first work approached Somerset Maugham and asked, "Mr. Maugham, I've just written a novel but have been unable to come up with an intriguing title. Your books have such wonderful titles—*Cakes and Ale, The Razor's Edge.* Could you help me with my title by reading the book?"

"There is no necessity for reading your book," replied Maugham. "Are there drums in it?"

"No, it's not that kind of a story. You see, it deals with . . ." "Are there any bugles in it?" "No, certainly not" was the response. "Well then," replied the famous author, "CALL IT 'NO DRUMS, NO BUGLES.'"

Unenthusiastic—*Mediocrity*

572   *I can't get too enthusiastic about this proposal.* At best it will have limited appeal. In fact, the only thing I can say on its behalf is what Abraham Lincoln said once when a man secured an audience at the White House to show the President a book he wrote.

Lincoln's comment would apply to many things, including the proposal in question: "FOR THE SORT OF PEOPLE WHO LIKE THIS SORT OF THING, THIS IS THE SORT OF THING THAT SORT OF PEOPLE WILL LIKE."

Research Lab

What is called science today consists of a haphazard heap of information, united by nothing.

—Leo Tolstoy

573   I thank the chairman. He was certainly generous in attributing so much progress to those in my and other allied fields. Modern technology is wonderful—it enables man to gain control over everything, except technology.

574   Really, though, the advances in automation are awesome —and they have been ever since the invention of Frankenstein.

575   It is gratifying to hear all those nice things about my work. We old scientists are like generals. We don't fade away, though. We just fail to react.

576   Really, though, I love my work. How else could one be considered doing something when he doesn't know what he is doing?

577   That's the great thing about us (scientists) (planners) researchers. We are the only ones who can go directly from an unwarranted assumption to a preconceived conclusion.

Discovery—*Technique*

578   *The most that can be said about our recent unhappy experience is that we have at least learned something.* We are like the noted botanist who gave instructions for a dish of mushrooms, which he had gathered himself, to be cooked for dinner expressly for his wife.

The latter, who was particularly fond of them, was highly delighted at her husband's thoughtfulness and thanked him with much gusto. At breakfast next morning he greeted her anxiously.

"Sleep all right?" he inquired.

"Splendidly," she answered.

"Not sick at all—no pains?"

"Why, of course not, dear," she responded in surprise.

"EUREKA," yelled the professor. "I'VE DISCOVERED ANOTHER MUSHROOM SPECIES THAT ISN'T POISONOUS!"

Gratitude—*Worthwhile*

579   *I don't know how we can thank the honoree for all he has done.* I am constantly amazed at the amount of time and activity he has put in. In that sense I express almost the same words as a man I heard about who was in an incident in a bar. He had turned to a woman just passing and said, "Excuse me, Miss, do you happen to have the time?"

In a screaming voice she responded, "How dare you make such a proposition to me?"

The man snapped to attention in surprise and was uncomfortably aware that every pair of eyes in the place had turned in their direction. He mumbled, "I just asked the time, Miss."

In a voice even louder, the woman yelled, "I'll call the police if you say another word!"

Grabbing his drink and embarrassed very nearly to death, the man hastened to the far end of the room and huddled at a table wondering how soon he could sneak out the door.

Not more than half a minute had passed when the woman joined him. In a quiet voice she said, "I am terribly sorry, sir, to have embarrassed you, but I am a psychology student at the university and I am writing a thesis on the reaction of human beings to sudden shocking statements."

The man stared at her for three seconds, then he leaned back and roared, "YOU'LL DO ALL THAT FOR ME ALL NIGHT FOR JUST FIVE DOLLARS?"

Internationalism—*Globalism*

580   *Modern communications have made the world into a neighborhood—what Marshall McLuhan calls "the global village."* The exploration of the moon has also reminded all countries of their common global destiny. An early hint to explorers of this newer and smaller world was found in the Antarctic explorations some years ago. Rear Admiral George Dufek, one of the first Americans actually to reach the South Pole, was examining the

icecapped landscape with Father Linehan, a geophysicist from Boston College. It was lunchtime, and in his provisions he found a roast-beef sandwich and offered it to Father Linehan, who said, "No, thank you—it's Friday, you know."

The undaunted admiral replied, "BUT, FATHER, IN ANTARCTICA ALL YOU HAVE TO DO IS STEP TWENTY PACES TO THE LEFT AND IT'LL BE THURSDAY."

Mistake—*Computers*

581   *I have always believed that decisions involving people require human insight as well as statistical input.* I recall one exchange former Defense Secretary Robert McNamara had with Congressman Ed Hébert.

The brilliance of Robert McNamara amounted almost to arrogance. What angered congressmen was his total reliance on the computer and his refusal to believe that his mathematically based decisions could be wrong. He was once summoned to appear before the House Armed Services Committee to explain why he had ordered the closing of 672 Army bases. Could he have made a mistake in the case of one or two? asked Representative Edward Hébert.

"No," said McNamara emphatically. Replied an exasperated Hébert, "SIX HUNDRED AND SEVENTY-TWO DECISIONS AND NOT A SINGLE MISTAKE? YOU'RE BETTER THAN JESUS CHRIST. HE HAD ONLY TWELVE DECISIONS TO MAKE AND HE BLEW ONE OF THEM."

Specialization—*Problem*

582   *Things are getting so specialized today that you get an answer to a problem only by referral.* I recall hearing about an avarian—that is, an expert on birds—who walked into a bar and found a customer asking the bartender how he could tell the difference between a male and a female love bird he had bought his wife. His wife was bugging him about it.

"Excuse me," said the avarian, "I'm an expert on birds. You get a pile of worms and separate them into male and female worms. The male love bird will take the female worms and the female will take the male worms."

Satisfied, the customer left. A bit later he called to ask a question. The avarian replied, "OH, FOR THAT YOU WOULD HAVE TO FIND AN EXPERT ON WORMS."

(I don't know where the expert is on the problem we have, but . . .)

Technocracy—*Planning*

583   *In this computer age we have learned that not all the statistical programming is enough without human decision.* For example, not long ago the passengers in a new ultra-modern supersonic transport plane had just settled back after take-off when they heard a voice from the loudspeaker.

"Good afternoon, ladies and gentlemen, this is a computerized flight. This plane operates electronically in a plotted flight pattern. Every detail in planning has been thoroughly tested. There is nothing to worry about. EVERYTHING WILL BE ALL RIGHT . . . ALL RIGHT . . . ALL RIGHT . . ."

(And everything will not be all right with us unless we . . .)

ADVICE: Try to simulate the monotone voice of the captain's recorded voice.

Tea Party

Woman once made equal to man becomes his superior.

—Plato

584   With that introduction you have made me feel like a real queen—Queen Victoria—of whom Disraeli said, "Don't just speak about her, lay it on with a trowel."

585   I was hoping that you would dispense with an introduction, but I guess you felt with a woman speaking she would need all the introduction she could get.

586   You remember what Sam Johnson said—a woman speaking is like a dog walking on his hind legs. You don't expect her to do it well; you're just lucky if she can do it at all.

587   I thank you for that introduction. You're almost as generous as my husband. He's a great booster. He says, "Dear, you're at home in so many fields: you're at home in environment, you're at

home in economics, you're at home in urban affairs, you're at home in social work, in fact you're at home in everything but home."

588 Well, actually, I guess I'm not at home as much as I would like. I'm on the road too much—the road to the cleaners, the market, and the drugstore.

589 In fact it seems as if we women spend all our lives delivering—obstetrically once and the car pool forever after.

590 I thank the chairman for his remarks about my recent efforts. In the last few weeks I have been very busy. It seems as if I've been all over the state campaigning for this amendment. Last night I returned home and told my husband I think it looks like we're going to sweep the state. "Good, but why don't you start with the kitchen?"

591 I guess my husband is no different from others. He doesn't like it if you rush home from a meeting and hand him one of those TV dinners. But that's unfair. I spoil him. You should see the good cake I give him. It literally melts in his mouth—while it's defrosting.

592 Seriously, I'm no Women's Libber. I'm not going to picket for equal pay. Just give me for housework the minimum wage by the hour.

593 You know, really, I like marriage. In fact, I can get sentimental about it. It's just that I didn't know that when my husband carried me across the threshold he was taking me to work.

594 It's not that I find housework demeaning. I'll gladly do the woman's work in the home—be a cook, seamstress, decorator—if I can just get my husband to be the repairman, the electrician . . .

595 You know, home is a place where everything sooner or later wears out—including your nerves.

Husband—*Details*

596 *Criticism is nothing new to me. As a husband you get used to that pretty early.* The best example of such conjugal criticism

came some years ago in Washington when my wife and I drove in a taxi down Pennsylvania Avenue one wintry night hoping to see the White House lit up. President Johnson was in his periodical economy drive, and he had all of the mansion's lights doused. My wife took it as a personal affront—and proof that men can't tell true economy from false.

As we came down Pennsylvania Avenue the White House was barely visible that blizzardy night, but not so the garden fountains. Dancing in blazing floodlights, they rose high and splashed merrily down again in complete denial of both winter and the President's concern for thrift.

"He's in Texas this week, isn't he?" asked my wife.

"Yes," I said.

"Just like a man," she sniffed. "HE TURNS OUT ALL THE LIGHTS AND THEN GOES OFF AND LEAVES THE WATER RUNNING!"

Husband—*Role*

597   *You women can do your part in building support even if it is only in your own neighborhood and your own home.* You must never underestimate your role there. A friend of mine has a son studying drama at Northwestern. He came home for the summer vacation and got a job with a summer theater. He reported triumphantly, "I've snagged my first part! Next week I'm going to play a husband who's been married for thirty years!" "Good start," approved his father. "Just you stick to it, AND YOU'LL GET A SPEAKING PART YET!"

Practical—*Basics*

598   *What we are really looking for when we select a president of this organization is not so much a charming front man or a great speaker but someone who can handle the basic everyday problems.* It reminds me of a morning television program I saw once where three women contestants were interviewed by the emcee. The emcee asked each of them what kind of man they'd prefer being shipwrecked with on a desert island.

"I'd want a fellow who was a wonderful conversationalist," said the first.

"That would be nice," said the second, "but I'd rather have a guy who knew how to hunt and could cook the things he caught."

The third smiled and said, "I'D SETTLE FOR A GOOD OBSTETRI-CIAN."

Priority—*Money*

599   *I think the first thing is to find out if we really know what we want.* We don't want to be like that deacon who was against getting a chandelier for the church. The women of the auxiliary of this Evangelical Baptist church had declared themselves in favor of installing a chandelier. After they had proposed it, a church conference was held to discuss the matter.

An old deacon, representing a faction that opposed this proposal, said in opposition, "We are against this here chandelier proposition for three reasons. In the first place we couldn't even order one—nobody would know how to spell it! And then even if we got it, there ain't anybody in our congregation that could play it. AND THIRD, IF WE'VE GOT A SUM OF MONEY TO LAY OUT, WE THINK WHAT THIS CHURCH NEEDS IS A NEW LAMP."

Salesmanship—*Solicitation*

600   *It is not enough to communicate our message.* We must identify with those interested and follow up with a request. We don't want to make the same mistake the members of the Methodist women's church circle in a Pennsylvania sin town made some years ago. People were disturbed because a widowed church member and her three small daughters were staying away from services. Finding the reason to be a lack of suitable clothes, the ladies' group corrected the situation in a generous manner. When the little girls still failed to appear at Sunday school, some of the ladies called to inquire about their absence. The mother thanked them sweetly for the clothing and explained, "THE GIRLS LOOKED SO NICE I SENT THEM TO THE PRESBYTERIAN CHURCH."

(And so after we make this effort, we don't want to waste our work by not following up . . .)

Stupidity—*Opposition*

601   *If the men have that idea of us they are not only all wet; they're saturated.* It is like the time some men hecklers tried to taunt Nancy Astor as the fashionable lady member of Parliament was propounding some of her proposals on women's rights.

A heckler in the back, referring to the necklace and many bracelets the bejeweled Lady Astor wore, jibed, "You have enough brass on you, Lady Astor, to make a kettle."

"And," replied Lady Astor, "YOU HAVE ENOUGH WATER IN YOUR HEAD TO FILL IT."

Women—*Difference*

602   *One of the earliest chapters in the history of the Women's Liberation movement came in the session of the French Chamber of Deputies in the 1920s.* It was a debate on whether or not French women were to be given the right to vote. A Socialist deputy ended an impassioned speech by saying, "It is a disgrace that the wonderful women of France, famous throughout the world for their chic, intelligence, and beauty should not have equal rights with men. After all, in this modern world there's very little difference between French men and French women."

At this point a little deputy in back of the room jumped to his feet and cried, "VIVE LA DIFFERENCE!"

Women—*Extracurricular*

603   *Burning bras is one thing but tearing down false distinctions is another.* A woman in a store in my town confronted the manager and asked why one of her colleagues, who had come after she and who did much the same sort of work, had a higher paycheck.

The store manager said, "But you've got to remember that she is married and has five kids."

And she replied, "I DIDN'T KNOW WE GOT PAID ON WHAT WE PRODUCED IN OUR OFF HOURS."

Women—*Faith*

604   *Whatever happens, I am sure we will prevail as long as we have faith such as the women had who were fighting for the women's vote.* I recall back in the days before World War I, two suffragettes had been placed in jail for willfully interfering with the police in the performance of their duty.

One of the two, a young girl who was involved in her very first encounter, was terribly frightened and could barely stifle her tears.

The other, a veteran of dozens of street demonstrations in favor of the great cause, said, "DON'T BE AFRAID. JUST HAVE FAITH IN GOD. *SHE* WILL PROTECT US."

Women—*Family*

605   *When we think of women's growing power in politics, I am reminded of the time a hostile reporter once accosted Winston Churchill immediately after an election in which the latter had retained his seat in Parliament.* The reporter said with a sneer, "I presume we may expect you to continue to be subservient to the powerful interests that control your vote."

To which Churchill replied, "I'LL THANK YOU TO KEEP MY WIFE'S NAME OUT OF THIS."

Women—*Fortitude*

606   *I'd like to pay tribute to the women's auxiliary in the same way Joseph Choate, ambassador to the Court of St. James's, once did.* He was called to make a toast to the Pilgrim Fathers at the annual Pilgrim dinner in London.

He paid tribute to those courageous Massachusetts settlers who braved the Indian threat, withstood the rigors of New England winters, and suffered the hardships of hunger and privation in founding the Plymouth colony.

"BUT LET US GIVE THOUGHT," he added, "TO THE PILGRIM MOTHERS WHO NOT ONLY HAD TO ENDURE EVERYTHING THE PILGRIM FATHERS ENDURED, BUT, MARK THIS, THEY ALSO HAD TO ENDURE THE PILGRIM FATHERS."

Women—*Politics*

607   *I regard the likelihood of my being in that position very dubiously.* It is like the time Senator Margaret Chase Smith was a guest speaker at the Women's Press Club. The topic got around naturally to women in politics and inevitably to women as Presidential candidates. The question—what would you do, Senator Smith, if you woke up one morning and found yourself in the White House? "THE FIRST THING I'D DO IS GO STRAIGHTWAY TO THE PRESIDENT'S WIFE AND APOLOGIZE, THEN I'D GO HOME."

Women—*Relief*

608   *As the cigarette commercial says, you've have come a long way, baby.* It reminds me of a case a state trooper recently told me about. This woman motorist was doing seventy miles an hour on a highway with a fifty-five-mile speed limit. She happened to glance in her rear-view mirror and spotted a state trooper on a motorcycle as he pulled out from behind a billboard she had just passed. He seemed to be catching up with her, so she put her foot down on the gas and zoomed up to eighty miles an hour, with the cop in hot pursuit.

Down the road she spotted a service station. Gunning the motor, she roared into the station, drew to a screaming halt, jumped out of her car, and dashed into the ladies' room.

After a little while she came out and saw the trooper flanking her car. She walked brightly over to where he was waiting and, with a big grin on her face, said, "YOU DIDN'T THINK I'D MAKE IT, DID YOU?"

(And for a long time we didn't think our first woman appointee would . . .)

Women—*Topic*

609   *This is certainly one of the most splendid dinners I have ever attended.* And if I have to single out the major reason that has made the occasion so enjoyable, I would go back to a comment by Justice Oliver Wendell Holmes. He was asked by his then law clerk, Dean Acheson, the following question: "If all the great statesmen of the last three or four centuries were brought together in one room, what would they talk about, divided as they would be by language, custom, and even centuries?"

Holmes said, "THERE IS ONLY ONE UNIVERSAL TOPIC THAT TRANSCENDS TONGUE AND TIME—THE BEAUTY OF THE WOMEN PRESENT."

Tour Bus

Too often travel, instead of broadening the mind, merely lengthens the conversation.
　　　　　　　　　　—Elizabeth Drew

Customs—*Knowledge*

610　*It pays to have some understanding of the usages and customs, the way they do business, the way they live.* I always remember how an American movie actor messed himself up in England. Anxious to break into English social circles, the actor got himself invited to an English hunt. After the weekend, he had the impression that he was being cold-shouldered. He called his friend Sir Thomas. "Tommy, you can speak frankly with me. What's happened? I'm being virtually ostracized."

"Well, old boy," Tommy replied, "you'll remember that fox hunt you went on last weekend? HERE IN ENGLAND IT'S CUSTOMARY TO CRY, 'TALLYHO!' WHEN YOU SIGHT THE FOX—NOT, I'M AFRAID, 'THERE GOES THE LITTLE SONOFABITCH!' "

Friend—*Help*

611　*Gentlemen, I rise to make a toast to one who has been a real friend.* I suppose one definition of friendship is the spirit that warms the cockles of one's soul. At least that's how an acquaintance of a colleague of mine views it. He was taking a vacation mountain climb with a native Swiss guide. On the windy, snowy slopes they temporarily lost their bearings for a bit and in the bitter cold were preparing camp when all at once they sighted the familiar Saint Bernard dog with the keg of brandy tied around his neck. Said the Swiss guide: "HURRAH, HERE COMES MAN'S BEST FRIEND!" "YES," said the vacationing American," AND LOOK AT THAT BIG FURRY DOG THAT'S CARRYING IT."

Improvement—*Import*

612　*I think we all could use a touch of class around here.* I think the presence of our new visitor is going to brighten up the place. It reminds me of a distinguished Englishman who was visiting Dallas. His host, who was treating the Englishman to a long dissertation on the wonders of the Lone Star State, drawled, "Maybe you don't realize, but you could put all of Great Britain into one little corner of our state."

"I dare say you could," said the Englishman dryly, "AND WOULDN'T IT DO WONDERS FOR THE STATE?"

Inevitability—*Sex*

613   *No matter what problem we talk about today, it always comes back to the energy crisis.* It recalls to me the time some years ago when the mayor of New York was hosting the newly arrived French Consul General. The mayor took him on a VIP tour ending at the Empire State Building. The mayor pointed it out proudly and boasted, "It's the tallest in the world. What do you think of it?"

The Frenchman gazed at it admiringly and commented, "It reminds me of sex."

"That's a strange reaction," said the Mayor. "How can the Empire State Building remind you of sex?"

The Frenchman explained simply, "EVERYTHING DOES."

(And everything today reminds me . . .)

Outlook—*Progress*

614   *When I am asked to assess the outlook for earnings in the next year, I am reminded of what a Washington cab driver said.* I was attending a conference in Washington and brought my family along. I took some time out from some of the sessions to see some sights. When we passed the National Archives Building, my nine-year-old daughter read out the inscription that comes from Shakespeare's *Tempest* that is engraved on the front of the building, "What is past is prologue." Then my daughter said, "Daddy, what does that mean?"

Before I could say anything, the driver boomed out, "HONEY, THAT MEANS YOU AIN'T SEEN NOTHING YET!"

Prediction—*Assumption*

615   *As I go out on the limb with these predictions, I can't help but think of a story a Detroit bus driver told me.* He was taking

a tour bus of passengers around Detroit. As the bus driver started to point out each of the famous sights, this know-it-all woman would beat him to the punch. As they passed one palatial estate, she said, "There is the Ford home, where Henry Ford lives." "No," the bus driver patiently corrected, "it belongs to Edsel Ford, not Henry." Then she pointed to another mansion. "And there—the Dodge estate of Phelps Dodge." "No," said the bus driver, "it's Horace, not Phelps."

Finally they passed Christ Church, one of the famous Episcopal churches, and she got up and said, "And there's . . ." She paused and the driver said, "GO AHEAD, LADY, YOU CAN'T BE WRONG ALL THE TIME!"

(And similarly, I hope I'm not going to be wrong all the time . . .)

Problem—*Dilemma*

616   *Either way we go, we are going to run into some real difficulties.* The question is, which will be more tolerable? Which can we more easily live with? A similar question faced a recent arrival in hell.

The gentleman had led a sinful life, but not that sinful, so when he was assigned to hell by the recording angel he was at least allowed the privilege of a choice—either the German hell or the Italian hell.

"But what is the difference?" asked the downcast arrival.

"In the German hell," explained the angel, "you spend half your time eating all the food you want, listening to music, and cavorting with girls. The other half of the time you are pinioned to the wall and beaten mercilessly, your nails and teeth are pulled out, and boiling oil is poured over you."

"And in the Italian hell?"

"In the Italian hell, you spend half your time eating all the food you want, listening to music, and cavorting with girls. The other half of the time you are put on the rack and stretched and then you are dunked in scalding water."

"But there's no difference."

"There is in some of the details. In the German hell, you have German food, German music, and German girls, whereas in the Italian hell you have Italian food, Italian music, and Italian girls."

"But both nationalities are first-class in those respects."

"Certainly. As for the more painful part, the tortures in the German hell are conducted in the usual German fashion, whereas . . ."

The gentleman quickly replied, "I'LL TAKE THE ITALIAN."

Problem—*Solution*

617 *It may come as some surprise, but the problem being so prominently mentioned is one that we don't have to worry about.* It reminds me of the flies that those expert Japanese samurai wielders can cut in mid-air. An American tourist heard of the incredible swordsmanship of the cultists of the ancient rite. While in Tokyo he made inquiries as to where the best swordsman was. The best was not available. Neither was the second best. But the American got a chance to see Japan's number-three samurai wielder. The swordsman let a fly out of the bottle. While it was in flight, he struck with the sword. Swish. The fly was cut in half. The American was impressed. He couldn't see that anyone could do better than that. But a little later he wangled an invitation to the number-two man. Again a fly was released from the bottle. The Japanese expert made two swishes with the sword. Incredibly, the fly was hacked and quartered in mid-air. Now he couldn't see how number one could do better than that. Finally his place on the waiting list went to the top. He was ushered into the presence of the best swordsman in Japan. Once again there was the ritual of opening the bottle with the fly. While it was buzzing above, the swordsman wielded a great chop. To the American's surprise, the fly kept in flight. The American said, "I don't see why you are number one. The number three sliced the fly in two and then I saw the number two cut it in two passes to quarters. But you missed completely."

"MISS, DID I?" said the number-one swordsman. "I ASSURE YOU THAT FLY WILL NEVER PROPAGATE AGAIN."

(And similarly, one thing we aren't going to have to worry about . . .)

COMMENT: This is a three-stage build-up story. It calls for gestures.

Provincialism—*Perspective*

618 *The problem with that idea is that it is narrowly conceived.* It is not so much that it is wrong as that it doesn't take in other considerations. It is like the haberdasher in my home town,

Mr. Rosencrantz. When he returned from Europe, his partner in a men's clothing store hung on his every word. "And I was even in a group that went to the Vatican," reminisced Rosencrantz, "where we were blessed by the Pope."

"The Pope!" exclaimed the other partner. "What does he look like?"

"A very pious man, reverent, spiritual, almost saintly," Rosencrantz answered. "I FIGURE A SIZE THIRTY-EIGHT SHORT."

Question—*Stupidity*

619　*I hope the audience will take advantage of the rare opportunity they have now to question the panelists.* Let's make the most of it. Some of the questions I have heard at sessions like this remind me of an experience of Samuel Hopkins Adams's, the veteran newsman, who, always willing to try anything once, accepted an invitation to a nudist party a few years ago. Describing the experience to his friends the next day, he said, "They certainly didn't do things by halves. Even the butler who opened the door was completely nude."

"How did you know it was the butler?" he was asked.

"WELL," said Mr. Adams, "IT CERTAINLY WASN'T THE MAID."

Timing—*Late*

620　*Our timing on this project leaves much to be desired.* It reminds me of the time I was visiting Windsor outside London. A bus took a group of us to Runnymede. One passenger demanded of the guide, "What happened here?"

"This is where the Magna Carta was signed."

"When?" asked the American.

"1215," replied the guide.

Looking at his watch, the tourist said to his wife, "MY GOSH, DEAR, WE MISSED IT BY THIRTY MINUTES!"

Woman—*Safety*

621　*I read in a magazine article the other day where a noted world traveler was talking about the customs of women.* "Ideas about modesty are unusual and varied," he said to this group. "In Turkey, if a girl is surprised in her bath, she will cover her face every time. And a Chinese woman, under the same circumstances, will hide her feet. But the American woman . . ."

"Yes? Go on," urged one eager listener.

"Well," said the traveler, "THE AMERICAN WOMAN WILL ALWAYS KEEP THE BATHROOM DOOR LOCKED!"

(Well, I don't know about the bathroom door, but a woman is a fool today who doesn't lock . . .)

Walls of Bureaucracy

The perfect bureaucrat is the man who manages to make no decisions and escape all responsibility.

—Brooks Atkinson

622 It's always nice to be described in an introduction as a high public official—but that's just another name for a bureaucrat without tenure.

623 Someone asked me, though, before the dinner, why I'm still in Washington and I quoted Benjamin Franklin, who said, "Never seek, never refuse, never resign an office."

624 As I begin this speech, I think I should tell you something of bureaucratic procedure in Washington. No one ever delivers a speech that he wrote and no one ever writes a speech he delivers.

625 Seriously, though, I want you to know that bureaucracy is not a phenomenon of the twentieth century. The Chinese 3,000 years ago had a word for "bureaucrat." It was a picture character of a roof with two mouths under it. So don't think it's something new when you catch us bureaucrats speaking out of both sides of our mouth.

626 And if you have difficulty following what I have to say, remember, I have to abide by the bureaucratic guidelines—when in charge, ponder; when in trouble, delegate; and when in doubt, mumble.

627   Sometimes I get a little provoked when people attack the competence or the intelligence of the bureaucrat. After all, in a sense we all work for the government—but we get paid for it.

628   Seriously, though, where would we be without the bureaucracy? Because of us there is no danger of our government ever being overthrown. There's far too much of it.

629   Now is that time of the year when we see a lot of visitors in Washington—people coming down to see their government *in action*—and every year it's getting harder to tell whether that's one word or two.

630   But it is hard being a bureaucrat—it's not easy finding a problem in every solution.

631   Really, even though the work of the bureaucrat is long and hard, I can't complain. We in government get lots of fringe benefits—a good pension, tenure, health-care benefits, parking space —and the best of all the fringe benefits, that of spending someone else's money.

632   Seriously, we do get a lot of fringe benefits—like all the public holidays. People in private business, for example, don't get off Columbus's birthday. I guess the reason we bureaucrats celebrate it is that he started out not knowing where he was going, when he got there he didn't know where he was, and he did it all on borrowed money.

633   Whenever I speak I find people who think Washington frustrating. They feel they can't get through—can't get themselves heard. They ought to remember what John Kennedy said about Washington—"It's a city of Southern efficiency and Northern charm."

634   And it's been that way right from the beginning. Why do you think the planner Pierre L'Enfant laid it out as a city going around in circles?

Action—*Delay*

635   *I don't know what's holding up action on this project.* But I think it's time somebody stopped playing around and got down

to business. I remember one time in 1957 when the U. S. Post Office was deeply embroiled in censorship and refused to deliver certain books and magazines, a great many people felt that censorship was the business of legal courts and not of the post office.

Senator Gale McGee, when asked by a reporter what his plans were for the upcoming session of Congress, said, "I'M GOING TO INTRODUCE A RESOLUTION TO HAVE THE POSTMASTER GENERAL STOP READING DIRTY BOOKS AND DELIVER THE MAIL."

(And similarly, I think we ought to stop playing around with appointing study groups and making reports and get down to action. . . .)

Commitment—*Pledges*

636 *Gentlemen, all of you have made commitments to this cause and we are going to hold you to those pledges.* We are going to take the same action as a local minister to whom an Internal Revenue agent made a visit. "Reverend," the IRS agent said, "one of your parishioners, a Mr. L. Harris, has claimed on his tax return that he made a two-thousand-dollar contribution to your church. Do you know if that's true?"

"Well," the minister answered, "don't worry. IF HE DIDN'T, HE WILL."

(And we are going to remember your offer . . .)

Complicated—*Paperwork*

637 *The paperwork required to obtain such an approach would awe even the most experienced bureaucrat.* The situation recalls the time Leon Henderson, head of OPA, was asked by FDR, "Leon, what about the constitutionality of this legislation, and why isn't the Department of Labor included?"

Henderson said, "Mr. President, I sent you a memorandum on those points."

FDR replied, "Leon, ARE YOU UNDER THE IMPRESSION THAT I READ THOSE MEMORANDA OF YOURS? WHY, I CAN'T EVEN LIFT THEM."

Criticism—*Pedantry*

638 *All of us get a little tired of some of the bureaucratic nit-picking that goes on under the name of processing, approval,*

and review. We can all sympathize with the way Winston Churchill once handled such a criticism from Whitehall, the British Pentagon. Whitehall had sent back one lengthy memorandum by Churchill on defense preparedness with this reprimand in one of the sentences: "Do not end sentences with a preposition." To which Churchill wrote underneath and sent back, "THIS IS PEDANTIC NONSENSE UP WITH WHICH I SHALL NOT PUT."

Introduction—*Accuracy*

639   *The generous introduction I received reminds me of the time I heard David Bell, JFK's budget director, make a presentation of fiscal estimates for a particular bureau of the Treasury Department.* The estimate he made to the Senate Appropriations Committee was a little over 366 billion dollars. A week later Bell was called back to testify to the committee. The chairman said, "Mr. Director, we found your computation in error. The total should be 350 billion." Mr. Bell replied, "GIVE OR TAKE 10 OR 15 BILLION DOLLARS, THE PRESENTATION WAS SUBSTANTIALLY CORRECT."

(And give or take a little excess, the introduction was substantially correct. . . .)

Planning—*Mistake*

640   *Even the best-planned operations can sometimes go awry.* At least we did not have the problem the people at Parke-Bernet had in New York. They were awaiting a huge piece of sculpture to be placed on 76th Street in front of the entrance to the famous art-auction house. The work depicting Aphrodite bringing culture to the shores of the New World was a magnificent sculpture. The bare-bosomed Aphrodite gave abundant evidence of her generous charms in beauty and love. The only problem was that the authorities found Aphrodite a bit too well endowed; her bosom protruded over into city property, violating the city ordinances. Fortunately the battle of the bulging breastworks was resolved by an agreement that Parke-Bernet pay twenty dollars a year bosom-rental space.

(And similarly, our mistake has not been that costly. . . .)

Qualifications—*Expertise*

641   *I must confess when I first assumed this job I had some doubts about my qualifications, but then I recalled an exchange*

between Sargent Shriver and his Peace Corps director for Central America. Shriver, who at that time was directing both the Peace Corps and the War on Poverty agencies, received a memo from his regional director recommending a Peace Corps administration for Guatemala. Shriver approved the appointment but added, "But what does he know about Guatemala?" The return memo said, "NOT MUCH, SARGE, BUT WHAT DO YOU KNOW ABOUT POVERTY?"

Taxation—*Bureaucracy*

642   *The best illustration of why we don't seem to get our money's worth for our tax dollar happened at a state banquet given by Frederick the Great of Prussia.* The monarch asked those present to explain why his revenues continued to diminish despite incoming taxes.

An old Prussian general said, "Your Majesty, let me show you." Asking for a piece of ice, the old general lifted it for inspection and then handed it to his neighbor and requested that it be passed on hand to hand to the king. By the time the ice reached Frederick, it was about the size of a pea. The king got the idea—"TOO MANY HANDS FROM START TO FINISH."

Taxation—*Fear*

643   *Although I have frequently heard the saying "Nothing is more certain than death and taxes,"* I wasn't aware of the theological connection until I was told of this ecclesiastical examination by St. Peter at the gates of entrance. Three men were applicants. The first man said, "I was a minister of the Gospel for forty years."

"Step aside for further consideration," he was told.

"I was a minister also," reported the second man, "although for only thirty years."

"Step aside for further consideration," he was also directed.

Then the third candidate stepped up. "I," he said, "was not a minister, just a government worker with the Internal Revenue Service for ten months."

"Step right in," said St. Peter, bowing low.

"But, sir," objected one of the other two, "how is it this government clerk is permitted to enter the pearly gates before two ministers?"

"Well," said St. Peter, "THE WAY I LOOK AT IT IS THAT THIS IRS

AGENT SCARED THE DEVIL OUT OF MORE PEOPLE IN TEN MONTHS THAN EITHER OF YOU DID IN A LONG LIFETIME!"

ADVICE: I have also heard this story used about cab drivers.

Taxes—*Waste*

644   *People are beginning to sense that they are not getting the full value of their tax dollar out of bureaucratic Washington.* This was dramatically brought home to me by the story a few years ago of a little boy who wrote a letter to God. Eventually it found its way to the post office, and the postal authorities brought it to the attention of Postmaster General Edward Day. The letter said that since his father died his mother was having a hard time making ends meet, and wouldn't the Lord see fit to send his mother one hundred dollars to help out? The Postmaster General and his staff was so moved that together they got up fifty dollars and mailed it to the little boy's mother. Two weeks later another letter arrived from the little boy.

"Dear God, thank you so much for all you have done, but we need another one hundred dollars. AND IF YOU DON'T MIND, WHEN YOU SEND IT TO MAMA, PLEASE DON'T ROUTE IT THROUGH WASHINGTON, BECAUSE THE LAST TIME THEY DEDUCTED 50 PERCENT."

(And so we find that local services run from Washington . . .)

ADVICE: Good story to use about taxes or bureaucratic waste.

INDEX

Subject Index

A NOTE ON USING THE INDEXES

Throughout the book, the jokes are numbered. In the indexes the numbers shown refer to these numbered jokes except in the cases of unnumbered material. Then a page number is given, and "p." in **bold-face type** precedes the number.

Name Index

295

About the Author

James C. Humes is a lawyer, public speaker, and former state legislator who has served in the White House and State Department. He has written presidential speeches as well as speeches for corporation executives, governors and senators. He now practices law from his offices in Philadelphia and Washington.